IDEOLOGY

Publication of the Advanced Seminar Series
is made possible by generous support
from the Brown Foundation

School of American Research
Advanced Seminar Series
Douglas W. Schwartz, General Editor

Contributors

Robert McC. Adams
Smithsonian Institution

Robert L. Carneiro
Department of Anthropology
American Museum of Natural History

Geoffrey W. Conrad
William Hammond Mathers Museum
Indiana University

George L. Cowgill
Department of Anthropology
Arizona State University

Arthur A. Demarest
Department of Anthropology
Vanderbilt University

David A. Freidel
Department of Anthropology
Southern Methodist University

Susan D. Gillespie
Department of Anthropology
Illinois State University

David C. Grove
Department of Anthropology
University of Illinois

Alan L. Kolata
Department of Anthropology
University of Chicago

David J. Wilson
Department of Anthropology
Southern Methodist University

IDEOLOGY

and Pre-Columbian Civilizations

Edited by
ARTHUR A. DEMAREST AND GEOFFREY W. CONRAD

SCHOOL OF AMERICAN RESEARCH PRESS
SANTA FE, NEW MEXICO

School of American Research Press
Post Office Box 2188
Santa Fe, New Mexico 87504-2188

Distributed by the University of Washington Press

Library of Congress Cataloging-in-Publication Data:

Ideology : and pre-Columbian civilizations / edited by Arthur A.
  Demarest and Geoffrey W. Conrad.—1st pbk. ed.
      p.   cm.—(School of American Research advanced seminar
  series)
    Includes bibliographical references and index.
    ISBN 0-933452-82-9 (cloth) : $35.00.—ISBN 0-933452-83-7
    (paper) : $15.00
    1. Indians—Philosophy—Congresses. 2. Indians—Politics and
  government—Congresses. 3. Indians—Economic conditions—Con-
  gresses. 4. Ideology—Congresses. 5. Ethnoarchaeology—Latin
  America—Congresses. 6. Marxian archaeology—Latin America—
  Congresses. 7. Latin America—Antiquities—Congresses.
  I. Demarest, Arthur A. II. Conrad, Geoffrey W. III. Series.
  E59.P45I44   1992
  970.01'1'01—dc20   92-14578
                                                           CIP

CONTENTS

ACKNOWLEDGMENTS

We wish to acknowledge the generosity and hospitality of Douglas W. Schwartz and his staff at the School of American Research, who gave us the opportunity to exchange information and ideas in exceptionally pleasant surroundings. We owe special thanks to Jane Kepp for her patience and persistence in seeing this book to completion, and for her editorial assistance and advice during its preparation.

We want to express our appreciation to June-el Piper for her meticulous copy-editing. The task of cross-referencing manuscripts and bibliographies and ensuring accuracy and stylistic uniformity was truly herculean, and we thank June-el for her efforts and her patience. We are grateful to LeRoy E. Demarest for his cover illustration.

As organizers and editors, we want to thank all the contributors to the advanced seminar and this book. Their willingness to write and debate made the SAR seminar an exciting and productive event, while their willingness to rethink the issues and refine their arguments produced a publication of which we are truly proud. We are especially grateful to Jonathan Haas, Mary Helms, and John Monaghan, who made many valuable contributions to the seminar and to the ideas in this volume.

We are grateful to the students and staff of the department of anthropology at Vanderbilt University and to the staff of the William Hammond Mathers Museum, Indiana University. We owe special thanks to Mary Pye, Tracey Ferrell, and Sandra Warren, who spent many long hours on the preparation of the seminar and this volume. We also thank our families and friends for their patience, tolerance, and support during the hectic periods that went into the preparation of this book.

Arthur A. Demarest
Geoffrey W. Conrad

IDEOLOGY

ARCHAEOLOGY, IDEOLOGY, AND PRE-COLUMBIAN CULTURAL EVOLUTION

THE SEARCH FOR AN APPROACH

ARTHUR A. DEMAREST

During the past three decades, archaeologists struggled with issues of methodology, cultural causality, and epistemology. We moved from the relative security of cultural ecology to the methodological scrutiny of "processual" archaeology and, finally, to the "postprocessual" age of supreme self-doubt. The latter has culminated in a rejection of evolutionism (e.g., Hodder 1986; Trigger 1982, 1989; Yoffee 1979) and in "critical theory," which in some cases rejects positivism itself (cf. Conkey and Specter 1984; Hodder 1985; Trigger 1989). In a sense, archaeological debate in the 1970s and 1980s was a condensed recapitulation of the past three centuries of Western philosophy: reaction to the extreme positivism of the New Archaeology led to a series of ever less assured, more introverted epistemological debates.

Yet there is some question about the impact of these theoretical debates on field practice. Throughout the 1960s, 1970s, and 1980s, monographs produced by large-scale, multidisciplinary field projects reconstructed long periods of prehistory based on a form of cultural ecology and settlement archaeology that was not notably different in theoretical premises from the approaches developed by Julian Steward and Gordon Willey in the 1950s. Most applications of the more sophisticated approaches were limited to narrow case studies, ethnoarchaeological researches, and historical archaeology. A cynic might doubt that the philosophical debate has had any relevance to the actual reconstruction of prehistory. Nevertheless, something has been gained from the turmoil, even in the less contemplative arena of major field projects. Many directors and interpreters of the "big digs" have become more aware of the incompleteness of most materialist approaches. They are striving to find some clues for addressing the issues, flaws, and biases revealed by contextual, Marxist, and postprocessual archaeology without succumbing to antipositivistic despair.

It is within this context, and in this spirit, that an advanced seminar on the role of ideology in pre-Columbian cultural evolution called together in 1987 a group of archaeological field directors concerned with ideology. The goal was to address the complex issue of the role of ideology in culture change. The problem was how to address this issue in the context of pre-Columbian prehistory. The participants included directors of regional field projects that had reconstructed episodes of the rise and expansion of complex societies: David C. Grove (Chalcatzingo, Mexico), George L. Cowgill (Teotihuacan, Mexico), David J. Wilson (Santa Valley, Peru), David A. Freidel (Cerros, Belize, and Yaxuna, Yucatan), Alan L. Kolata (Tiahuanaco, Bolivia), Geoffrey Conrad (Chan Chan and Osmore, Peru), and myself (Petexbatun, Guatemala). Their approaches to ideology reflected both varying theoretical positions and a realistic understanding of the limitations of the field. Ethnographer and theorist Robert L. Carneiro and Old World archaeologist and historian Robert McC. Adams provided alternative perspectives, commentary, and critique.

No definitive common answers or uniform perspectives were intended as a goal—indeed, the theoretical range of the participants precluded this possibility. The intent was to make archaeologists look beyond ecology and economics in each of their respective regions. They have done so here in trial reconstructions of the role of ideology in major episodes of culture change. The results are useful in themselves as broader reconstructions of culture history. They also provide a glimpse of how religion and ideology can be viewed in culture-historical reconstructions.

Before these individual contributions are introduced, it might be useful to place the seminar within the context of the recent history of the debate on ideology and its role in cultural evolution. This initial commentary must, inevitably, begin with a discussion of various definitions of, and perspectives on, ideology.

DEFINITIONS AND THEORETICAL PERSPECTIVES

There is no clear consensus in anthropology on the meaning of the term *ideology*. Definitions vary according to the writer's vision of the role of ideology in culture change. In this book, each author defines ideology in his or her own terms, yet all stress the paradox of the contrast and connections of ideology with the economic or material base of societies. Most see an important role for ideology in episodes of culture change, but they do not see ideology as the dominant force in culture process.

Definitions of ideology are constructed in terms of its perceived function (or lack thereof) in society and its development. The positions taken in this book include those of Marxists, structuralists, cultural ecologists, and idealists—each with his or her own perception of ideology. For example, an "orthodox" Marxist view sees ideology as no more than "a phantasmic representation of the relations of production, the echoes of the life process" (Marx and Engels, cited in Bottomore 1956: 75). Some researchers keep discussions of ideology very close to the traditional Marxist concept of exploitation: "a complete Marxist view of ideology sees systems of ideas as means by which competing classes and interest groups present their views and justify them so as to manipulate and control others" (Gilman 1989: 68). Other Marxist perspectives see a more dynamic role for ideology, and some structural Marxists even hold that

> religious ideology is not merely the superficial, phantasmic reflection of social relations. It is an element internal to the social relations of production. This belief in supernatural abilities, a belief shared by the dominated peasantry and the dominant class alike, was not merely a legitimizing ideology, after the fact, for the relations of production; it was a part of the internal armature of these relations of production (Godelier 1978a: 8–10).

Friedman (1975) goes even further and argues that in the Marxist analysis of historical transformations, ideology can sometimes be the critical variable.

Systems theorists and cultural ecologists like Rappaport, Flannery, and Orlove (and David Wilson, this volume) also examine ideologies as dynamic elements in culture change and see them as information-regulating mechanisms. These theorists envision ideational systems as information processors that relate a group's possible adaptive responses to its natural and social environment. Ideologies link system variables via decision-making feedback processes (e.g., Orlove 1980). This position resolves the fruitless debate between superstructural and infrastructural dominance and concludes that materialist and idealist approaches in anthropology find a "common ground through a more thorough interpretation of culture and ideology as systems which mediate between actors and environments through the construction of behavioral alternatives" (Orlove 1980: 262).

Linkages and feedback systems, however, make causality itself highly problematic, as Adams notes in his commentary in this volume. Wilson addresses this problem in his systemic model of the role of ideology in Santa Valley prehistory. He believes that the general issue of causality and the specific role of ideology can only be addressed in systemic models by narrowing discussions to particular historical contexts. Kolata reaches this same conclusion on the interpretation of causality from a very different structural-Marxist perspective. Contexts, then, set parameters for analysis and define the relative importance of change in specific institutions at a given time. Those perspectives avoid the irresolvable questions (and the tautologous definitions) regarding the relative explanatory weights of ideology, economics, or politics.

In my own somewhat eclectic approach, I move the definition of ideology more specifically toward religious belief, and I extend the concept of ideology beyond religion and ritual only in the sense of including less formalized and explicit symbolic systems and behaviors. I generally follow Sharer and Ashmore's conception (1987:406): "Ideology encompasses the belief and value system of a society. Religious beliefs come most readily to mind as examples of ideological systems, but art styles and other symbolic records also provide information about the ways human groups have codified their outlook on existence."

In retrospect, however, I find that in actual application in my chapter, I tend to emphasize only those aspects of ideological systems that have a *political* impact. It is also apparent that my general perspective is greatly influenced by cultural ecology. Again, it is the general theoretical position of the scholars, not carefully crafted definitions, that guide their analyses of ideology. This pattern is characteristic of most of these papers, and the authors often discuss ideologies in ways that differ from their own initial definitions. Aspects of ideology that do not affect politics or economics are acknowledged to exist, but they are not incorporated into the models.

In the end, almost all of the participants are interested primarily in the evolution, or "historical transformation," of political systems. For example, Conrad, although espousing a somewhat "idealist" position in his paper, examines the use of ideology in political propaganda. On the other hand, Freidel (this volume) argues for the unity of elite and nonelite ideologies and, thus, a role for ideology that, in some sense, transcends politics. Still, it is the effect of ideology on power relations—not ideologies or cosmologies in and of themselves—that concerns us here, since the changes, expansions, and collapses of the civilizations discussed in this volume are, in the end, the successes and failures of *political* systems.

BACKGROUND: THE RETURN OF IDEOLOGY

In the history of pre-Columbian studies, prehistoric archaeology, evolutionism, and the study of ideology have been treated separately. Although the issue of the role of ideology in historical or evolutionary development is currently fashionable, little substantive progress has been made in addressing ideology within the context of major *prehistoric* episodes of culture change. Studies of pre-Columbian ideology have generally been carried out within the isolated and synchronic framework of the reconstruction of specific ancient religions. These studies have been based on historical, ethnohistorical, and iconographic data rather than field archaeology. Furthermore, the issues of long-term culture change and cultural evolution usually were not of central concern to those researchers.

Meanwhile, scholars interested in long-term cultural and historical process have generally (either implicitly or explicitly) rejected religion or ideology as a major factor in cultural evolution. This neglect or rejection of ideology parallels the history of evolutionism in American anthropology. The return of evolutionism to American archaeology in the 1950s came with the introduction of cultural ecology and materialist perspectives in the works of Julian Steward (1955), Leslie White (1959), V. Gordon Childe (1954), and others. In general, these neoevolutionists stressed the development of technology and material forces in cultural evolution. The cultural materialist school that followed in the 1960s explicitly rejected a major role for ideology in cultural evolution (Harris 1964, 1968; Sanders and Price 1968). Indeed, an interest in ideological factors in prehistory has often been denounced as characteristic of "obscurantist" or "reactionary" approaches (e.g., Harris 1979; Paulsen 1981).

Pre-Columbian archaeologists have usually followed the lead of materialist thinkers on ideology. Occasionally they have explicitly viewed religions and beliefs as either epiphenomenal or as a mere "legitimation" of economic and political realities (e.g., Bray 1978; Carrasco and Broda 1978; Kurtz 1978). Alternatively, some have seen religious institutions and rituals as manifestations of a hidden, ecologically adaptive rationale. For example, underlying ecological causes—relating to alleged demographic pressures—have been invoked to explain Aztec warfare (Cook 1946), Inca expansionism (Isbell 1978; Paulsen 1976), and Aztec cannibalism (Harner 1977; Harris 1977).

More often, archaeologists have *implicitly* applied a materialist paradigm by simply ignoring the issue of ideology. This neglect is understandable; the methodological breakthroughs of the past 30 years have been largely related to chronology, subsistence remains, and settlement patterns. Ecological reconstruction and the reconstruction of ancient economies became the major focus of research projects in the New and Old Worlds. Building on the early work of Steward (1937) and Willey (1953), large-scale archaeological projects studied settlement patterns and interpreted them in terms of ecology, hydraulic systems, population dynamics, and systems of exchange (e.g., R. McC. Adams 1965; Deevey et al. 1979; Harrison and Turner 1978; Sanders, Parsons, and Santley 1979; Wolf 1976; Wright and Johnson 1975). The results of this research were used to build regional, materialist culture histories (e.g., R. E. W. Adams 1977; MacNeish 1964, 1967; Sanders and Price 1968; Sanders, Parsons, and Santley 1979; Willey 1953; Wolf 1976).

It soon became apparent, however, that a purely ecological approach might not be enough. For example, the Near Eastern settlement pattern studies of R. McC. Adams and others (Adams 1965; Adams and Nissen 1972) concluded that population growth and irrigation could not be considered the dominant factors in the rise of Sumerian civilization. Instead, social, political, and ecological factors all interacted to bring about complex society in the Near East (Adams 1966, 1969, 1972, 1981). These studies also hinted that the research focus on individual valleys, basins, or other ecological units might be obscuring the interregional, interethnic, and even "international" interaction that was very important in the rise of all of the Near Eastern civilizations (Adams 1981; Kohl 1978; Lamberg-Karlovsky 1974, 1975; Wright 1985). In the New World, doubts arose concerning purely materialist interpretations even in the very ecologically oriented Valley of Mexico projects (Blanton 1976a, 1976c). Meanwhile, Wittfogel's irrigation or "hydraulic" hypothesis was contradicted by the chronology and nature of irrigation in the Valley of Mexico and the Near East (Adams 1965, 1972, 1981; Brumfiel 1976; Parsons 1976; Sanders, Parsons, and Santley 1979:281).

By the 1970s, many archaeologists had become concerned that the materialist paradigm, although essentially correct, was incomplete:

> If thinking human beings are the generators, as well as the carriers, of culture it seems highly probable that, from very early on, ideas provided controls for and gave distinctive forms to the materialist base and to culture, and that these ideas then took on a kind of existence of their own, influencing, as well as being influenced by, other cultural systems. If this is so, then it is of interest and importance to try to see how ideas were interrelated

with other parts of culture and how they helped direct the trajectories of cultural and civilizational growth (Willey 1976: 205).

Archaeologists must cease to regard art, religion, and ideology as mere "epiphenomena" without causal significance. . . . [These] "epiphenomena" . . . lie at the heart of society's environmental and interpersonal regulation, and as such cannot be omitted from any comprehensive ecological analysis. . . . (Flannery 1972: 400; see also Flannery 1977).

IDEOLOGY IN PREHISTORY: STRUGGLING FOR AN APPROACH

The current interest in ideology is not, as some have labeled it (e.g., Harris 1979; Mignon 1986), an "idealist" rejection of cultural ecology or of technoeconomic factors in cultural evolution. In fact, Marxist approaches to archaeology have been the most aggressive in their recent attempts to incorporate ideology as a force in prehistory (e.g., Cohen and Toland 1988; Friedman 1974, 1975; Friedman and Rowlands 1978; Godelier 1978a, 1978c; Miller and Tilley, eds. 1984). In field studies, archaeologists of cultural-ecological bent have also begun to incorporate ideology into their interpretations (e.g., Blanton 1976a, 1976b, 1976c, 1978, 1980; Cowgill 1975a, 1975b, 1979; Drennan 1976; Flannery 1972, 1977; Flannery and Marcus 1976b; Puleston 1977, 1979; cf. Orlove 1980). Most of the studies in this volume, although in no sense orthodox, are influenced by either Marxism or cultural ecology or both. None of these studies support an "idealist" proposition that ideology was the "prime mover" in cultural evolution. The very purpose of most of these discussions, and of the advanced seminar, is to seek ways to combine ideology with the study of ecological, economic, and political factors involved in culture change.

Few large-scale archaeological studies have tried to explore the role of ideology in culture change. Most studies that have addressed this problem deal with ethnohistorically and historically known empires rather than prehistoric societies. For example, Godelier (1978a), Schadel (1978), Fritz, Michell, and Nagaraja Rao (1985), and Conrad and I (1984; Demarest and Conrad 1983; Demarest 1976, 1984b) develop evolutionary reconstructions using religion as a critical factor, but all of these studies deal with Conquest period empires. Similarly, the most conceptually elegant studies of symbolic systems and ideology in the material record have been ethnographic and ethnoarchaeological studies, where the data base is even richer (e.g., Braithwaite 1982, 1984; Donley 1982; Glassie 1975; Hall 1979; Hamell 1983; Hodder, ed. 1982; Lewis-Williams 1986; Pearson 1982, 1984; Tilley 1984). The challenge for archaeological studies of ideology has always been to reconstruct the nature and effects of *prehistoric* belief systems. Recent efforts to struggle with ideological evidence have included a number of studies by the contributors to this volume (Conrad 1981; Cowgill 1979; Demarest 1978, 1984b; Freidel 1981a; Freidel and Schele 1988a; Grove 1973; Kolata 1983b). Other attempts to look at ideology and cultural evolution in a prehistoric context include insightful studies by Ashmore (1986), Coe (1981a), Drennan (1976), Flannery and Marcus (1976b), Fritz (1978, 1986), Helms (1979), Keatinge (1981), Knight (1986), Pader (1982), and Renfrew (1982).

Recent examinations of the role of ideology in specific prehistoric regions, however, are characterized by little theoretical unity. Most of the New World studies share only a heavy reliance on direct historical analogy to the Conquest period systems, as well as the use of iconographic and some epigraphic evidence to guide these analogies. We have not developed central themes or general frameworks for interpretation. Groping for a theoretical perspective is also characteristic of the diverse set of approaches in this volume. It reflects the current, general uncertainty in archaeology about the complex issues of causality and culture change.

Recent studies by European scholars have had greater unity in theoretical and interpretive frameworks—most center around neomarxist approaches and the concept of political "legitimation." In the ethnographic studies and theoretical essays of the 1970s, neomarxists and structuralists began to consider the role of ideology and political legitimation in the emergence of early states (Carrasco and Broda 1978; Claessen and Skalnik 1978; Friedman 1974, 1975; Friedman and Rowlands 1978; Godelier 1978a, 1978c). There followed a series of attempts to consider the role of ideology in culture change using both ethnographic and archaeological case studies (see especially Cohen and Toland 1988; Hodder 1982; Hodder, ed. 1982; Miller and Tilley, eds. 1984). These attempts emphasize the role of ideology in legitimation of political power and exploitive economic arrangements. They vary, however, in that some see ideology as a powerful agent in culture change, whereas others view it as a set of institutions narrowly limited to a role of legitimation of the established political and economic order. Indeed, some of the Marxist-influenced approaches can be criticized for a priori imposition on ideology of a specific chronological order and a "legitimating" causal role in interpretations of change.

Other recent Marxist or quasi-Marxist approaches, although they use some of the same terminology, are broader in their interpretations of the role of ideology. Following Godelier, Miller and Tilley assert that "ideology and power are inextricably bound up with social practices; they are a component of human *praxis,* by which is to be understood the actions of agents on and in the world, serving as an integral element in the production, reproduction, and transformation to the social" (Miller and Tilley 1984: 14). These more recent approaches differ only in their adherence to Marxist terminology from the more eclectic studies of Schaedel (1978), Conrad (1981), Freidel (1981a), Demarest (1976, 1981, 1984b), and many of the papers presented in this volume. They all share the view that ideology can be a dynamic force that has varying structural effects in the initial formation of state systems. Given the rather thorough reworking of Marxist concepts in studies like those of Godelier (1978a, 1978c) and Miller and Tilley (eds., 1984), little seems to be gained by retaining Marxist terms loaded with variable and controversial preexisting meanings. The archaeological papers presented here freely borrow useful concepts from Marxism and combine them with other productive approaches. These recent studies seem to be moving, albeit in disarray, toward similar conclusions regarding the range of roles that ideology can play in cultural systems and their development.

THE SCHOOL OF AMERICAN
RESEARCH ADVANCED SEMINAR:
PRE-COLUMBIAN ARCHAEOLOGISTS JOIN THE FRAY

Direct interpretation of prehistoric evidence of ideology represents a major challenge to archaeology, but it is a challenge that must be met. If considerations of the role of ideology in cultural evolution are to have any lasting impact on pre-Columbian studies, they must begin to move back beyond the ethnohistoric period, beyond theoretical and methodological discussions, and beyond narrowly focused studies of patterning in iconography or artifacts. The issue of the role of ideology should also be addressed in terms of the critical cultural transformations at the major centers of the pre-Columbian world (e.g., the Valley of Mexico, the Titicaca basin, or the north coast of Peru).

The essays in this volume attempt to address these challenges. Seven of the studies presented here are by field directors involved in archaeological excavation projects. These scholars have studied important centers of the pre-Columbian world, and their recently completed or ongoing field projects constitute major data bases that can be used to improve our understanding of New World prehistory. These archaeologists were asked to address the evidence from their period and region of expertise to try to ascertain the role of ideology in cultural evolution. The result is a speculative but, we hope, realistic series of perspectives on the role of ideology in culture change and its interplay with ecological, economic, and political forces and institutions. The diversity in the perceived role and nature of ideological factors in each study reflects both the variable role that ideology can play and the varying theoretical orientations of each of these scholars.

The papers in this volume address the issue of the role of ideology in some of the major transformations of pre-Columbian society. Drawing on two decades of research on the Early and Middle Formative (e.g., Grove 1968, 1974a, 1974b, 1981a, 1981b; Grove, ed. 1987; Grove and Gillespie 1984), Grove and Gillespie document the interregional exchange systems of this so-called Olmec period. They discuss how ideological interaction in the Early Formative (1500–1000 B.C.) helped to transform Mesoamerican civilization in the subsequent Middle Formative era (1000–500 B.C.). The continuing elaboration and diversification of Olmec period ritual systems influenced the ideological systems of later Formative and Classic times. Exchange patterns, iconography, and analogy are all used to try to sketch the essential elements of this first interregional ideology of Mesoamerica, emphasizing its dynamic impact on political systems.

A very different scenario is presented in Wilson's consideration of the initial rise of civilization in coastal Peru (1000 B.C.–A.D. 400). There, the interplay between conflict and cooperation was played out at a regional rather than interregional level. Wilson's decade of settlement pattern studies on the north coast of Peru (1983, 1985, 1987, 1988) shows that a shift in ideology was one of the factors involved in the absorption of regional polities by the expanding Moche state. Although Wilson rejects Carneiro's classical circumscription model, his own approach represents another version of cultural ecology. Causality is viewed in terms of interactive feedback and the growth of systems as a whole, rather than as a unidirectional relationship between broad categories of phenomena (economic, ideological, etc.). The settlement patterns of ceremonial centers and fortresses are analyzed to reveal that an ideology of *intra*valley cooperation combined with a political dynamic of *inter*valley conflict to define a single regional process of cultural evolution.

With regard to the full state-level societies of the Classic period, the essays on Tiahuanaco, Teotihuacan, and the Maya display the range of variation that was present in pre-Columbian states and their ideologies. Kolata's research at Tiahuanaco (1983b, 1986, 1987) reveals an expansionistic urban phenomenon of unexpected proportions. Between A.D. 0 and 600 the site of Tiahuanaco became the center of an economic juggernaut, with a state apparatus that reworked both the political economy and the ecological landscape of the southern Andes. Drawing on Godelier's structural-Marxist perspective, Kolata describes how Tiahuanaco's ideological system may have functioned as one element in its overpowering imperial machine. His theoretical perspective draws on neomarxist concepts and emphasizes political ideology at the state level. Analyzing all types of iconography, settlement data, and exchange systems, Kolata reconstructs the structure and impact of the ideology that helped Tiahuanaco to expand and redefine the Andean world.

In contrast, the Mesoamerican states of Teotihuacan (200 B.C. – A.D. 900) and the Maya area (A.D. 0–900) appear to have been less economically centralized and less powerful polities than those of the Andes. Two decades of research at Teotihuacan have detailed the growth of that city and its regional polity (e.g., Cowgill 1974, 1983; R. Millon 1981; Millon, Drewitt, and Cowgill 1973). Cowgill cautiously draws on this established archaeological and chronological base to show ideology's role in that process of growth. He also cites recent surprising discoveries from excavations in the center of Teotihuacan (e.g., Cabrera and Sugiyama 1982; Cabrera, Rodríguez, and Morelos 1982b) and new iconographic interpretations (e.g., Langley 1986; C. Millon 1988; Pasztory 1988) to challenge some commonly accepted characterizations of the Teotihuacan state. Cowgill documents the changing role of ideology in holding together the complex economic, religious, and military forces that constituted the Teotihuacan polity. His emphasis on factional diversity and ideological reintegration stresses both the variability of ideologies and their potential functions.

Freidel and I present two theoretically distinct perspectives on Maya civilization. Based on archaeological, iconographic, and epigraphic studies (e.g., Freidel 1979, 1981a, 1986a, 1986d; Freidel and Schele 1988a, 1988b), Freidel reconstructs the ideological structures of Maya society. He documents in detail the ways in which the ideology of sacred kingships sustained the political structure of the major Maya states of Palenque and Copan. Freidel sees the Maya realms as polities unified by a powerful world view in their political, economic, and religious activities and institutions. He argues that the vast corpus of Maya art and architecture reflects a successful ideological unification of that society—a unity based on a concept of kingship that placed political leadership squarely in the center of Maya cosmology.

My own chapter draws on recent archaeological and epigraphic interpretations in the Petexbatun region that indicate a dynamic instability, competition, and conflict inherent in Maya political structures (e.g., Freidel 1979, 1986d; Matheny 1980, 1987; Demarest 1978, 1984a, 1986; Mathews 1985; Culbert 1988a; Demarest and Houston 1990). I agree with Freidel that Maya states were held together by ideological forces, but I see this cohesion as a reflection of economic weakness and dependency on ritual in these polities, which limited their size and set up cycles of recurrent collapses. Comparing Maya dynamics to Southeast Asian states, I argue that ideological dependency defined the nature and the limitations of Maya polities. Our divergent views reflect different theoretical positions—my own, an uneasy amalgam of cultural ecology and ideology; and Freidel's, more purely structuralist and idealist in orientation. The papers also represent different responses by two Mayanists to the unprecedented flood of new evidence and interpretations from the ongoing revolution in Mayan epigraphy and archaeology.

Finally, Conrad brings us back to the ethnohistoric horizon with a new consideration of how and why the Inca empire was successful in its rapid imperial expansion. His essay underscores the diversity of theoretical approaches now being applied by archaeologists to the issue of ideology by drawing on modern propaganda theory (e.g., Doob 1935; Ellul 1965; Jowett and O'Donnell 1986; Lasswell et al. 1979; Liverani 1979). Through a comparison of propaganda from the Assyrian empire to Hitler's Germany, Conrad sketches the nature and qualities of effective propaganda and shows how the Inca central cults embodied these qualities. He addresses the current concern with causality and circumstance in historical change in his consideration of the "accident of empire" that resulted in Inca expansionism.

In our opinion, a useful discussion of the issue of the role of ideology in culture change requires a cultural-materialist critique and counterpoint. Robert Carneiro enthusiastically performed this task in the seminar discussions and in this volume. He provides a very different perspective on the issues of causality in culture change and the role of material and ideological forces in these transformations. Relying on ethnographic as well as archaeological examples, he has tried to keep seminar participants honest about their interpretations of the relative weight of ideological factors in pre-Columbian cultural evolution. Although his positions differ from my own and from those of most of the seminar participants, he points the way toward more productive syntheses of the many different theoretical stances popular in contemporary archaeology.

In his concluding overview, Robert McC. Adams takes a comparative look at these issues from the perspective of an Old World archaeologist, historian, and theoretician. He assesses the seminar topic broadly and analyzes the dynamics of the seminar itself as they reflect general theoretical orientations and epistemological trends. Adams's emphasis on methodology and epistemology brings us back to earth and helps us to remember the speculative, or at least contestable, nature of many of our fundamental definitions and understandings of the issues involved. He then shows us how historians and archaeologists working with the far richer data in China, the Near East, Rome, and Europe have learned to specify their assumptions cautiously and precisely because of the complexity and pluralistic nature of historically known states and empires. Adams ends the volume on an appropriately balanced note—he exhorts us to proceed with caution and without the recurrent overarching assumption that human societies are uniform, organic wholes with corresponding uniform ideologies.

Taken together, the essays collected here, and the seminar interaction that produced them, are a microcosm of the theoretical turmoil in contemporary archaeology. Despite the limitations of the evidence, archaeologists are now willing to tackle issues that are even challenging historians and ethnographers. It remains to be seen whether our data and interpretive tools will enable us to succeed. Still, progress in addressing complex issues, such as the role of ideology in cultural evolution, cannot be made by limiting our study to the better-controlled historical and ethnographic evidence. Perhaps the scholars here have at times overstepped the limitations of their respective archaeological and ethnohistorical records, but they are merely pressing a cautious field to extend itself into the most exciting concerns of modern anthropology and history. Archaeologists have a unique, long-term perspective on history and cultural evolution. We must try to bring this broad and deep body of evidence and interpretations into the ongoing debate on the role of ideology in culture change.

2

IDEOLOGY AND EVOLUTION AT THE PRE-STATE LEVEL

FORMATIVE PERIOD MESOAMERICA

DAVID C. GROVE
AND SUSAN D. GILLESPIE

The evolution from simple farming societies to complex chiefdoms characterized by differential access to resources, land, labor, and services took place in Mesoamerica during the Formative (Preclassic) period. The concern of this chapter is the role played by ideological as well as material factors in that evolution. We recognize that investigations of ideology using archaeological remains confront the fundamental problem that "Mesoamerican archaeology has absolutely no coherent and consistent theoretical framework" for analysis and interpretation of data related to the ideological realm (Flannery 1976:331). Nevertheless, when processes of culture change are being examined, the role of ideology cannot simply be ignored, for causes will not have social effects "except via human perception and evaluation of them" (Hodder 1986:13).

In our discussion of the Formative period archaeological record we will be dealing with ideology primarily in terms of how conceptions of cosmic and social order structure behaviors and give meaning to events, as well as the role events may have played in reconstructing those concepts. Our use of the term *ideology* follows Geertz's (1973:90) definition of religion as a symbolic system that acts to establish powerful, pervasive motivations in people by formulating a general order of existence, a model for perceiving their world. This definition has the advantage of dealing with symbols—objects, beliefs, and customs—as well as motivations and behaviors, including those involved in culture change.

The relationship between perception and behavior provides a means for understanding culture change. The assumption that ideology merely legitimates the status quo, and that it "dupes" the masses into accepting the dominance of their masters, treats humans as automatons bereft of creativity and incapable of independent thought (Hodder 1986:25–26). In fact, ideological systems are not merely derivative of other aspects of culture, nor are they static. They are constantly redefined and transformed by the dialectical processes involved in fitting the constructed order of existence to actual historical events (Drennan 1976:347; Sahlins 1985:138). This process of the transformation of ideology and its effects on future human behaviors is an integral part of cultural evolution: "If we can understand the ideological structures of phase *a,* then we can begin to examine how the change to phase *b* was produced, and given meaning" (Hodder 1986:27).

This chapter concentrates on the Formative period in western Mesoamerica and particularly the Gulf coast, the Valley of Oaxaca, and central Mexico. Equally important developments occurred elsewhere in Mesoamerica during that time but are not discussed here. Two factors have influenced our discussion. The first is simply the limited quantity and quality of archaeological data relevant to an understanding of ideology in this early time period. The second is our perception that most scholars have generally misunderstood the few data available. Interpretations of Formative period developments have usually been Olmec-centric and thereby assume a precocity and priority for Gulf coast Olmec culture. A variety of artifacts across Mesoamerica have been identified as somehow Olmec-related, which has led to hypotheses of widespread Olmec cultural influences as the basis for most Formative period achievements. The Olmec-centered model may be incorrect, however, since it is becoming evident that other regions had independent and equally important early cultural developments (e.g., Demarest 1989; Flannery and Marcus 1976b; Flannery, Marcus, and Kowalewski 1981; Grove 1989b; Marcus 1989).

This chapter first focuses on the Early Formative (ca. 1500–900 B.C.) and begins with a discussion of public architecture, which is used to demonstrate early and widespread cultural complexity and to suggest some ideological correlates for its pan-regional importance. Next, the evidence of Early Formative long-distance exchange is examined, for it has long been recognized that this exchange was a probable mechanism in the spread of various abstract concepts from one region to another (e.g., Flannery 1968b). The exchange data are compared to the contemporaneous distributions of certain pottery motifs taken by scholars to represent a diffused "Olmec" belief system, and a lack of correlation is shown.

Only after presenting these data do we turn the discussion to the Gulf coast Olmec manifestation. We consider why the Olmec have been thought to be superior to other early Mesoamerican cultures, and we argue that actual differences were not necessarily ones of degree but instead reflect two markedly different ideological systems. The chapter then turns to the Middle Formative (900–500 B.C.) to consider the changes Mesoamerica underwent after 900 B.C. in terms of ideological transformations. It concludes with a brief observation on the legacies of the two Formative period ideological systems in later cultures.

THE EARLY FORMATIVE PERIOD (1500–900 B.C.)

PUBLIC ARCHITECTURE AND THE CREATION OF SACRED SPACE

One useful archaeological indicator of evolving social complexity throughout Formative period Mesoamerica is the marked increase in public architecture, built by or for the community at large. Beginning about 1500 B.C., evidence of public architecture emerges in the archaeological record in a variety of forms. In the Valley of Oaxaca during the Tierras Largas phase (1500–1150 B.C.), the people of San José Mogote built special houselike public structures distinguished from residences by their lime-plastered floors (Flannery and Marcus 1976a: 210). On the tropical Pacific coastal plains of Chiapas, several Ocos phase (1500–1100 B.C.) villages include what may be Mesoamerica's earliest "temple mounds," such as the "three meter high central mound surrounded by a quadrangular arrangement of very low platforms or house mounds covering several acres" at the site of Paso de Amada (Lowe 1977: 211; see also Ceja Tenorio 1985). On the Gulf coast, the Bajío phase (ca. 1350–1250 B.C.) inhabitants of San Lorenzo, Veracruz, began enlarging and leveling a natural hill, eventually creating a large artificial plateau that apparently served as public space for mound architecture (Coe 1970: 22–24, 1981b: 124). In west-central Mexico, at Teopantecuanitlan, Guerrero, a very different form of public architecture has been found to date to ca. 1400–900 B.C.—a large, rectangular, clay-plastered sunken patio (Martínez Donjuan 1982, 1986).

After about 1200 B.C., public architecture became increasingly important and abundant in western Mesoamerica, and each region appears to have followed a different, independent evolutionary path. The construction of ritual-use structures at San José Mogote, Oaxaca, included public buildings on raised stuccoed platforms (Flannery and Marcus

1976a: 211). Mound architecture was apparently present at Gulf coast Olmec sites (see Diehl 1981) and on the Chiapas-Guatemala coast (Clark
et al. 1987; Lowe 1977) but is poorly represented in the present archaeological sample. To the north, in the temperate highland valleys of central
Mexico, public mound architecture was uncommon but has been documented at Chalcatzingo, Morelos (Grove 1984: 41; Prindiville and Grove
1987), and at Teopantecuanitlan, Guerrero, where it complemented the
sunken patio, both embellished by this time with stone facing (Martínez
Donjuan 1986).

Although the creation of public space and architecture is a sign
of evolving social complexity, the material and ideological motivations
stimulating those labor efforts cannot easily be extracted from the archaeological record. The presence of raised mounds and public buildings
demonstrates to some degree formalized group behaviors, and the architecture can be inferred to have functioned in part as a stage or backdrop
for ritual displays that were important for the community to witness and
verify. In their initial stages, these constructions need not have been
associated exclusively with chiefdom-level societies. They may reflect
community-based labor carried out for the ultimate benefit of the local
group in general. These public works projects help to reinforce community solidarity and ties with the land. They may also have an ideological
content; these projects identify sacred space within the landscape and
thereby legitimate community "rights" to the land by metaphorically con-
verting nature and wilderness to culture and community, and perhaps by
linking the people to supernatural patronage.

In chiefdom-level societies with multilevel settlement hierarchies, public architecture is normally restricted to the highest-level sites (e.g.,
Spencer 1987: 371). In fact, site hierarchies are frequently first recognized
archaeologically by the presence and quantity of public architecture,
which creates the possibility of self-validating the public architecture cri-
terion for identifying hierarchies. When public architecture and site size
are used as major criteria, multilevel settlement hierarchies are recognizable for the Ocos phase on the Chiapas coast (Clark 1987a; Clark and
Salcedo Romero 1989; Clark et al. 1987), the San Lorenzo phase on the
Gulf coast (although data on regional settlement patterns are virtually
nonexistent), the Tierras Largas phase in the Valley of Oaxaca (Flannery,
Marcus, and Kowalewski 1981: 65–67), and the Tlatilco culture manifestation (ca. 1100 B.C.) in the Valley of Mexico–Morelos region (Hirth
1987: 348–52; Porter 1953: 34; Sanders, Parsons, and Santley 1979:
94–97, map 5).

INTERREGIONAL EXCHANGE IN THE MAINTENANCE
OF CHIEFTAINSHIP

As Elman Service (1975:293) and others have documented, chiefs (or other high-ranking officials) do not maintain their position by physical force but via continual "gift" exchanges with their followers ("clients") within their sphere of influence. Service has noted that the redistributive authority of a chief rests on his ability to be generous and fair in his allocation of resources, and thus, "a leader is created by his followers, not by their fear of him but by their appreciation of his exemplary qualities" (1975:293). Chiefs also coordinate and control interregional exchange with their peers—other chiefs—and these interactions may involve different kinds of materials with values that are not necessarily based on their utility (e.g., Helms 1979). In fact, the value of exchange materials may be directly proportional to their use as symbolic markers of chiefly rank; thus, some understanding of the role of perceptions of value must form part of any discussion of interregional exchange.

Many archaeologists recognize that intensive and extensive interregional economic interaction was a primary factor in the evolution of complex culture in western Mesoamerica (see Hirth 1984). As noted above, some have suggested that the Gulf coast Olmec stimulated much of that interaction, which resulted in a restructuring of local ideological systems to reflect Olmec ideas (e.g., Bernal 1969:130–43; Coe 1968:91–103). We believe that this hypothesis is not supported archaeologically. Although source analysis data and iconographic evidence do indicate that extensive interaction took place in Mesoamerica, the nature of the exchange relationships is unclear. It is difficult to determine to what extent trade in certain resources, such as obsidian, was controlled by chiefs, and the available evidence reveals that there was no single ("Olmec") network of interaction along which both goods and ideas flowed.

Nonperishable evidence for Early Formative long-distance exchange consists primarily of obsidian and iron-ore mirrors. Greenstone was a rarity at that time. Whereas obsidian has an obvious utilitarian value, and was the material of choice for cutting tools, the other two items lack similar intuitively economically useful characteristics. Their value may have been based in the specific meanings attached to mirrors and to the color green in Mesoamerican belief, as well as in the fact that they were available from very limited, often far-distant sources and thus were accessible to only a privileged few. Hence the perception of value is crucial to understanding their function in the society.

It is often suggested that unequal access to these limited items was a source of power for chiefs, but in fact the argument should be reversed. What the chiefs possessed was an unequal access to certain statuses in the society (see Fried's [1967: 109] definition of "ranked societies"). We suspect that one of the material correlates for those statuses may have been the right to control or display certain items, only a few of which are preserved archaeologically.

Obsidian. The most ubiquitous nonperishable material relevant to an understanding of long-distance exchange, and the material for which there is also the greatest quantity of source analysis data, is obsidian. Four major obsidian source regions served most of Mesoamerica (fig. 2.1): highland Guatemala (El Chayal, San Martín Jilotepeque, Ixtepeque, Taju-

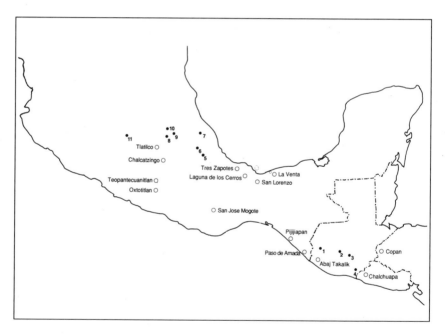

Figure 2.1. Major Formative period Mesoamerican sites and obsidian sources (numbered) mentioned in the text. Obsidian sources in highland Guatemala are (1) Tajumulco, (2) San Martín Jilotepeque, (3) El Chayal, and (4) Ixtepeque; in the Puebla-Veracruz region, (5) Pico de Orizaba, (6) Guadalupe Victoria, and (7) Altotonga; in north-central Mexico, (8) Otumba, (9) Paredón, and (10) Pachuca; and in west Mexico, (11) Zinapecuaro.

mulco), Puebla-Veracruz (Pico de Orizaba, Altotonga, Guadalupe Victoria, etc.), north-central Mexico (Otumba, Paredón, Pachuca), and west Mexico (Zinapecuaro). Several sources remain unidentified, and not all known sources are considered here.

During the Early Formative period, sites along the Chiapas coast acquired obsidian almost exclusively from the Guatemalan sources (Clark and Lee 1984; Clark and Salcedo Romero 1989). The Gulf coast Olmec center of San Lorenzo also obtained obsidian from a Guatemalan source (21 percent, El Chayal) as well as from sources in Puebla-Veracruz (63 percent, Guadalupe Victoria and Orizaba) and central Mexico (5 percent, Otumba and Paredón) during San Lorenzo subphase A (1150–1000 B.C.).[1] In the Valley of Mexico, 74 percent of the obsidian used by Early Formative settlements came from the closest central Mexican sources: Otumba, in the Teotihuacan Valley, and Paredón (Boksenbaum et al. 1987: table 3). Curiously, although these sources could have provided more obsidian than the amount necessary to fulfill local utilitarian needs, another 10 percent of the obsidian came from Zinapecuaro in west Mexico, and 1 percent came from Altotonga, Veracruz (Boksenbaum et al. 1987: table 3).

The obsidian from the Valley of Oaxaca provides an important data base with which interaction between Oaxaca and central Mexico and the Gulf coast can be hypothetically compared. The basic Valley of Mexico obsidian source complex of Otumba-Paredón (36 percent), Zinapecuaro (20 percent), and Altotonga (8 percent) is found at Early Formative Oaxacan villages, and exchange with central Mexico is confirmed by other data. Oaxacan villages also received obsidian from Guadalupe Victoria, Veracruz (28 percent), the major supplier for the Olmec at San Lorenzo, and exchange between Oaxaca and the Gulf coast likewise has other confirmation (e.g., Flannery 1968b; Pires-Ferreira 1975: table 3; Pires-Ferreira and Flannery 1976).

If the Guadalupe Victoria obsidian can be taken as a measure of a Gulf coast Olmec exchange link with any of the other regions, then it is significant that no obsidian from Guadalupe Victoria appears in even minor quantities at any central Mexican Early Formative site. Furthermore, only a small percentage of San Lorenzo's obsidian came from the central Mexican sources of Otumba (5 percent) and Paredón. Significantly, the two external sources important in the Valley of Mexico obsidian profile, Zinapecuaro and Altotonga, do not appear at San Lorenzo until after 1000 B.C. (San Lorenzo subphase B; Cobean et al. 1971: table 1), long after alleged Olmec influences appear in the Valley of Mexico. Conversely, in highland

Guatemala, where source analyses *do* indicate important Gulf coast interaction (which brought El Chayal obsidian to the Olmec chiefs at San
Lorenzo), "Olmec influences" are absent.

In all reconstructions of obsidian exchange patterns, the quality of the
data must be considered. Only small samples of the obsidian from a site
can be subjected to analysis, and these quantities may only poorly reflect
the reality of numerous discrete exchanges that took place during the
lengthy time period usually being studied. Resulting observations and
interpretations are thus based on very minimal data. Nevertheless, even
with these limitations in mind, and even if the obsidian data only mini-
mally reflect general exchange interactions, the characterizations fail to
support the assumption (e.g., Bernal 1969: 130–43; Coe 1968: 91–103)
that prior to 1000 B.C. there was a significant Gulf coast Olmec–central
Mexican exchange network through which ideological ideas and symbols
from the Gulf coast were transferred to the Valley of Mexico.

The obsidian data obviously provide no easy answers concerning the
nature of Early Formative exchange systems; rather they illustrate the systems' complexity. Obsidian exchange between sites and regions seems to
have been highly variable through time. The presence of both Zinapecuaro and Altotonga obsidian at Valley of Mexico sites, even though the
nearby central Mexican sources could have fulfilled all needs, indicates
that nonutilitarian factors may have been involved in the interaction, and
that obsidian exchange cannot be thought of only in terms of "cost-
effective" linear distances. Although obsidian was used by nearly all
members of a society, some obsidian artifacts—particularly blades—were
possibly acquired and redistributed by the chiefs (Clark 1987b: 280). Furthermore, a general temporal correlation is evident throughout western
Mesoamerica between the appearance of blade technology and certain
pottery motifs described below (Boksenbaum et al. 1987). Still needed
are data on possible differential distributions of obsidian within local site
hierarchies, and within sites themselves (e.g., Clark and Lee 1984: table
11.5), as well as on exploitative settlements at or near sources, all of which
might clarify suspected limits to access and distribution.

Iron-Ore Mirrors. During the time span of the Early and Middle Formative
periods, polished iron-ore mirrors, both flat and concave, became increasingly important as indicated by their numbers, geographic distribution,
and social contexts. The use of mirrors as status markers began as early
as the Barra phase (ca. 1500 B.C.) on the Pacific coast of Chiapas (Clark
1987a: 6; Clark et al. 1987: 17). Although concave mirrors are usually

thought to be "Olmec" in origin, Carlson's (1981:130) characterization of a "pan-Mesoamerican mirror tradition" is more appropriate. The only good evidence for mirror production is found in the Valley of Oaxaca, where mirrors were manufactured at San José Mogote during the Early Formative period with ores obtained from nearby sources (Pires-Ferreira 1975:37–61, 1976b). Oaxacan mirrors have been found in the Mixteca region, in the state of Morelos, and at the site of San Lorenzo, Veracruz (Pires-Ferreira 1975:60–62, 1976b; Grove 1987d:380, table 23.2), and thus help to document Oaxacan-related exchange networks. The restrictions in access to sources, manufacture, and exchange demonstrated by Pires-Ferreira (1975, 1976b) strongly suggest that the process was under chiefly control. How that control was effected remains to be determined.

Greenstone/Jadeite. In western Mesoamerica, greenstone was rarely used until the Middle Formative period (see below).

Perishables. Interregional exchanges undoubtedly included numerous perishable items that have escaped archaeological detection. The sixteenth-century *Codex Mendoza* provides tantalizing evidence of the movement of such items as feathers, jaguar pelts, textiles, and cacao beans, which during the Formative period might have passed between regions via chiefly interaction. Again, the San José Mogote excavations have provided the best archaeological data on the long-distance exchange of perishables, many of which apparently had ritual uses. Objects recovered include a turtle carapace (drum), macaw feathers (entire wings, with bones), conch shells (trumpets), a crocodile mandible, and fish and stingray spines (perforators) (Drennan 1976:341–44, tables 11.3, 11.4; Flannery and Marcus 1976b:380, figs. 3, 5). The spines were presumably used for ritual bloodletting, an act of significant consequence in the construction and maintenance of cosmic and social order (see below).

Shared motifs on pottery. Far better evidence of interregional interaction in western Mesoamerica results from the use by most Early Formative societies of a shared set of abstract motifs on their local pottery. Frequent designs include the "were-jaguar," "fire-serpent," and "paw-wing" (fig. 2.2; also see Flannery and Marcus 1976b:381, fig. 6; Joralemon 1971). The widespread nature of these motifs, which occur from the Gulf and Soconusco coasts in the south to central Mexico in the north, has led to their designation as a "horizon style" (Lowe 1977; cf. Grove 1992).

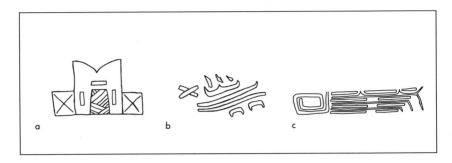

Figure 2.2. *Early Formative motifs on ceramic vessels from Las Bocas: a, "were-jaguar" (from Joralemon 1971:fig. 123); b, "fire-serpent" (from Joralemon 1971:fig. 102); c, "paw-wing" (from Joralemon 1971:fig. 112).*

Interestingly, the motif complex is thus far absent from both highland and lowland Guatemala and Yucatan, but it has been found in Honduras (Fash 1982; Healey 1974; Schele and Miller 1986:75, pl. 28–30).

Although similarly decorated vessels are present at Early Formative Gulf coast Olmec sites (e.g., Coe and Diehl 1980:162–85), good contextual data (i.e., houses or burials) are lacking. In the Valley of Oaxaca and at Tlatilco culture sites in central Mexico, however, this pottery is frequently found associated with burials as well as in general household refuse. At San José Mogote, Pyne (1976) and Flannery and Marcus (1976b; Marcus 1989) note a differential distribution in certain pottery motifs across the village and suggest that these discrete distributions may indicate the motifs served as lineage or descent markers. Burial data from Tomaltepec, Oaxaca (Whalen 1981), and Tlatilco in the Valley of Mexico (Tolstoy et al. 1977: table 5; Tolstoy 1989) suggest the motifs served a similar function there as well. As Marcus (1989) has noted, the two common motifs at San José Mogote ("were-jaguar" and "fire-serpent") may possibly reflect the basic cosmological opposition of the Oaxacan world view, earth and sky, and this important opposition would have been well suited for symbolizing kin-based separations within the society.

The interpretation of the shared design set as social markers differs from the earlier assumption that the motifs are "Olmec style," and by inference that they originated with the Gulf coast Olmec and hence demonstrate borrowing from, or interaction with, that area. In fact, Gulf coast origins for any of the motifs have yet to be demonstrated archaeologically

(see Grove 1989b for a discussion of the motifs and their regional variations). This is also true of the white-slipped baby-face figurines traditionally thought to be Olmec. The presumption by scholars of an Olmec
priority for these pottery motifs and figurines was stimulated in large part
by the elaborate archaeological discoveries at La Venta and the observation of similar symbols on various monuments and jades, which are now
known to postdate the ceramics (see below).

Based on present archaeological data, the widespread ceramic motifs
and baby-face figurines are best understood and dealt with as a shared
symbol system whose individual icons may have originated in diverse
regions and societies (Grove 1989b). It is clear that small agrarian communities were undergoing tremendous changes during the Early Formative period in means of production, land use, and the integration of social
groups within larger population concentrations. Societies would have
searched for order at a time of social disorder. Based on the Oaxaca data,
we suggest that across western Mesoamerica the intracommunity use and
intercommunity sharing and manipulation of this symbol system on the
most common and accessible portable artifacts—ceramics—were one
means of establishing and communicating order.

OLMEC: A POLITICAL IDEOLOGY MADE MANIFEST

The tropical Gulf coast witnessed an apparently rapid and precocious
evolution that culminated ca. 1200 B.C. in the archaeological culture
known as Olmec. San Lorenzo and La Venta are the two Olmec centers
for which the best archaeological data are available, and until recently,
only San Lorenzo had yielded any substantial evidence of pre-Olmec occupations.[2] Archaeologists therefore have looked to that site for explanations of the Olmec "phenomenon" and the development of Mesoamerica's
"first chiefs."

Using analogies with present-day agricultural practices, Coe (1974,
1981b: 182–84) has suggested that although the low hillsides would have
provided the main horticultural lands for most families at San Lorenzo,
the prized lands were the river levees, which are capable of extremely
high yields. Coe argues that control of the prime lands by one family or
group could have provided the stimulus for acquiring economic, political,
and social control. Following Carneiro (1970), he has hypothesized that
coercion and "circumscription" were involved in restricting control of the
levee lands to a small minority, who then parlayed their greater access to

crop yields into political power. This hypothesis has not yet been confirmed archaeologically, nor does it preclude alternative pathways for the development of the Olmec elite at San Lorenzo.

Any attempt to understand the Olmec manifestation in Formative prehistory requires an examination of the one factor that differentiates the Olmec "achievement" from developments in other regions of western Mesoamerica: the construction and use of monumental stone art (colossal heads, tabletop altars, statues, and stelae). Just as Mayanists today study Classic and Postclassic period artworks and inscriptions to improve their understanding of the ideology of those periods (e.g., Demarest and Freidel, chapters 6 and 7, this volume), archaeologists studying the Gulf coast monuments likewise offer valuable insights into Olmec concepts of rulership and power—concepts that gave meaning to the control exerted by the Olmec elite.

Images displayed on Olmec monuments include both supernatural representations and portraits of specific persons. Colossal stone heads appear to have been one of the earliest important monument types and are realistic depictions of specific personages, apparently various Olmec chiefs. Headdress motifs on these and other portrait carvings served as identifying emblems, probably naming devices of the individual chiefs (Coe 1977:186; Grove 1981b:66). The creation of these early monuments must have resulted from powerful motivations, when the enormous expenditure of labor is considered. Much of the stone came from the Tuxtla Mountains area (Velson and Clark 1975; Williams and Heizer 1965), more than 60 kilometers from San Lorenzo and nearly 120 kilometers from La Venta. The stone came from an area most likely under the control of another Olmec center (Laguna de los Cerros or Tres Zapotes), which implies early elite interaction.

Useful for improving our understanding of the nature of Olmec chieftainship are the tabletop "altars" showing seated personages. These massive carvings frequently depict the identified ruler seated within a niche carved into the altar's front face, beneath a projecting tabletop ledge. The ledge is often carved with motifs indicating that it symbolizes the earth's surface. The niche below the ledge is thus the "cave"—the entrance into the underworld, the realm of supernatural powers in Mesoamerican belief (Grove 1973, 1981b:64).

This depiction of the chiefs seated at the entrance to the underworld displays their pivotal position in the cosmos as mediators between society and the supernatural forces associated with rain and fertility, over which they were believed to have influence. In other words, the chief was figuratively positioned at a critical point within the general order of existence—linking humanity and divinity—as shown by the position of his portrait at the juncture between the earth's surface and the underworld. This meaning was reinforced by the fact that the "altar" is really a throne, the ruler's direct means of contacting the supernatural infraworld; when seated on the throne, he placed himself at that cosmological threshold (Grove 1973, 1981b:64). Thus, the altar was his "seat of power," his visual charter for rulership. Although chiefs elsewhere in Mesoamerica may have made similar statements about their ability to influence supernatural forces, using platforms or other public architecture as a stage-setting, the Olmec are set apart by their emphasis on depicting the individual chiefs, in stone, as permanently in contact with otherworldly power.

The iconography of Olmec monuments makes explicit an ideological concept that may have been pan-Mesoamerican: the chief was elevated above society by his sacred quality. This elevation may be a clue to the process of cultural evolution from an earlier, more egalitarian stage. As Service (1975:291) notes, even in nonranked societies, individuals are exalted for their personal differences. One difference might result from a societal belief in heightened access to supernatural power by certain persons who are often called shamans in the literature. Service suggests that these perceptions of inequality could lead to the development of permanent hierarchies and unequal access to power of other kinds. That appears to have been the case for the Olmec because the monuments depict individual chiefs in positions of access to cosmic power apparently denied to other persons, and they involve materials and ritual space under elite control.

The fact that the Olmec people provided the labor to transport and carve those monuments to glorify specific individuals indicates not merely that the ruler was powerful, but that his status was part of the symbol system that motivated the creation of "public works projects" with definite ideological (nonmaterial) content. Motivations other than utilitarian need or the threat of physical force could have accounted for public participation in the erection and display of the monuments, especially for a shamanic ruler: "A priest-chief can be an awesome figure, his own supernatural powers augmented by the power of his ancestors who are now gods in an hierarchical pantheon—and thus potentially frightening to be sure" (Service 1975:296). The people were probably not coerced by simple fear into creating these monuments; on the contrary, they quite likely perceived their work as an opportunity to acquire prestige for themselves by enhancing the prestige of their leader and community, as well as a religious act to strengthen their own position vis à vis the supernatural world. By their labors and participation in the rituals in which the monuments were used, the salient features of their ideology were made manifest, and the role of the ruler in the parallel structure of the cosmos and society was confirmed (see, for example, Feeley-Harnik 1985:293).

Furthermore, the monuments themselves may have been perceived to incorporate some form of power associated directly with the chief portrayed on them. This inherent power would have served to reinforce the messages of the monument and helped to place the forces of the supernatural realm in support of the chief's proclamations and actions. At the death of a chief his monuments were evidently broken and buried to neutralize any remnant supernatural power they may have contained (Grove 1981b:64–65). The personalized power of the chief was apparently concentrated in the attributes of the monuments identifying his persona—his unique facial features and naming devices—for these parts of the monuments suffered the greatest mutilation. Statues were decapitated and colossal heads defaced. The altars, the seats of power that displayed the chief permanently in contact with the supernatural world, were mutilated by smashing their corners and tabletop ledges, and they are the most damaged of all the types of monuments.[3] From these and other data it seems probable that monument mutilation and burial was the final participatory ritual by which the people expressed their beliefs concerning their relationship to the chief and the nature of his right to rule.

In addition to the primary representation of the chief in contact with underworld forces, secondary messages on altars indicate his relationships with other elites. Subsidiary personages are shown in bas-relief on the sides of some altars, and two themes are apparent in the relationships of those personages to the chief. On some altars the ruler seated in the frontal niche holds a supernatural "baby," and in one instance persons displayed on the altar's sides also hold similar babies (La Venta Altar 5). Exactly what these babies symbolize is still uncertain, and at this point they are best interpreted as symbols related to rulership. The subsidiary figures may represent the chief's distribution of authority among his more important clients, thereby insuring their loyalty to him. Alternatively, they may represent kinsmen or ancestors who shared his elite rank by virtue of their kinship ties, suggesting that an entire descent group, rather than a single chief, may have held a status denied to the nonelites (the typical situation in chiefdoms or ranked societies).

Stone statues of personages holding supernatural babies or other objects also occur separately, without an altar. Although the precise chronological position of these monuments is unclear,[4] they may indicate an important development in chiefly ideology in which the visual charter for rulership, explicit on the altars showing the chief at the cave entrance, was abstracted into the form of portable hand-held objects. These objects include the supernatural babies, scepters or bars, and the so-called torches and knuckle-dusters (see Grove 1987e).

Another secondary message is found on altars on which the chief, depicted within the niche, holds a thick rope, which passes along the base of the altar to the subsidiary personages on the sides. Of particular value in understanding its meaning is the San Lorenzo altar labeled Monument 14. Although the chiefly figure in the niche has been badly effaced and eroded to the extent that he cannot be identified by name motif, the secondary personage carved to his left is recognizable by both facial features and bird-claw headdress motif as the ruler portrayed by La Venta Colossal Head 4 (Grove 1981b:66). The depiction of a ruler from one major Olmec center on the monument of a second Olmec center is clearly significant, for it serves to link the chiefs and sites together. Grove (1981b:66) suggests that the rope symbolized the Mesoamerican metaphoric "rope of kinship" (rather than an alternative interpretation, the capture of prisoners, since the individuals are not bound by the rope). The monument thus suggests a chiefly network based on real or fictive kinship, binding the elites of different sites to one another and further sanctioning their separate statuses from their subjects.

IDEOLOGICAL TRANSFORMATIONS IN THE MIDDLE FORMATIVE (900–500 B.C.)

At about 900 B.C., a gradual societal transition becomes apparent in the archaeological record across western Mesoamerica. The change is particularly evident in decorated ceramics and other portable objects, which were sufficiently changed that their differences have been used by archaeologists to define the boundary between the Early and Middle Formative periods. The Early Formative iconographic motifs on pottery gradually disappear, as do clay baby-face figurines. Middle Formative ceramic assemblages generally become plainer. Vessels usually lack fancy designs, and instead, many are decorated around their rims with a variety of simple linear motifs called the "double-line-break" (Dixon 1959; Plog 1976). Figurines are frequently simpler and less well modeled.

The change to plainer ceramics cannot be understood as an isolated phenomenon but must be seen in conjunction with the rapid rise in prominence of jadeite and greenstone objects, many of which carry abstract symbols. These objects include items of personal adornment, celts, perforators, and baby-face figurines. Quality greenstone sources are uncommon, and the only known jadeite sources for Mesoamerica are in the Motagua Valley region of Guatemala. For most of western Mesoamerica, therefore, greenstone had to be acquired via long-distance exchange networks. Archaeological contexts and ethnohistorical data indicate that greenstone objects were generally restricted to the elite.

Although scholars often associate jadeite and greenstone with the Gulf coast Olmec, the earliest archaeologically documented use of these materials may be at Copan, Honduras, in the southern Maya area (Fash 1982; Schele and Miller 1986: 75, pl. 17). Greenstone is rare in Early Formative contexts anywhere, and the Olmec do not seem to have linked into jadeite and greenstone exchange networks any earlier than did the peoples of the Valley of Mexico (Tlatilco culture) or Oaxaca—ca. 900 B.C. The greatly increased popularity of greenstone in the Middle Formative may have been due to the desire by nascent chiefs for new symbols to consolidate their positions further. As part of the overall Middle Formative transition, exchange networks in all commodities became restructured, and resource acquisition and craft production came increasingly under elite control (Parry 1987: 133–34; Pires-Ferreira 1975, 1976a, 1976b).

In view of the timing of the introduction and popularity of greenstone into western Mesoamerica, its restricted availability, its manufacture into articles of ritual rather than utilitarian function, and the fact that green is known to have been a sacred color in later periods, it is significant to note that greenstone now became the major medium for the expression of iconographic motifs.[5] The Early–Middle Formative transition saw a nearly complete transfer in the display of the shared symbol system from one medium, ceramics, available to all, to another, greenstone, available to a few. This change appears to indicate that across western Mesoamerica the access to and control over ritual and cosmological symbols, probably relating to social order and the integration of kinship groups, was taken over by a limited number of high-ranking people.

The elite presumably succeeded in another major achievement: reserving for themselves the authority to oversee kin-group relations among their constituents (Service 1975: 295). This authority to maintain social order was paralleled by increased responsibilities of the chiefs in the maintenance of cosmic order, as discussed below. The gradual evolution of this type of power has been demonstrated ethnographically, as for example among the Bashu of Zaire (Packard 1981), whose chiefs evolved from a low-level ritual status into persons responsible for regulating relations among social groups, correlated with their ability to regulate relations between society and the cosmos.

MIDDLE FORMATIVE GULF COAST

The Gulf coast Olmec elite's continued emphasis on monumental art, extensive use of greenstone, and massive consumption of raw materials clearly distinguish them from the rest of Middle Formative Mesoamerica. For example, the Complex A excavations at La Venta (Drucker 1952: 36–79; Drucker, Heizer, and Squier 1959) uncovered secondary mounds surrounded by walls of massive upright basalt columns, a columnar basalt tomb, huge buried mosaic "supernatural masks," tremendous buried offerings of more than 100 tons each of imported serpentine blocks, cruciform greenstone celt offerings, greenstone figurines, and iron-ore mirrors. The lack of similar monumental buried offerings elsewhere in Mesoamerica should not be simplistically interpreted as a quantitative difference between a "more advanced" Olmec society and "less complex" others. A major factor to consider is that the Gulf coast Olmec had different conceptions than their counterparts of how social and cosmic order intermeshed, and how elite status was related to supernatural power (Gillespie 1992). The Late Middle Formative constructions and spectacular buried offerings at La Venta should be seen as a consequence of the Early Formative Gulf coast ideological trajectory that emphasized elite control over the importation of stone for ritual purposes on a truly public scale, as well as a preoccupation with the underworld as a source of supernatural power personally associated with the chiefs.

Several changes are notable in Middle Formative Olmec monumental art. Stelae appeared at about 700 B.C., most likely as a medium to communicate more narrative statements. Probable lineage references associated with the standing personages shown on La Venta's Stelae 2 and 3 appear as ancestral name motifs embedded in their tall headdresses. The embedded motif in the headdress on Stela 2 appeared several centuries earlier on Colossal Head 1, and the desire of the Stela 2 ruler to relate himself to that putative ancestor may explain the repositioning of Colossal Head 1 beside Stela 2 (Grove 1981b: 65–67). These data strongly suggest that the elite had made a further major achievement in the consolidation of their status: the successful transfer of office to a successor, most likely via a lineage tie. These transfers are characteristic of true chiefdoms

(Service 1975:293). Elite status, and the ability to contact infraworld forces, had thus become ascribed by that time.

Another significant change is the display on monuments of the chief holding new kinds of power objects as symbols of office. Recent iconographic analyses have suggested that many of those objects are associated with bloodletting (Andrews 1987; Grove 1987e; Joyce et al. 1990), part of a ritual complex which extends back in time to at least the Early Formative. Based on what is known for the Classic Maya (e.g., Schele and Miller 1986; Stuart 1984b), bloodletting was a means of communicating with ancestors and supernaturals. During the Early Formative, bloodletting was apparently carried out on a household level (Flannery and Marcus 1976b), indicating that any descent group could contact its ancestors and ask them to intercede with the supernaturals on behalf of their descendants. In the Middle Formative, however, although bloodletting continued at the household level, the elite seem to have taken some control of the ritual. They restricted for themselves the use of certain bloodletting instruments, including imported stingray spines and sharks' teeth, and introduced new perforator forms in greenstone. Some objects with bloodletting associations, such as "knuckle-dusters" and "torches," essentially became material symbols for chieftainship in monumental and portable art (Andrews 1987; Grove 1987e).

NON-OLMEC WESTERN MESOAMERICA

The continued lack of a stone monument tradition in non-Olmec Middle Formative period societies indicates that as they evolved in complexity, and though they interacted with the Olmec in pan-Mesoamerican exchange networks, they continued to maintain different means of manifesting the role of the elite in the cultural order, "uninfluenced" by Gulf coast beliefs. Despite the resulting anonymity of their chiefs, elite actions within those societies can be discerned in the archaeological record. Public mound architecture increased in quantity throughout the Middle Formative. Apart from the architectural sequence for the Valley of Oaxaca (Flannery and Marcus 1976a), however, its development in western Mesoamerica is still poorly understood.

One pattern is the widespread use of a basic template or layout of major public architecture: a large mound or pyramid facing a plaza (public space) that is flanked by one or two long, linear mounds. This pattern is found by ca. 700 B.C. on the Pacific coast of Chiapas (Love 1991); in the Chiapas highlands (Lowe 1977:fig. 9.4); on the Gulf coast at San

Lorenzo (Coe and Diehl 1980:map 2), La Venta (Drucker, Heizer, and Squier 1959:fig. 4), and Laguna de los Cerros (Bove 1978:map A); and in Oaxaca at San José Mogote (Flannery and Marcus 1976a:215). A variation of the template is also found at Chalcatzingo, Morelos, in the central highlands (Grove 1984:fig. 9; Prindiville and Grove 1987). Since the public architecture at those sites would have been planned and directed by the elite, the widespread occurrence of the shared template suggests that networks of elite interaction were in place. It also evidences the interregional sharing of ideological concepts and rituals involving the chief or his lineage, particularly because his and other elite residences were often within this precinct. Used in the cultural shaping of sacred space, this template may have been a model of the perceived cosmos (Lathrap 1985) within which chiefs displayed their pivotal roles.

Bloodletting was another widespread chiefly ritual activity in both non-Olmec and Olmec Mesoamerica, and bloodletting symbolism occurs on some of the greenstone objects (e.g., celts and perforators) used and controlled by chiefs in numerous Middle Formative societies.[6] Although non-Olmec societies appear to have held ideas about rulership that did not motivate representations in stone of the ruler in contact with supernaturals, their chiefs did serve as cosmic mediators via the blood they ritually sacrificed on behalf of their people. It is conceivable that this method of mediation, which focused attention on the sacred and powerful qualities of the chief, was attractive to emerging elites throughout Mesoamerica. Indeed, the portability of the bloodletting objects and iconography accessible via elite networks may have facilitated the transmission of that concept of chiefly power between many societies.

THE RESTRICTED SPREAD OF OLMEC IDEOLOGY

To this point we have argued that substantial archaeological evidence of Gulf coast Olmec "influence" on other societies is lacking, and we have interpreted the shared symbol systems, both nonelite (Early Formative) and elite (Middle Formative), as the material correlates of social processes more complex than simple "core-periphery diffusion." During the Middle Formative period, however, archaeological evidence is evident for the limited appearance of a distinctively Olmec trait—monumental art depicting elite personages—beyond the Gulf coast. This type of art appears at two groups or "chains" of sites. The first chain, in central Mexico, comprises the sites of Chalcatzingo, Morelos (Grove 1984, 1987a), and Teopantecuanitlan (Martínez Donjuan 1982, 1986) and Oxtotitlan (paintings) in

Guerrero (Grove 1970). The second chain, along the Pacific coast, consists of Pijijiapan, Chiapas (Navarrete 1969, 1974); Abaj Takalik, Guatemala (Graham 1982); and Chalchuapa, El Salvador (Boggs 1950; Sharer, ed. 1978). Based on the presence of narrative scenes and certain other stylistic traits, these monuments appear to date to the late Middle Formative or ca. 700–500 B.C. (Grove 1987b:426–30, 1989a), although Graham (1982) and Navarrete (1969, 1974) have proposed that some Pacific coast monuments are slightly earlier.

The sites listed above that have been intensively investigated were all found to have been important centers prior to the appearance of monumental art. They are located in regions with no previous stone-carving traditions, and their monuments incorporate some of the basic canons of Gulf coast Olmec art. Some differences in thematic content and iconography have led to the designation of their style as "frontier" (Grove 1984:109–10, 1987a:436; Grove and Kann 1980) to distinguish it from Gulf coast Olmec art. The major difference is that the frontier style frequently makes explicit concepts that were only implied on monuments at La Venta and San Lorenzo. This change is presumably due to a perceived need to communicate messages to an audience unfamiliar with the sociocosmic model for the "general order of existence"—at least as expressed via the new medium, monumental art.

There seems little doubt that the frontier monuments occur as the result of interaction between elites of the already established centers and those of the Gulf coast. The Middle Formative period witnessed the rise in complexity of numerous chiefdoms across western Mesoamerica. Archaeological survey data indicate a marked population increase, which would have created greater demands for both local and nonlocal resources. Source analysis data reveal ever-widening networks of resource acquisition. Grove (1984:161–64; 1987a:436–440) has therefore suggested that the appearance of Olmec-influenced art outside the Gulf coast may be tied to long-distance economic alliances. The frontier art phenomenon occurs along two corridors leading to important nonutilitarian resources apparently controlled by elites—greenstone (Guerrero) and cacao and jadeite (Chiapas-Guatemala coast)—and may represent the adoption of the Gulf coast ideology by the elites to verify these relationships.

The alliances introduced into those regions an alien ideology associated with conceptions of rulership, along with its material correlates. Ethnohistoric examples of similar alliances and the subsequent borrowing of iconography have been discussed by Helms (1979). Together with the appearance of the frontier art are the first depictions outside the Gulf coast of identifiable rulers in stone portraiture and, at Chalcatzingo, in ceramic figurines as well (Gillespie 1987; Grove 1987b: 423–24; Grove and Gillespie 1984). That ideology, requiring public displays of chiefs' portraits in stone or clay, was transitory, lasting perhaps only a century or two at these centers. Other regions, equally important and at equivalent levels of sociopolitical complexity, continued as before with essentially "anonymous" chiefs.

FORMATIVE PERIOD LEGACIES

Despite the acceptance at several central Mexican Middle Formative centers of a strikingly different ideology, the long-term impact of the Gulf coast–inspired conceptions relating chieftainship to the cosmology, along with its concomitant frontier-style art, was negligible. No monument tradition continued in central Mexico after the decline of Chalcatzingo and Teopantecuanitlan at the end of the Middle Formative, and later societies were apparently not motivated to maintain the portrayal in permanent media of identified rulers. Even the large public architecture at Late Formative central Mexican nucleated centers, such as Cuicuilco, is probably derived from roots other than the Chalcatzingo-Teopantecuanitlan manifestation. In the Late Formative period, monumental stone art became important in Oaxaca and on the Pacific coast, but it appears to lack any strong thematic continuity with earlier Gulf coast art. At Monte Albán, Oaxaca, the theme was conquest (Marcus 1976b, 1976c), and the Pacific coast monuments (e.g., Parsons 1986), including those of Izapa (Norman 1973), seem to lack the major Gulf coast focus on the identified ruler and his power symbols.

On the Gulf coast, chieftainship seems to have emerged from an earlier shamanic role as mediator with underworld forces. The chief's link to superhuman power was communicated via stone monuments, which also emphasized the idiosyncratic characteristics of the individual chiefs. In other societies, the ruler was not the focus for permanent public display, and thus their chiefs are anonymous. Yet they were probably just as important and powerful as their Olmec counterparts, and they may also have been viewed as mediators between the secular and sacred worlds. Their control over public labor is demonstrated by the creation of massive public architecture. Across Mesoamerica, pyramids and plazas emphasized and made permanent the setting aside of sacred space for elite use and provided for public participation (at least as spectators) in rituals that constructed and reinforced societal conceptions on the nature of rulership.

Those two disparate conceptual systems, models of a "general order of existence" motivating different expressions of the relationship of the ruler to supernatural power, were further elaborated in the Late Formative and succeeding periods. They thus may have served as ideological trajectories with determinative effects on the organization of the earliest states in Mesoamerica. The Classic period Maya developed further a conceptual system first manifested by the Olmec, stressing the identified ruler and his acts of kingship, which they then permanently fixed in time using hieroglyphic writing and the Long Count calendar. In contrast, the later central Mexican ideology of rulership and power as expressed in architecture and monumental art seems to have emphasized the sacred center (e.g., Monte Albán, Teotihuacan, Tenochtitlan) more than the sacred king.

─────── *Notes* ───────

1. Percentages are based on Pires-Ferreira (1975:table 3), which did not include Paredón ("Group A", Cobean et al. 1971), Orizaba, or unidentified sources in the calculations; thus, regional percentages are actually greater. Percentages and sources vary through time; see Cobean et al. (1971:table 1) and Boksenbaum et al. (1987:69, table 3).

2. Recent excavations at La Venta have discovered pre-Olmec occupations at that Olmec center as well (González Lauck 1988; Rust and Sharer 1988), although the data are not yet published.

3. An important observation by Porter (1989) indicates that at least two of San Lorenzo's colossal heads had been recarved from tabletop altars. He suggests that altar "mutilation" may have been the initial act of transforming an altar into a colossal head. This intriguing hypothesis does not account for all of the destruction suffered by altars or by the other types of stone monuments, but it does merit further testing.

4. Although some tabletop altars appear to be contemporaneous with the colossal heads in the Early Formative, there are reasons to believe that La Venta's two major altars, No. 4 and No. 5, as well as statues of persons holding supernatural babies, were carved in the Middle Formative period.

5. It is probably not coincidental that the first appearance throughout much of Mesoamerica of green obsidian from the Pachuca, Hidalgo, source correlates closely with the increasing utilization of greenstone beginning in the Middle Formative (Boksenbaum et al. 1987:table 3; Cobean et al. 1971:table 1).

6. The Middle Formative iconographic motifs, including those dealing with bloodletting, appear to be a further extension of the shared symbol system of the Early Formative. Each region of Mesoamerica manipulated and innovated that system in distinct ways, and presently its origins are not traceable to the Gulf coast Olmec.

3

MODELING THE ROLE OF IDEOLOGY IN SOCIETAL ADAPTATION

EXAMPLES FROM THE SOUTH AMERICAN DATA

DAVID J. WILSON

In these days of "postprocessual archaeology" it might seem somewhat foolhardy to argue that an ecologically informed systems-hierarchical model along lines similar to those proposed in the 1970s (e.g., Flannery 1972; Harris 1979; Rappaport 1971) might well provide the best means of hypothesizing about the critical role of ideology in the rise of complex irrigation-based societies. Indeed, given the virtual lack of any concrete Chavin-related iconography in the Cayhuamarca period system, the earliest complex society for which we currently have evidence in the Santa Valley on the north coast of Peru (Wilson 1983, 1987, 1988), it might seem wiser to focus on the iconographically rich areas of highland Chavin de Huantar or the coastal Nepeña and Casma valleys to examine the possible role of ideology in the development of societal complexity in the prehispanic central Andes.

Since 1979–80, the period of the Santa Valley Project fieldwork, I have switched my research focus to a settlement pattern study of the Casma Valley (and hope soon to publish preliminary results of this work). Nevertheless, for two reasons I shall concentrate in this chapter on the lower Santa Valley. First, Santa is a region about which arguments can be made for the overarching regulatory role of early ceremonial-civic centers and (presumably) ideology—in spite of the absence of the rich iconographies, such as those of Chavin (ca. 1000–350 B.C.) or Moche (ca. A.D. 400–650), which have given Andeanist scholars a basis for arguments about prehispanic ideology (e.g., for Chavin, see Burger 1988; Lathrap 1974, 1977, 1985; Patterson 1971; for Moche, see Donnan 1976;

Hocquenghem 1987). One cautionary note, however, concerns the danger of imputing content and function to an artifact or motif of presumed ideological nature and, in the end, making up "just so" stories about ancient systems of belief (e.g., see Yengoyan 1985 for a critique of Hodder 1982, 1983, ed. 1982). With this caveat in mind, I shall be more concerned here with a discussion of the possible systemic role of ideology than an attempt to get at its specific content.

Second, arguments have already been proposed by Lathrap in particular about the nature and role of tropical forest ideology in the development of Chavin culture, both in the highlands and on the coast. To attempt to add anything of substance to his provocative and often brilliant analyses surely would be foolhardy. Lathrap's work, especially, teaches us an important point: namely, that significant long-term cultural connections exist between the Amazonian lowlands and the Andean highlands as well as between these areas and the coast (see also Kroeber 1927 and Tello 1960 for examples of earlier arguments of a similar nature).

Recent work by other scholars emphatically underscores the importance for Andean archaeologists of knowing the ethnographic data from both the Amazonian lowlands and the Andean sierra. For example, in their use of ethnographic analogy based on current Aymara practices in the Bolivian high plains, Morrison (1978) and Reinhard (1987) have constructed the first really plausible arguments about the probable function of the lines and geoglyphs of the Nazca area. As another example, it seems apparent from a study of the Jivaro ethnographies (e.g., Harner 1973) that the preparation and cultural function of *tsantsa* trophy heads might well provide a cross-cultural basis for understanding similar trophy heads from the Early Intermediate period Nazca culture (ca. 350 B.C.– A.D. 700; Proulx 1971). A final intriguing example of probable strong connections in time and space involves the *vagina dentata* myths that establish part of the charter for relations between the sexes among some Amazonian groups (Sullivan 1988). A textile from the coast of Peru depicting a Chavin-related female staff god (fig. 3.1) clearly provides grounds for arguing that a similar myth existed at a very early time period in the central Andes. In sum, apparent parallels in myth and ideology connect prehispanic and traditional modern groups across broad geographic areas and through several thousand years of cultural development in South America.

Granted that these parallels exist, what has been lacking in the recent South Americanist literature is the use of systems-hierarchical models to construct an argument that an important mutual causal relationship exists

Figure 3.1. Painted textile with Chavin iconography, from the Ica Valley, Peru. (Redrawn from Roe 1974:fig. 14)

between ideology and other societal and environmental variables in cultural adaptive systems. I shall use selected examples from both the systems and the South Americanist literature to argue for the utility of a systems-hierarchical approach. It is important to emphasize at the outset that the following discussion is aimed more at throwing light on *how we think* about the functioning of adaptive systems than at attempting to "explain" once and for all just how a particular system really functioned. Indeed, it is probably the issue of explanation in ethnology and archaeology that has most soured many scholars toward accepting a systems-hierarchical approach as a useful heuristic device for carrying out analyses of anthropological data (e.g., Plog 1975). But, as we shall see in the case of the Yanomamö, the most useful discussions, whether by Chagnon (1973, 1977, 1979) or Harris (1975, 1977, 1979, 1984), usually involve arguments of complex mutual causation that imply or explicitly invoke a heuristic model of hierarchically organized variables.

It is not my intent in the following discussion to provide a complete review of the systems and South Americanist literature. Rather, I shall focus on those aspects of systems-hierarchical approaches that I have found most useful in thinking and teaching about the complexities of *possible* causal interrelationships in the systems of selected recent and ancient South American groups.

DEVELOPMENT OF A
SYSTEMS-HIERARCHICAL MODEL

One of the most useful, not to mention controversial, models proposed by an anthropologist in an attempt to make sense of causation and functioning in cultural systems is that of Harris. In his book *Cultural Materialism: The Struggle for a Science of Culture* (1979), Harris outlines the emic and etic complexities of a model (depicted in fig. 3.2) that makes several reasonably straightforward assertions. First, cultural systems can be usefully seen as composed of three hierarchical levels: infrastructure, structure, and superstructure. Second, these three levels are in turn composed of five basic subsystems: mode of production, mode of reproduction, domestic economy, political economy, and the superstructure. Third, the origins of critical aspects of the structural and (especially) the superstructural subsystems lie overwhelmingly in the infrastructure (for a similarly layered but much more complex model, see Rappaport 1971).

Using this model and a great variety of apparently supportive data, Harris has consistently argued that primary causation in all cultural systems is from the bottom up. Indeed, because of this assertion and what might be seen as the trivialization of superstructure through inclusion of such things as art, music, dance, literature, and advertising, many ideologically oriented anthropologists find it easy to reject Harris's cultural-materialist perspective outright. In this sense, then, Harris's model of primary causation has to be modified to be acceptable to anthropologists who see causation either as entirely top-down or in the mutual interplay between higher and lower levels in a system, with ideology or "ultimate sacred postulates" (Rappaport 1979) acting as critical regulatory variables in systemic functioning. Other drawbacks of Harris's model involve the exclusion of the physical and social environments at any specific level in

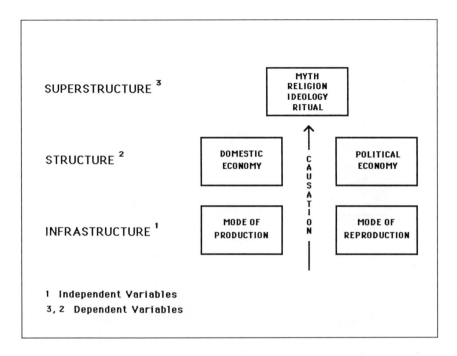

Figure 3.2. Model depicting Harris's cultural materialist theory of a human adaptive system.

the system, although presumably infrastructure either includes the physical environment or acts (*sensu* Steward 1955; cf. Netting 1968) as a point of interaction, or interface, between the environment and higher levels of the cultural system.

In my opinion, among the most useful features of Harris's model are (1) the assertion that no model of a cultural system can exclude consideration of both the physical environment and subsistence adaptations to it; (2) the limited number of critical subsystem variables it postulates, thus potentially keeping analysis from becoming totally counterintuitive (never mind that "real" systems probably are); and (3) its specificity in naming the subsystem variables.

In his classic paper on "The Cultural Evolution of Civilizations," Flannery (1972) provides what is certainly the best known counterargument to Harris's latter-day version of the technologically and infrastructurally focused bottom-up models of Marx and Steward. As shown in figure 3.3, Flannery's model is hierarchical, like Harris's, but convincingly argues that causation is complex and circular; in other words,

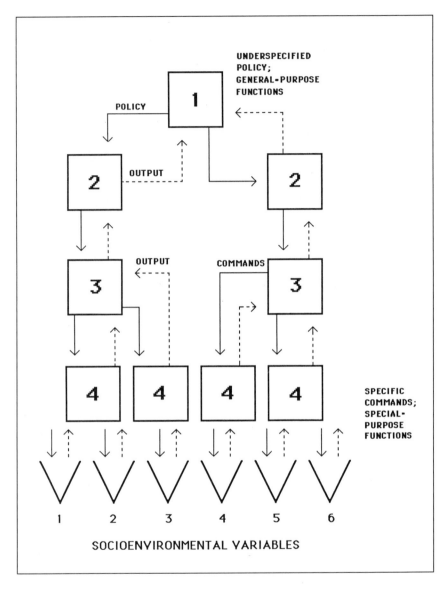

Figure 3.3. Flannery's generalized systems-hierarchical model.

it potentially involves the causal primacy of a variable or variables at any level in a system. Moreover, in terms of the day-to-day functioning of a given system at a single point in time, it is as important to understand the role of top-down policy and regulation as it is to know what the environment is like and how people get their food (the bottom-up, or "output," part of the model).

Another important feature of Flannery's model is the assertion that we must understand not only how a culture adapts to its organic and inorganic physical setting but also how it maintains equilibrium or adapts through feedback and change to aspects of its social environment. In a very real sense "ecology" thus becomes more than just counting calories or focusing on Harris's "guts, wind, sex, and energy"; rather, it also includes an examination of how a cultural system adjusts to and regulates all critical aspects of both its social and its physical environments. Indeed, the single drawback of this useful model may be its lack of specificity in the labeling of component variables at the various levels in the system. It is one thing to be convinced that complex cultural systems are ordered as shown in figure 3.3 and quite another to actualize the model and apply it to the study and analysis of the real-world systems in which we are interested.

Figure 3.4 illustrates the most recent version of my ongoing attempt not only to bring together the best features of Harris's and Flannery's models, but also to add several features to the model not present in either of the two earlier ones. As in Harris's model, the three basic levels of infrastructure, structure, and superstructure are present and the names of the component variables at each of these levels are specified. As in Flannery's model, the mutual causation among all levels is specified in terms of policy and output. Following Flannery, both the physical and social environments are included, but, rather than being specified as V_1, V_2, etc., they are separated, with physical environment shown as the underlying aspect of cultural infrastructure and social environment indicated at the edge of the model. Following Steward's work, I have added settlement pattern to the upper part of infrastructure to take into account site distributions in relation to the physical and social environments. (For example, for cultural ecologists, site distributions of Amazonian interriverine groups should be dispersed, with a hostile intersite social environment representing an important aspect of adaptation to a protein-scarce physical environment.)

Following assertions of such systems theorists as Rappaport and Flannery, I have added both ritual and leadership to the model to indicate

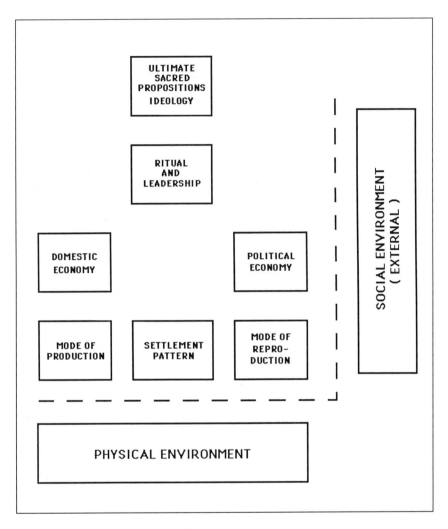

Figure 3.4. The model proposed in this paper, combining elements of models by Harris, Flannery, and others.

specific real-world activities involving system regulation. These concrete regulatory activities are seen as being informed in a very critical and real sense, however, by ultimate sacred propositions (to use Rappaport's term, *ultimate sacred postulates*) or by ideology in a general sense.

Although a systems-hierarchical model has utility in that it provides a theoretical basis for hypothesis testing in the field, as implied earlier in this paper I think it is equally useful as an intellectual and pedagogic tool for analyzing arguments in the literature about both recent and prehistoric groups. Does this mean that use of the model somehow miraculously changes our old "linear" arguments into beautifully circular systemic arguments about causation and functioning? I would emphatically argue that it does not. And yet, as we shall see presently, some of the best arguments about causation among ecosystemic variables of cultural adaptive systems ultimately suggest this type of "circular" causation—the ultimate result of which, I think, imparts to the investigator a sense that *explanation* is perhaps indeed being achieved in addition to mere description. I speak here as a reasonably unrepentant positivist. In other words, following Harris, I believe that it is possible to achieve not only mere description of a system but limited problem-specific explanation as well. (I shall not go further into this issue here, except to note that adequate achievement of description and explanation must surely involve proper choice of field methods in the context of hypotheses generated from overarching anthropological theory.)

APPLICATION OF THE MODEL
TO THE YANOMAMÖ CASE

A student in one of the anthropology classes I taught some years ago at the University of Michigan-Flint once told a nutritionist friend that, using Chagnon's data and Harris's arguments about that data, her professor was arguing for a clear connection between the nature of a group's nutrition, warfare, and ultimate sacred propositions about relations between the sexes. The nutritionist could not believe that this "you are what you eat" argument could be made, but then, of course, he had neither read Chagnon and Harris on the Yanomamö nor had he been exposed to the complex chains of (usually linear) causation that are part and parcel of systems-hierarchical reasoning.

Harris's (1975, 1977, 1984) version of Chagnon's argument about the Yanomamö is illustrated in figure 3.5, using the composite model outlined in the preceding section. Harris asserts that Chagnon argues for a chain of causation involving a top-down (and therefore totally misguided, in Harris's opinion) account of why the Yanomamö go to war and how this behavior affects other aspects of their society. Although the issue of Chagnon's argument is now somewhat clouded by the fact that he has become a sociobiologist (e.g., Chagnon 1979), one has to agree with Harris in terms of his basic assertions.

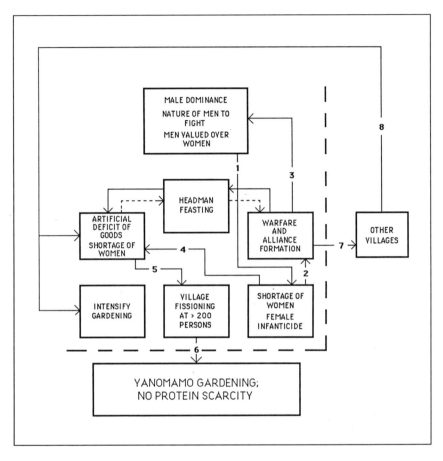

Figure 3.5. Model of Harris's characterization of Chagnon's top-down argument about the Yanomamö.

In any case, according to Harris the argument starts at the level of ideology, which reinforces male dominance over women, the inherent nastiness and fierceness of men, and the greater value men have over women in society. This ideology "causes" (see "1" in fig. 3.5) the shortage of women through preferential female infanticide, which then brings about the need ("2" in the model) both for raids to obtain more women and for alliance formation to protect the allies against the raided groups and other enemies. This behavior further reinforces ideology ("3"), which closes the loop.

The shortage of women causes not only fights over women (in the

category of "domestic economy") but also the creation of artificial shortages of goods, which makes alliance formation with other villages necessary ("4" in the figure). Fights over women lead among other things ("5")
to village fissioning (in the "settlement pattern" category). Artificial shortages, in turn, lead to a need to intensify gardening. Village fissioning, on
the other hand, keeps the Yanomamö from creating protein scarcities (i.e.,
overhunting) in the subsistence environment ("6" in fig. 3.5). The upshot
of Chagnon's argument, according to Harris, is that the entire Yanomamö
system is not an adaptation to anything infrastructural; rather it represents a system driven by (rather peculiar) ideological beliefs.

Harris's own arguments about the Yanomamö can be understood by
reference to the model shown in figure 3.6. The ultimate cause of the
Yanomamö system that Chagnon describes becomes the result of a *deus*

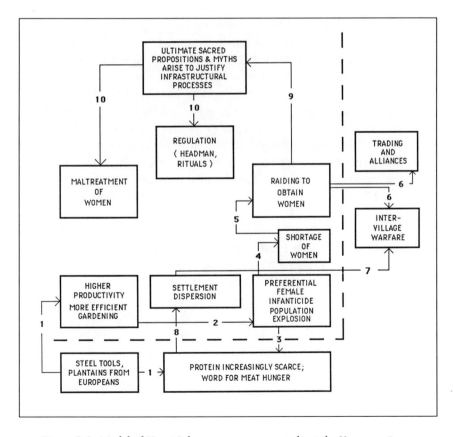

Figure 3.6. Model of Harris's bottom-up argument about the Yanomamö.

ex machina introduction to the Yanomamö area from the outside world of steel machetes and plantains. This addition to the technology and subsistence base brought about higher productivity and more efficient gardening, and it directly degraded the environment as well. Changes in the mode of production, in turn, have created a population explosion, which has resulted in protein scarcity. This explosion (acting through protein scarcity, although not indicated on the model) thus brought about the need for preferential female infanticide, the only really effective way to control population growth. The resulting shortage of women creates a need for both raiding some villages and forming alliances with others. As figure 3.6 indicates, the chain of causation goes on, causing further changes in other variables. The upshot of Harris's version of the Yanomamö, in any case, is that all system variables at the level of structure and superstructure are ultimately dependent on what is happening at the level of infrastructure. In specific terms, then, protein scarcity has brought about the creation of an ideology that values men over women and reinforces the nasty, chauvinist treatment that men mete out to the women. In this argument infrastructure thus takes total precedence over the higher levels of the Yanomamö cultural system.

The "democratic" way to resolve the dilemma about what really causes the Yanomamö to be the way they are is to view both Harris's bottom-up and Chagnon's top-down arguments as valid. Causation in this case is an interplay between higher-order and lower-order variables. Indeed, Harris's argument works well to explain the *origins* of the Yanomamö predicament, whereas Chagnon's argument shows how ideology helps to regulate and justify their adaptive behavior. An equally important point to make, however, is that the model helps to explain the two rather complex arguments that Chagnon and Harris make about causation in Yanomamö society. Even more important is that ideology seems clearly and significantly connected to lower-order variables in both arguments, irrespective of where the chain of causation starts.

Thus, if nothing else, we may draw two conclusions from the data on one of the best-studied indigenous groups in South America: (1) it is not possible to understand a group in the absence of information about its ideology; and (2) however complex the relationships between ideology and other societal variables, there is clearly a mutually causative chain of relationships among all systemic variables, including ideology. To the extent that ideology is a regulating and reinforcing variable, it cannot therefore be seen as an epiphenomenon.

Whether this last statement is, as I suspect, true for all groups in South

America and other areas of the world is not as important as the conclusion that the role of ideology in societal functioning thus has become an empirical question. Its adaptive role cannot therefore be rejected out of hand. Indeed, in a general sense the use of a systems-hierarchical model may provide more convincing proof of ideology's adaptive role (either to students or to cultural-materialist doubters) than a complex verbal argument involving realms of text but no graphic representation of the chain of causation. As stated earlier, the value of these models therefore probably lies more in the realm of explaining a researcher's argument than in providing the ultimate explanation of why people behave the way they do.

APPLICATION OF THE MODEL
TO THE NORTH COAST OF PERU

Both the materialist and the social aspects of the model proposed in the preceding section make it logical to begin the discussion of the role of ideology in the Santa Valley area with a brief overview of reconstructed aspects of the physical and social environments (see Wilson 1983, 1987, 1988 for more detailed support for this reconstruction). All valleys along the Peruvian littoral consist of narrow oases entirely dependent on the water that flows down from the adjacent Andean cordillera. Figure 3.7 shows that each of the valleys in the lower Santa region is separated from neighboring ones by stretches of desert ranging from 15 to 25 kilometers wide; the valleys are also separated from habitable sections of the Andes by comparable distances involving at least one or two days' hard walk.

Although the prehispanic people of each valley thus lived in essential isolation from neighboring valleys, we have good archaeological evidence for continual interaction between valleys. This interaction appears to have included possible trade with areas to the north and east (based primarily on strong similarities among the ceramic assemblages of Santa, Viru, and the adjacent Callejón de Huaylas in the periods prior to the Moche state, or before ca. A.D. 400) and probable warfare with areas to the south (an argument based on data discussed below, as well as on strong dissimilarities between the Santa assemblages and those of valleys to the south in the pre-state period).

As in the Yanomamö villages, basic subsistence items and most other resources potentially available in each of these valleys were probably quite similar. It is therefore difficult to surmise what might have caused the apparently peaceful relations between the Santa and valleys to the north. It is possible, however, that inhabitants of Santa Valley needed allies in

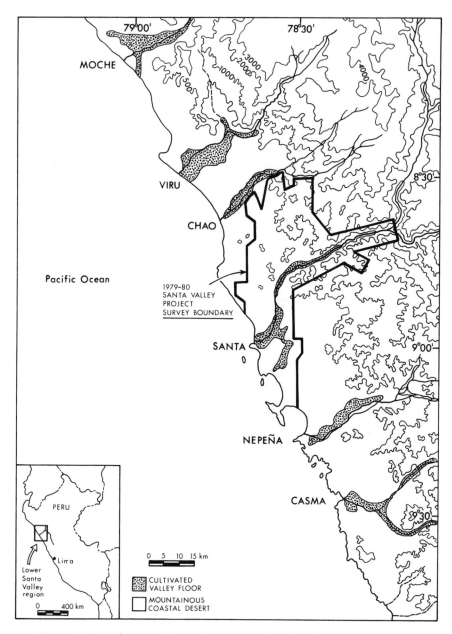

Figure 3.7. *North coast of Peru, showing Santa and nearby valleys.*

the face of conflict with villages to the south. Indeed, since we know that the Yanomamö artificially create scarcities to bring about the necessity for intervillage trading and alliances, it is possible that the inhabitants of Santa Valley and their apparent allies to the north specialized in similar ways to bring about a context for interaction. If so, then surely this interaction was reinforced by appropriate ideologies just as is the case with the Yanomamö.

It is less difficult to suggest possible reasons for conflict between the Santa Valley and valleys to the south. Because of its deep penetration into the Andes, the Santa River provides on a year-round basis more than ten times the amount of water necessary to irrigate all cultivable land. In sharp contrast, each of the other valleys of the area penetrates much less deeply into the cordillera and consequently has much lower average volumes of seasonal water flow. Moreover, modern studies show that the water regime in these rivers is often unpredictably erratic. Thus, given the population growth that characterizes all of these valleys in the pre-state periods (e.g., see Willey 1953 on Viru; Proulx 1973 on Nepeña), the low, erratic seasonal flow in these other valleys may have been occasionally inadequate to raise enough crops to feed all the people in the valley. Indeed, we know from modern studies in the Viru Valley (Holmberg 1952) that a body of ritual and ideology is focused on the anxiety connected with potential fluctuations in maize productivity.

From all these considerations, I have therefore argued (Wilson 1987, 1988) that the strong difference in water regimes between the Santa and other valleys provides the best context in which to understand the warfare that clearly occurred in the earliest part of the sequence (the issue of the nature of this warfare, whether internecine or interregional, is discussed below; unfortunately we do not yet have data to suggest why the Santa did not experience conflict as well with the water-scarce valleys to the north). For a society in another valley that was experiencing a food "pinch" (e.g., because of inadequate food storage to protect the inhabitants from an unpredictable lean period), the Santa would have been an attractive focus of continual raiding.

Elsewhere (1987, 1988) I have discussed in detail the conclusions of my analysis of the pre-state settlement data in the Santa Valley. Since these conclusions are critical for reconstructing the nature of pre-state ideology in the valley, it is useful to summarize them briefly. The settlement data from each of the four pre-state ceramic periods (only the first and last of the four are illustrated here) provide strong support for the assertion that warfare occurred throughout this long period between ca. 1000 B.C. and

A.D. 400. Indeed, a variety of data suggests not only that warfare was endemic but that it was always interregional, not internecine. These data include the following: (1) each Santa Valley pre-state period is characterized by numerous widespread fortresses; (2) the great majority of fortresses and settlements are located on hills of the more easily defended middle and upper valley areas; (3) the settlement groupings of each period are almost all sharply different in estimated population numbers, thus disallowing the "balance of power" necessary for continual warfare to occur without ending quickly in conquest; (4) pottery assemblages among most settlement groups are quite similar, suggesting strong within-valley socioeconomic interaction; and (5) study of the modern traditional canal network of Santa and nearby valleys indicates that the subsistence infrastructure of local groups could not long have existed (certainly not during the entire 1000-year pre-state sequence) in the context of continual within-valley hostilities.

None of this host of empirical evidence against the "coercive theory" of pre-state internecine warfare, however, has yet convinced Carneiro and his followers that pre-state warfare did not occur among neighbors and kin in the same valley (e.g., Carniero 1988; Roscoe and Graber 1988). I cannot outline in detail the arguments against the coercive theory here, but I will make several observations in the spirit of the ecological focus of this paper. First of all, it is hard to imagine more different infrastructural systems than that of Amazonian groups reliant on extensive subsistence techniques involving slash-and-burn agriculture and that of coastal Peruvian groups focused on irrigation canal networks connecting most areas of a valley. The former adaptation selects for widely scattered villages, village autonomy, intervillage warfare, and often an ideology of hostility to other villages. The latter adaptation selects for concentrated groupings of villages, supravillage coordination of defense and subsistence activities, intervillage neutrality (if not peace), and as argued below, an ideology of local and valleywide cooperation.

Surely, if nothing else, ecological anthropology and the systems-hierarchical model discussed in this paper tell us that different infrastructures (i.e., Amazonian slash-and-burn vs. coastal Peruvian irrigation) will lead inevitably to different kinds of societal systems and different kinds of warfare. The point is that, although Amazonian (and Andean) ethnology may tell us a lot about what ancient coastal societies and their ideology might have been like, the specific nature of the prehispanic coastal adaptation is an empirical question not necessarily subject to arguments based on conditions obtaining solely in a tropical rain forest context.

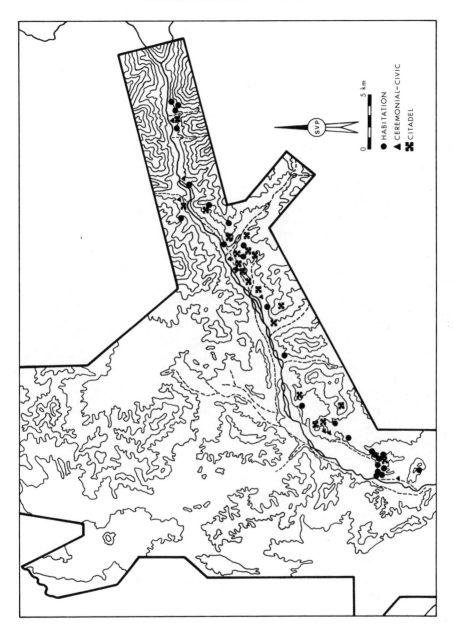

Figure 3.8. Settlement pattern map of the Cayhuamarca period system (ca. 1000–350 B.C.).

If we assume that the external politics providing part of the pre-state adaptive context of Santa Valley involved continual raids by valleys to the south, and apparently a resulting need to have allies to the north, it is interesting to examine the settlement patterns of two of the four pre-Moche periods with a view toward constructing arguments about the systemic role of ideology. As figure 3.8 indicates, a very interesting settlement pattern occurs in the Cayhuamarca period (ca. 1000–350 B.C.), the first system in the sequence characterized by agricultural subsistence. As mentioned, fortresses are found essentially everywhere in the system. Moreover, both these sites and the numerous habitation sites tend to be located at substantial distances from the valley floor. In sharp contrast, ceremonial-civic centers (fig. 3.9) are found in fewer numbers and either on the valley floor or near it. In addition, each of the principal site groupings has at least one ceremonial-civic center.

The fact that these centers are few, evenly distributed, and associated with every settlement grouping—not just in the Cayhuamarca period but in every other pre-state period as well (e.g., fig. 3.10)—suggests that supravillage coordination was necessary both in local domestic activities

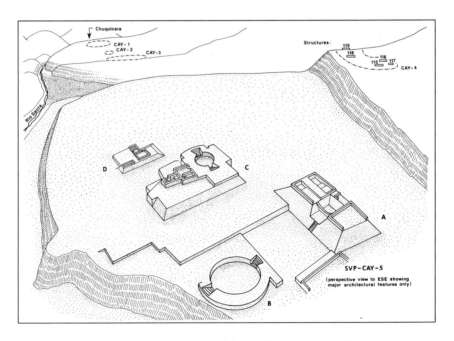

Figure 3.9. Ceremonial-civic center of the Cayhuamarca period, showing nearby sites in the uppermost valley.

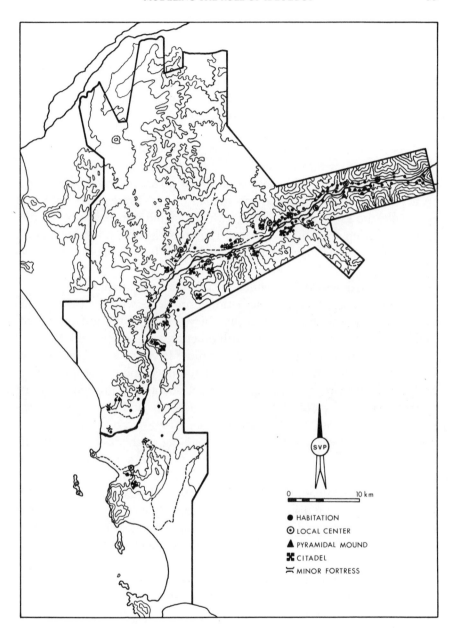

Figure 3.10. Settlement pattern map of the Late Suchimancillo period system (ca. A.D. 200–400).

and to defend against continual raids by hostile valleys to the south. Structures of a probable civic and religious nature, including circular sunken courts and pyramidal platforms, are usually among the main features found at these centers. As mentioned earlier, we did not find on these sites the rich body of iconographic symbols that characterizes the pottery and architecture of other nearby areas.

What, then, can we reconstruct of the ideology of this pre-state system? As summarized in figure 3.11, we can establish the nature of the physical context: a narrow oasis valley surrounded by unusable desert, with an ample year-round water supply that provided predictable crops on a year-to-year basis. Valleys to the north and south probably were essentially the same as the Santa, with the significant exception of the sharply differing availability of water. The unpredictable water regimes of other valleys may not have enabled adequate production of crops for storage, however, and the sociopolitical context may quickly have become one of continual hostilities in which the other valleys attempted to control Santa Valley as a way to mitigate periodic problems with their own food supplies. These hostilities in turn may have required the inhabitants of Santa Valley to establish alliances with other areas.

Because population growth was continual in Santa as well as nearby valleys, the context was set not only for the development of intervalley warfare but also for a corresponding local adaptation involving supravillage coordination of defensive activities. In addition, population numbers were already higher than could be supported by one local agricultural system if everyone lived in just one big, highly defended site. It was thus necessary to disperse to the extent possible, yet not too far from the forts. Thus, an additional function of local ceremonial centers probably involved coordination of subsistence activities as well as allocation of land and (perhaps) redistribution of foodstuffs. Given the nature of the settlement hierarchy and the presence of more formal dwellings on some sites (including the ceremonial centers), it is likely that a chiefly elite developed as early as the Cayhuamarca period.

We may hypothesize, then, that the ideology of the pre-state Santa Valley developed out of a structural and infrastructural context involving the need to cooperate with neighbors, make alliances with some valleys, and engage in conflicts with others. The archaeological data thus tell us a great deal about the infrastructural and structural contexts for the development of ideology: namely, that both local cooperative activities and external conflict (and possibly alliances) probably were occurring. If the systems-hierarchical model and ethnographic data on the clear

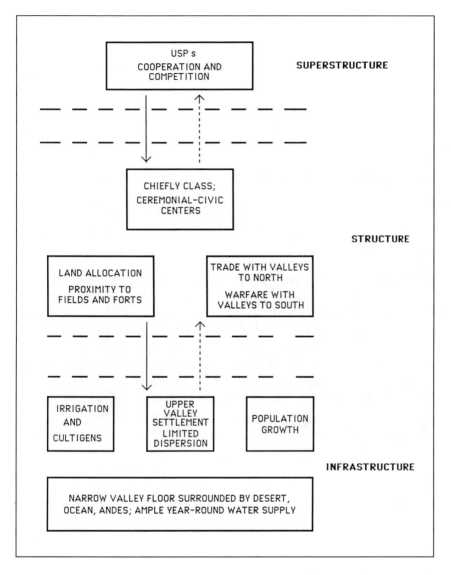

Figure 3.11. Model of the pre-state Santa Valley, showing hypothesized general causal relationships between levels in the subsistence-settlement hierarchy (USP = ultimate sacred propositions).

connection between ideology and lower-order variables mean anything, then, we can infer that local ideologies of valleys like Santa involved loving your neighbors, tolerating your allies, and hating your enemies. The architectural facilities at ceremonial centers must have been developed primarily with the idea of fostering these feelings and adaptive activities. We thus can say something quite significant about the nature of even this earliest of prehispanic ideologies. We cannot, however, say anything about the specific kinds of iconographic symbols that reinforced these notions. Nevertheless, the centers themselves clearly are the symbols of an overarching ideology worked out to help people to survive and prosper in an increasingly complex and difficult world.

It is appropriate to close this discussion of North Coast ideology with a brief overview of the first period of multivalley state formation in Santa and other nearby valleys. If pre-state ideologies and activities were local, or valleywide, prior to state formation, then the rise of the Moche state represents the first period in the sequence when not only external conquest occurs but an external ideology is imposed as well. As figure 3.12 shows, the settlement pattern of the Guadalupito period (ca. A.D. 400–650) illustrates the results of this conquest: in contrast to the primarily upper valley–oriented and heavily defended system of the pre-state periods, settlements now are located mostly in the more productive and easily farmed lower valley area. No defensive facilities are present.

The largest center to this point in the sequence is constructed on the north side of the valley mouth, and it contains the two largest pyramidal mounds built during any period in the entire prehispanic sequence. Secondary centers are distributed throughout the valley, and one of them (El Castillo; Wilson 1988) was covered with murals depicting militaristic iconography that I have argued was aimed at serving the ideology of the Moche state: namely, to ensure that potential recalcitrants at the local level were constantly aware of the dangers of rising up in rebellion against it.

A pottery vessel from the Santa Valley made in the Moche style (fig. 3.13) commemorates the state's taking of prisoners, presumably from one of the provincial valleys like Santa or perhaps one farther to the south (it is hard to imagine that a local potter would commemorate the conquest of Santa itself given the long-standing tradition of fiercely defending its autonomy). In any case, for the first time in the sequence one sees the clear imposition of an ideology that is external to the local adaptive system: In fact, I suspect that the state cared very little about the ecological integrity of the provincial systems that local ideology and ritual had maintained intact for 1400 years. One sign of this indifference is the massive

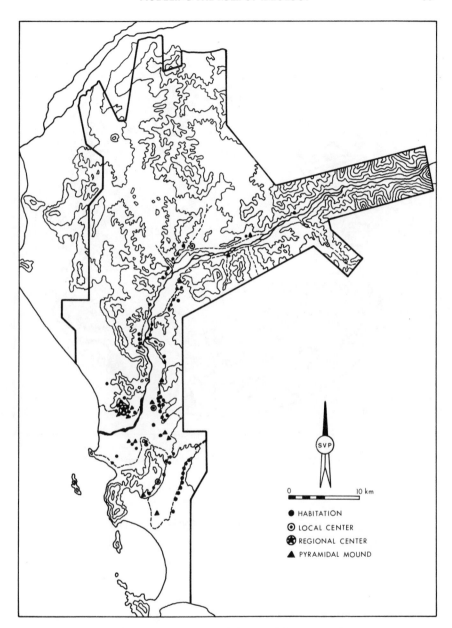

Figure 3.12. Settlement pattern map of the Guadalupito (Moche) system
(ca. A.D. 400–650).

*Figure 3.13. Moche iconography on a flaring funerary bowl from the Santa
Valley.*

build-up of settlements and population all along the desert margins of the
lower Santa Valley, which I have argued represents the Moche state's
policy of extracting the maximum productivity possible out of the provinces, irrespective of the danger of oversalinization (which may well have
occurred as indicated by the settlement pattern of the following Early
Tanguche period, which is primarily middle-valley focused; Wilson 1988).

To conclude this section, one aspect of long-term continuity in central
Andean traditions that supports assertions about local cooperative activities in prehispanic times should be mentioned. Work on individual land-
holdings today in traditional parts of the central Andes is carried out in
the context of the institution of *ayni,* or mutual assistance (Mishkin 1946).

When an individual needs help in fields or with domestic activities, nearby neighbors will join in to help with the expectation not only that they will be given food, drink, and coca for their efforts but that, when the time comes, the individuals they have helped will return the favor. In many areas of the central Andes, local cooperative projects—such as road building or canal cleaning—are carried out by all able-bodied workers for the good of the entire community (e.g., for the Viru, see Holmberg 1950). Given the widespread nature of this tradition in coastal and highland Peru, and the assertions about the continuity of important institutions presented above, an argument of local cooperation in any coastal Peruvian valley from the very start of agriculture is not without substantial merit. These institutions could not be maintained without an appropriate ideology, or "ultimate sacred propositions" to reinforce it, as has been argued for the prehispanic Santa Valley. Indeed, the long-standing presence of this type of institution provides further reasons to question the "coercive" argument that neighbor fought neighbor in the same local valley in ancient times.

We also know that the Inca cleverly took advantage of the widespread central Andean tradition of *ayni* through the institution of *mit'a,* which involved in a sense a "command performance" for local laborers to report for duty on a corvée project. The state, in turn, created a sort of fictive reciprocity by "wining and dining" these laborers while they were forced to work (Rowe 1946). The research of the Chan Chan–Moche Valley Project (Moseley 1975) has made it clear that the same *mit'a* principle was involved in building the huge adobe-brick pyramids at the Moche capital, specifically as evidenced by columns containing adobes with discrete sets of maker's marks on them. The fact that the adobes were marked seems clearly to indicate that Moche state labor principles grew out of a previously existing tradition of *ayni*-type local cooperation and reciprocity. Indeed, the adobes with maker's marks we found atop the main pyramid of the Moche state in Santa Valley also suggest that Santa had similar long-standing pre-state traditions of *ayni* cooperation and, of course, a corresponding ideology.

SUMMARY AND CONCLUSIONS

I have attempted to show that reconstruction of the ideology of emerging complex prehispanic societies can be carried out effectively within the context of reference to (1) local and continental ethnographic data, (2) explicit use of a systems-hierarchical heuristic, and (3) appropriate archaeological data. In South America, as in many other areas of the world, substantial cross-cultural continuity of institutions and belief systems is evident through time and across space. Archaeologists should therefore study the relevant ethnographic data to discover additional illuminating parallels between ethnographic and archaeological data. Moreover, reference to the ethnographic data is especially important because it probably affords the best chance of showing that important adaptive connections do exist between lower-order variables and the higher-order ideology of a cultural system—and of showing that causality may be a two-way street involving interaction among various systemic variables.

I have also argued that explicit use of a systems-hierarchical approach provides perhaps the best way of convincingly demonstrating that these adaptive connections exist, since they usually are not directly apparent. They often involve interaction through one or many intervening variables, at least as "chains of causation" are presented in arguments in the literature. Another important point should be made about the use of these models: namely, we must not throw out the systems "baby" with the nonexplanatory "bath water" that is usually considered to accompany it, because these heuristic devices do help us to understand complex arguments about the origins and functioning of variables in a cultural adaptive system.

At the same time, use of these models is the best way to make a case for the causal interplay between both higher-order and lower-order variables; that is, their use makes it clear that causation is neither just bottom-up nor all top-down. Indeed, since we will probably never be able to quantify (let alone qualify) satisfactorily the causal importance of a variable at any single hierarchical level, nor will it be easy to identify the starting point of a "loop of causation," it seems better to fall back on the democratic assertion that causation is equally top-down and bottom-up. We must be ecological anthropologists/archaeologists, not cultural materialists (bottom-uppers) or symbol-oriented ideologists (top-downers).

Systems-hierarchical models are thus our best chance of achieving cross-cultural and processual explanation since, in studying and attempting to relate traditional modern and prehistoric adaptations, we surely are dealing with ecosystems and their growth, maintenance, regulation, and demise. Anyone who reads the classic literature in ecology will be convinced that causality is systemic, circular, and hierarchical, and that it also involves trying to deal messily in most real-world cases with a huge variety of different kinds of data.

I am convinced that the application of an ethnologically informed, systems-hierarchical model to the data from Santa Valley and its neighbors makes clearer than mere reference to archaeological data how important the emergence of ceremonial centers was in the earliest agricultural systems of coastal valleys. Ceremonial centers in these systems represent a concrete manifestation of the rise of both supravillage coordinative and regulatory activities and, I think in a very real sense, the corresponding ideologies necessary to survive in a world that increasingly involved making very complex choices about cooperation and conflict. Given the great time depth of the Andean institutions of reciprocity—ecologically adaptive at the local level and fictive, but state-maintaining, at the interregional level—it comes as no surprise that some pre-state coastal valley chiefdoms had developed an ideology of local cooperation from the start of agriculture.

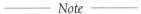 *Note*

I am indebted to students in several seminars on state origins, especially Susan Garrett and James Kendrick, for suggestions in developing the systems-hierarchical model presented in this paper. John Harris, another graduate student in our department, kindly spent a number of hours designing the systems graphics on his computer from my rather rough sketches. Finally, I wish to thank several anonymous reviewers who forced me to realize that the first version of this paper needed substantial revision; I hope that following their suggestions has made this final version more explicit in terms of my thinking about the role of ideology in the earliest complex adaptive systems. Nevertheless, having read and reread much of the current nonecological (top-down) literature on reconstructing prehistoric ideology, I remain convinced of the utility of the more explicitly programmatic approach of systems-hierarchical thinking.

4

ECONOMY, IDEOLOGY, AND IMPERIALISM IN THE SOUTH-CENTRAL ANDES

ALAN L. KOLATA

> . . . economic conditions are merely a contributing
> factor to historical developments; human psychology
> is another factor, and even both together cannot
> supply more than statistical laws for the evolution of
> human society. . . . The empiricist knows that the
> chance elements can never be completely eliminated
> from historical occurrences and that it excludes a
> strict predictability even of major historical trends.
> Hans Reichenbach,
> *The Rise of Scientific Philosophy*

More than five decades ago, Sorokin (1941) characterized the differences between the philosophical principles of medieval and postmedieval Western society in terms of the contrast between "ideational" and "sensate," or materialist, frames of reference. The ideational culture, according to Sorokin (1941:19–21), acknowledges the existence of a "supersensory reality" beyond the immediately observable, whereas the sensate culture recognizes only that "the true reality and value is sensory."

This classificatory contrast in philosophical principles played out in Western intellectual history succinctly encapsulates the distinction in fundamental postulates that separates the ideational from the materialist paradigms in contemporary anthropology. Both seek to explain stability and change in the evolution of human culture. The ideational paradigm, in effect, claims that the mental templates of humans generated by endless chains of individual, actor-based decisions, whether idiosyncratic or prescribed by ethnic or group interests, play essential roles in promoting behaviors that enhance survival and reproduction. Therefore, proponents of this approach argue that these mental templates must be incorporated into any general theory of culture change (see Kehoe 1975 for an argument to this effect).

The sensate or materialist paradigm, on the other hand, seeks to define the causal agents that promote or inhibit social reproduction solely within the material and biological conditions of life. Price (1982: 709), a vigorous advocate of the materialist position, characterizes the contrast between these competing paradigms in a similar fashion: "Idealist paradigms, in their most general form, presume that behavior is caused by ideas, beliefs, values, cognitions, and comparable mental templates; explanation of behavior must therefore be stated in terms of these parameters. Materialism by contrast affirms that the causes of behavior are most parsimoniously sought with consistent reference to the material conditions of life." Price (1982: 710) comments, with respect to the materialist position, "by direct deduction from the paradigm, material processes and phenomena are held to be preeminently implicated in the causation of similarity and difference, stability and change."

According to the somewhat austere program of the cultural materialists, belief systems, ideas, values, and cognitive categories in themselves rank rather near the bottom in the hierarchy of causal agents that explain human behavior. Mostly these mental templates are relegated to the class of epiphenomenal entailments of human behavior that, according to the committed materialist, is generated fundamentally by the interaction between processes of [Darwinian] natural selection and the technoeconomy of production. The material conditions of life, the technology and social organization of production, and the dynamics of population biology essentially define the significant explanatory universe of the materialist paradigm.

Given the apparent dialectical nature of intellectual inquiry, it should not be surprising that in recent years a significant and growing number of archaeologists have begun to recoil from the perceived uncompromising reductionism of the unalloyed materialist program (Bender 1978; Conrad 1981; Conrad and Demarest 1984; Hodder 1982; among others). Although the intellectual backlash against materialism has taken various eclectic shapes, certain pivotal, shared themes form the armature of what I have termed here the ideational paradigm. Ideationalists (my shorthand portmanteau term of convenience for materialist counterparts) maintain uniformly that we can no longer sustain a methodological justification for constricting the meaning of empiricism to direct sensory perception, that is, to the directly observable. This sally across the decks of positivism, the principal philosophical strut of the materialist method, derives its motive force from the notion that human culture is grounded in symbolic processes that are meaningfully constituted and ultimately determined by an underlying programmatic framework of rules and codes: the deep-seated, perduring mental schemata of biologically successful human populations.

The goal of the ideationalists is precisely to investigate these symbolic processes, which, they maintain, hold adaptive significance for humans, through the analysis of their external cultural manifestations in palpable, ordered sets of symbols and forms of social relationships. In this regard, Kehoe (1975:6) trenchantly comments: "symbols themselves are concrete—available to sense perception—while their associative linkages are thoroughly abstract and multivalent."

These "thoroughly abstract," multivalent, associative deep-structure features of human culture reveal themselves not through the method of direct observation, but through the systematic comparison of the content, context, and transformation of correlative symbolic sets. As Kehoe (1975:5) emphasizes, quoting Edwin Ardener (1971:459), "the bringing of one system into relationship with another by transformational links is the nearest thing available to testing. . . . In zones where positivism cannot reach, the testing of system against system is the only hope for advance."

The ideationalist argument is deceptively simple: (1) human decisions, values, and perceptions form and order a cognitive web of social relations; (2) these cognized social relations generally promote reproductively successful human behavior; and (3) archaeologists may gain access to and understanding of this core cognitive dimension of human culture through the controlled spatial and temporal analysis of tangible, materially expressed symbolic sets. These insights are unremarkable on the face of it, and not terribly controversial. The ideationalist program remains afflicted, however, by serious methodological problems of operationalizing these insights, epistemological problems (particularly in nonliterate societies) of verifying hypotheses focused ultimately on the intangible cognitive dimensions of human culture, and interpretive problems of defining the precise causal linkages between mental schemata (beliefs, values, perceptions) and adaptive, on-the-ground human behavior in the material world.

Even if the materialists, turning momentarily away from their psychological dependence on the sensate, were to concede the methodological and epistemological points by accepting the importance of mental templates and their accessibility in the archaeological record, fundamental disagreement would remain concerning the causal implications of belief systems, ideologies, values, and perceptions. The cultural materialist position on this issue is unambiguous: "apart from behavior associable with them, ideas cost nothing. . . . It costs no more to think one thing than another, unless the difference entails distinct behaviorial consequences. For this reason cultural materialism tends to treat ideas and beliefs as epiphenomenal to behavior" (Price 1982:725). In short, in the materialist pantheon of prime movers, belief systems and ideologies barely register: the material conditions of life, specifically environment, demography, and the technology of production, reign supreme. Predictably, ideationalists remain cold to the materialist blandishments and correctly emphasize the dramatic behavioral consequences that may flow from reformulations or rapid transformations of political and religious ideologies.

We are left, then, at an apparent philosophical and conceptual impasse. If the polemics of the materialist and ideationalist paradigms are to be taken at face value, we are forced to assign causal priority to either the material or the cognitive domain. If, however, we reject this theoretical polarization by acknowledging that mental schemata and the material conditions of life are mutually interpenetrating, mutually implicatory elements of any explanatory framework, then we must also discard the embedded notions of an a priori hierarchy of causative agents. This theoretical perspective, of course, emphasizes the role of history in accounting for variability and change in the constitution of social formations. In a given historical context, the evolutionary trajectory of a specific population may be conditioned principally by environmental limitations or technological possibilities, by demographic forcing, or by radical shifts in belief systems. The immediate task of the archaeologist, then, is an empirical one: to generate context-specific data that define causal parameters affecting given populations. This task is the analytical step of separating the part from the whole—of specifying, for instance, the role of a particular religious or political ideology or of special group interests in structuring the relations of production in a given social formation (Godelier 1977, 1978a, 1978b).

A focus on the historically specific variables does not vitiate the attempt to build general theory. Rather, it brings a realistic, if complicating, element of empirical variability to the explanatory enterprise. From this perspective, the seach for general causal parameters may still proceed, but the possible permutations of variables implicated in the processes of culture change increase dramatically, and, as Reichenbach notes in the epigram to this chapter, the prospects for strict predictability, even of major historical events and movements, are dim: we can, at best, suggest some "statistical laws for the evolution of human society."

Once the analytical step of discriminating the structure of the various material and cognitive components of a given social formation has been taken in a reasonably comprehensive fashion, the truly difficult question of how these components are related remains. As Friedrich (1986: 28) comments, the ultimate question becomes "just how does this [mutual interpenetration of component parts] work out in actual social contexts, cultural idea systems, and in history?" From the perspective of the debate between the materialist and ideationalist paradigms this question can be further specified: just how, and to what extent, do the material conditions of life articulate with mental schemata to form and regulate successful, adaptive human behavior in actual social and historical contexts?

In what follows, I will offer a trial synthesis, or tentative model, of the articulation between economic and ideological behavior in one specific social and historical context: the emergence and organization of an expansive, predatory state formation in the south-central Andes. The specific focus of this contextual inquiry will be on the state of Tiwanaku and its immediate successors in the Lake Titicaca Basin. The purpose of this exercise is to contribute one tangible portrait of the potential mechanisms of interpenetration between the economic and ideological dimensions of state societies in the Andes.

POLITICAL ECONOMY AND IDEOLOGY

Before I embark on a specific discussion of the economic, political, and ideological structure of Tiwanaku society as they can currently be reconstructed, it is appropriate to interject an explicit definition of two terms that constitute the substantive subject matter of what follows: *political economy* and *ideology*. I will offer these definitions as analytical categories for the purpose of constructing the argument, although it should be recognized from the nature of the argument itself that the definitions are in part arbitrary, and therefore that the effective boundaries between what we refer to as political economy or as ideology are blurred by their very interaction.

By political economy, I mean the aggregate processes of production, distribution, and consumption by which populations reproduce the biological and cultural bases of their society. The core elements of this meaning of political economy are the mechanisms of resource production and resource allocation: the stress, in effect, is on the production and flow of energy through the interaction of human labor, technological capacity, and the given physical environment. However, these generically economic mechanisms may entail and entangle a variety of processes that do not necessarily partake intimately in the technoeconomy of production itself: the emergence and promotion of class stratification and status legitimation together with the panoply of tangible markers that reify change in social circumstance, the pursuit of economic self-interest by individuals and groups, and the generation of religious and cult behavior to modulate group action.

By ideology, I follow the pragmatic meaning formulated by Friedrich (1989:301) which, as he implies, is consonant with "scientific realism": "ideology is a system, or at least an amalgam, of ideas, strategies, tactics, and practical symbols for promoting, perpetuating, or changing a social and cultural order; in brief, it is political ideas in action. . . . Such sets of ideas for action arise from the creative engagement of individuals with practical problems and necessarily reflect or express the will and interests for control or change of some social group or class—notably its economic interests." Friedrich (1989:302) extends this definition of ideology by recapitulating the

> analytically priceless, mainly Marxist notion of ideology as a set, or at least an amalgam of ideas, rationalizations, and interpretations that mask or gloss over a struggle to hold onto or get power, particularly economic power, with the result that the actors and ideologues are themselves unaware of what is going on. In this second, critical meaning, ideology arises from the interests of a class, usually an economic class or an economically defined class, and it is thus historically embedded.

From this frame of reference, ideology is the projection of group interest. Here again in the analytical definition of ideology we find an ineluctable intermingling of ideas, political strategies, shrewdly constructed belief systems, and the promotion of group economic and social interests.

If we examine these two definitions of political economy and ideology, particularly as they might apply to state formations, we find a strong current of intersection that focuses on the attempts of elite interest groups to carve out and promote their domination over economically valuable resources, principally labor and territory. For many state societies, ideology functions as a kind of technology of production, not in the sense of producing tangible goods, but by motivating and regulating the mobilization of labor and by providing the rationale and rules for allocating the distribution and redistribution of surplus product. As Price (1982:725) remarks, we can assess the behavior manifested in ideology in terms of the work it performs. That is, from the materialists' perspective, we should, at least theoretically, be capable of quantifying the energy contribution that ideology as political ideas in action makes to the social system by measuring its on-the-ground economic effects. From this perspective, ideology as a technology of production that channels knowledge and information into directions prescribed by dominant groups furnishes a practical armature for the organization of the state's political economy, and, of course not coincidentally, a justification for, or legitimation of, the status quo.

IDEOLOGY AS A RELATION OF PRODUCTION

Godelier's (1977, 1978b) recent reflections on the role of ideology in the political economy of class-structured societies provide valuable correlative insights that complement and expand the treatment thus far described. These insights may be profitably applied to the Andean context I outline below.

Orthodox Marxist interpretations resolve social formations into an analytically distinguishable infrastructure, consisting of forces of production (technology, material means of production) and relations of production (resource allocation, distribution, consumption), and a superstructure, consisting of ideology, kinship systems, belief systems, and other similar mental "epiphenomena" determined by the material imperatives of the infrastructure. Godelier's (1977, 1978b:763–65) form of structural-Marxist analysis essentially collapses putatively superstructural elements, such as kinship and politico-religious ideology, downward into the infrastructure by recharacterizing these key elements as relations of production. That the appropriation, allocation, and distribution of basic resources in precapitalistic societies may have been organized fundamentally by relations of kinship, or by relations of status embedded in religious and political institutions, and that therefore these apparent elements of the Marxist superstructure may be considered functionally as relations of production, seems painfully obvious. Nevertheless, insights that seem obvious in retrospect often lay the groundwork for the best science.

COERCION AND CONSENT

A second critical insight turns on the relationship between the dominant and dominated groups in class-structured societies. Godelier (1978b: 767) remarks that "the power of domination consists of two indissoluble elements whose combination constitutes its strength: violence and consent." He then constructs the seemingly paradoxical proposition that "of these two components of power, the stronger is not the violence of the dominant, but the consent of the dominated to their domination" (1978b: 767). Again, ideology as a shared belief system assumes a central position in maintaining the consent or, better said, acquiescence of the dominated social classes to a hierarchical social order.

Given this construction, the question then arises, why would a dominated class consent to and actively participate in a belief system that serves the interests of an elite, dominating class? Godelier's solution to this conundrum makes great intuitive sense: participation in the society-wide belief system also enhances the economic interests of the dominated class. Specifically, Godelier (1978b: 767) hypothesizes that an elite ideology that reifies hierarchical relations of dominance and exploitation could only be promoted and perpetuated if these relations were cast in the form of an exchange of services between the elite and the dominated. The precise form of this hypothesized exchange of services may vary, but Godelier (1978b: 767) suggests that in the case of early, agrarian-based state formations the emerging elite class would offer esoteric knowledge of the supernatural realm, of "invisible realities and forces controlling (in the thought of these societies) the reproduction of the universe and of life" in exchange for the supplementary labor of the commoners. One could also conceive of a variety of other, more directly pragmatic services that an elite class could offer to commoners: adjudication of boundary disputes, maintenance of security, management of redistribution networks, and the like.

As Godelier acknowledges, however, even if dominated classes share to one degree or another the system of political and economic ideas, beliefs, and symbols promulgated by a dominant class, the threat and the power of coercion hovers in the background. It may be that the most successful (that is, stable, persistent) class-stratified societies arrived at the appropriate mix or balance of force and persuasion. Unmitigated terror leads, in time, to divisiveness, disgust, and revolt; ideological propaganda unreinforced by the potential for sanctions leads, in time, to fragmentation and the dissolution of the hierarchical social order (see

Conrad's contribution to this volume for a parallel, extended discussion of this point).

We arrive, then, at the point at which the foregoing theoretical insights with respect to the mutually interpenetrating, mutually implicatory nature of economy and ideology may be applied and tested in a specific historical context: the indigenous Tiwanaku state of the Andean high plateau. My approach will be to isolate first the basic structure of Tiwanaku's political economy and then to explore the contribution of ideology in constructing and regulating that economy.

THE POLITICAL ECONOMY
OF THE TIWANAKU STATE

Perhaps more than any other great city and center of state formation in the ancient Americas, the essential character of Tiwanaku's political economy remains an enigma. This enigma persists despite the efforts of a number of scholars to model Tiwanaku's presumptive networks of economic production, distribution, and consumption (Browman 1978, 1981; Lynch 1983; Núñez and Dillehay 1979).

At present, I believe that we can best conceptualize the contours of Tiwanaku political economy in terms of long-term interaction among distinct production zones in core and periphery regions. First, I would argue that the essential geopolitical core of the Tiwanaku state consisted of a politically and economically integrated agricultural heartland reclaimed from the flat, marshy lands that ring Lake Titicaca. The fields in this core area provided the bulk of the state's considerable subsistence needs and accommodated the natural expansion of its demographic base (Kolata 1983a, 1986). Large-scale herding of camelids in the adjacent high reaches of the *puna* (tundralike grassland) complemented intensive tuber and grain agriculture in the lacustrine flatlands, creating a powerful system capable of sustained yields (Tomoeda 1985; Yamamoto 1985). Although difficult to quantify precisely owing to the present lack of systematic research, it is evident from Tiwanaku middens tested to date that intensive exploitation of the lacustrine environment was a substantial, self-sustaining element of this pivotal productive system (Browman 1981; Kolata, Stanish, and Rivera 1987).

Second, the Tiwanaku subsistence economy, although grounded in intensive *altiplano* (high plateau) agropastoralism, was not restricted to the food crops and camelid herds that can be produced and managed at high elevations. A key element of the state's economic policy was colonization and the selective enclaving of populations in regions ecologically distinct from that of the high plateau. The direct effect of this policy was the establishment of agricultural provinces in zones at lower elevations (in *yungas*, or low-lying lands to the east or west of the *altiplano*) through which the residents of Tiwanaku settlements on the high plateau enjoyed unmediated access to large quantities of important warm-land crops, such as maize and coca.

Finally, a third element played a critical role in the economic success and integration of the Tiwanaku polity: long-distance exchange through the medium of organized llama caravans. This element of Tiwanaku political economy is forcefully stressed by Browman (1978, 1981) and Núñez and Dillehay (1979), who envision Tiwanaku as a pilgrimage center of great ritual prestige that became the nexus of multiple, far-flung caravan routes operated by loosely confederated ethnic groups. Although I cannot agree with this characterization of Tiwanaku as an inchoate confederation of ethnic groups bound solely by economic and religious mutualism rather than by political imperative, it is clear that caravan-based long-distance exchange was a dynamic, multiethnic, and certainly not entirely centralized sector of Tiwanaku economy.

Given that these geographically diverse, internally differentiated zones with varying productive capacities were integrated into the Tiwanaku macropolity, two pivotal questions rise to the fore: (1) how were these distinct systems and zones of production organized and managed? and (2) what, to paraphrase Godelier, was the mesh between the Tiwanaku state's multiple forces of production and its social relations of production? My tentative answers to these questions will implicate social, economic, and ideological institutions that were central to Tiwanaku's ability to monopolize surplus labor, to concentrate and reinvest economic surplus, and to dominate foreign territory politically.

THE AGRICULTURAL CORE OF PRODUCTION

The architects of the Tiwanaku state system of agricultural production constructed nearly 150 square kilometers of raised fields, serviced by an elaborate network of canals, aqueducts, dikes, and causeways, in two valleys immediately adjacent to the Valley of Tiwanaku. I have termed these two enormous valleys the northern and southern components of the Tiwanaku sustaining area (Kolata 1987). The northern component, in an area known locally as the Pampa Koani, contains approximately 75 square kilometers of these fields, and the southern component, which focuses on the Machaca–Rio Desaguadero zone, incorporates an additional 60 to 70 square kilometers.

Elsewhere (Kolata 1986) I have estimated that the raised fields in the northern component of the Tiwanaku sustaining area were capable of producing 60 million kilograms of potatos annually on a sustained yield basis, or enough to support a population of approximately 125,000. If we double that population to reflect the productive capacity of the southern component, it becomes abundantly clear that by at least the Tiwanaku III phase (ca. A.D. 200) Tiwanaku and its satellite settlements on the southern shores of Lake Titicaca had achieved economic autarchy and the ability to sustain substantial resident populations in concentrated urban settings.

The organization of this remarkable, high plateau agricultural hinterland underscores the exceptionally centralized, hierarchical character of the Tiwanaku polity in the Lake Titicaca Basin. Settlement patterns in the Pampa Koani region indicate unambiguously that agricultural production in that zone was directed explicitly toward the generation of surplus, and not with an eye toward local consumption (Kolata 1986). Throughout the 75 square kilometer zone, we have located fewer than 100 small habitation mounds dispersed among the field systems, which cannot account for more than a few hundred inhabitants. The bulk of these mounds do not appear to have been occupied permanently. Moreover, an important, centrally located cluster of massive platform mounds clearly served administrative and ritual functions for the region (Kolata 1986). The distribution and function of these settlements in the Pampa Koani region imply that (1) the labor to construct and maintain the extensive field systems must have been drawn from a wide, nonlocal region in a pattern attuned to the agricultural cycle of the seasons; (2) this labor was most likely extracted by the centralized authorities of the Tiwanaku state in the form of corvée through a mechanism similar to the Inca *mit'a* tax system (a rotational, periodic labor service levied on heads of households); (3) Tiwanaku established proprietary agricultural estates in which ownership and usufruct rights were vested directly in state institutions (or, perhaps more precisely, in the hands of the elite, dominant classes); and (4) these "corporate farms" or production zones were bound directly to the capital of Tiwanaku through a network of secondary and tertiary administrative centers. Dispersed, rural hamlets and individual households occur in the Tiwanaku area outside the zone of optimal lacustrine agricultural soils. These settlements were probably engaged in small-scale subsistence dry farming and "tethered" herding of camelids and undoubtedly, along with the commoner populations of the larger secondary and tertiary centers, provided a substantial proportion of the corvée labor for the state fields.

Tiwanaku's interest in reclaiming agricultural land was not restricted to the immediate sustaining hinterland of the capital. A pattern of strategically located, state-built administrative centers along the optimal lacustrine coast, similar to that documented for the Pampa Koani and its southern sustaining area counterpart along the Desaguadero, may be perceived in the entire circum-Titicaca region during Tiwanaku phases III–V, ca. A.D. 200–1100. This distinctive settlement pattern of substantial site-unit intrusions strongly implies that the Tiwanaku state imposed a regional political unification of the Titicaca basin with an eye toward expanding its agricultural production and thereby its fundamental sources of wealth, economic vitality, and political power.

IDEOLOGY AND IMPERIALISM IN THE TITICACA BASIN

With the expansion of Tiwanaku into the northern Titicaca basin no later than the Tiwanaku IV phase (ca. A.D. 400–800) we see clear evidence that one element of Tiwanaku imperial policy was the forced imposition of a state cult or ideology focused iconographically on the figure of the "Gateway God" and its correlative symbols. Demarest (1981) has convincingly demonstrated that the central figure of the Gateway of the Sun at Tiwanaku represented a manifold celestial high god that personified elements of nature intimately associated with the productive potential of *altiplano* ecology: the sun, wind, rain, hail—in brief, a personification of atmospherics that most directly affect crop production in either a positive or a negative aspect.

The essential agrarian focus of this state ideology is recapitulated in images on monumental stone stelae, such as the Bennett Monolith, which Zuidema (1985), in a fascinating and provocative interpretation, reconstructs as a 12-month, sidereal-lunar agricultural calendar. Zuidema suggests that his reconstructed Tiwanaku agricultural calendar was homologous with and lay at the origin of the calendrical principles embedded in the Inca state's unified *ceque* system cosmography (a radial system of ritual lines of sight that integrated Inca kinship and cosmology). Zuidema demonstrates that llama husbandry, rituals of llama sacrifice, and agricultural fertility were intimately associated with this calendrical system, reflecting social, symbolic, and ecological relationships between pastoralism and agriculture in the high plateau. As Zuidema (1985:16) notes, "while the crops are growing, the animals are kept away from the fields, but after harvest they are led into them [to permit llamas to graze on the remaining stubble and thereby through their dung regenerate the fertility of the fields]. . . . Thus, crops and animals alternate in the same fields."

Building on these observations, I would further hypothesize that the ancient and probably pan-Andean divisions of labor, status, productive strategies, property conceptions, and perhaps even of ethnic affiliations between pastoralists and agriculturalists were formalized by the Tiwanaku state into a unified ideological system that emphasized and commemorated in monumental public display the necessary, complementary interaction between these two great touchstones of the high plateau economy. Not surprisingly, the public monuments on which these intense images of ecological and productive complementarity occur, such as the Bennett Monolith, also represent idealized portraits of the ruling elite.

In fact, the entire message of the harmonious, rhythmic, symmetrical, cosmically sanctioned complementarity between farmer and herder occurs in standardized images on elements of royal costume, such as tunics, crowns, and sashes; on symbols of royal authority, such as scepters and staffs of office; and integrated into the principal, elite architectural ensembles at Tiwanaku and its secondary administrative centers. The intended meaning of the metaphoric association between images of agropastoral productivity and the representation of royal office, all framed in the context of calendrics, could not be more clear: the kings of Tiwanaku nourish and sustain the common people. Through direct intercession and identity with the divine forces of nature, they will guarantee the agricultural and reproductive success of the nation.

We can glimpse here the kind of reciprocal exchange of service between dominant and dominated classes proposed by Godelier as the root of social and economic differentiation: the elite are guarantors of reproductive success through divine intervention (the service on which Godelier focused) but also through manipulation of a pragmatic body of knowledge—an effective agricultural calendar. Furthermore, the elite classes, in effect, harmonized the potentially disruptive competition between farmer and herder by formally synchronizing productive strategies, adjudicating territorial disputes, and redistributing the very different work products of these two occupational pursuits.

From the critical-Marxist perspective, one could interpret the elite ideology as a shrewd, political idea in action: an appropriation and self-interested transformation of widely shared Andean folk concepts concerning

reciprocal exchange of products, labor, and marriage partners into a formalized coda of state beliefs that stressed the pivotal role of the king and
his court in structuring and mediating the complementary halves of social
production and reproduction. In short, from this perspective, the elite
classes were masking the underlying exploitative character of their relationship with commoners by appropriating the fundamental idiom of
kin-based reciprocity and subtly transforming it into a political and ideological notion of reciprocity that factored elite-brokered redistribution
into the social relations of production. In this transformation, in which
ideology takes the place of kinship as the armature of the social relations
of production, the elite were now conceived as the indispensable, key
players.

That the entire indigenous Lake Titicaca Basin population did not voluntarily embrace this Tiwanaku state ideology with messianic fervor is
made apparent in the archaeological record. Imposed Tiwanaku administrative centers organized around public architecture directly modeled
after the capital of Tiwanaku itself begin to appear around the circum-
Titicaca rim during Tiwanaku III times, and the pattern of massive site-
unit intrusions intensifies during the Tiwanaku IV phase. Perhaps even
more trenchant with respect to Tiwanaku's aggressive expansionism in the
Titicaca basin, we now know that a major stone stela from the site of
Arapa near Puno on the northern shores of the lake was broken at the
base in antiquity, transported more than 150 kilometers by raft, and incorporated into one of the palace complexes at Tiwanaku (Chávez 1975).

This stela was associated with the early, north Titicaca basin urbanized
culture of Pukara. The implication of this violent political and ideological
act is clear: in the process of subjugating the northern Titicaca basin, a
ruler of Tiwanaku ritually debased and appropriated a sacred emblem of
the concentrated spiritual power or, in Andean terms, *huaca* of the Pukara
nation and, in so doing, demonstrated both the ideological and the secular superiority of the Tiwanaku state. This ideological act of *huaca* capture
is not rare in the Tiwanaku archaeological record. In excavations during
the 1989 season at Tiwanaku, a second Pukara-style sculpture of a puma-
masked, crouching figure holding a trophy head was encountered at
the base of the ruined west staircase of the Akapana temple. The Semi-
subterranean Temple at Tiwanaku contains an eclectic assemblage of
stone stelae and sculptures carved in various styles, representing temporal, spatial, and ethnic variability, which were carefully arrayed in subsidiary positions around a centrally located, monumental *axis mundi*: the
7-meter-tall Bennett Monolith, which, as we have seen, visually encoded

the essential tenets of Tiwanaku state ideology and cosmology (Ponce Sanginés 1961, 1969).

This process of co-opting local deities and *huacas* in the process of politically incorporating new territories is a familiar one that is replicated in the annals of Inca ethnohistorical accounts. When the Incas subjugated a new territory, the principal *huacas* were brought to Cuzco and housed in a special, central shrine supported by the peoples of the conquered provinces (Rowe 1982:109). The provincial *huacas,* although honored and worshipped in a traditional manner in Cuzco, were, in effect, held hostage to the imposed solar-focused state cults of the Inca. Frequently, as in the case of the powerful lord of the Chimu state deposed by the Incas, the secular authorities of conquered provinces were held in captivity in Cuzco along with their nation's spiritual icons, where they were treated with elaborate royal hospitality that served to underscore their new status as subjects in thrall to their Inca overlords.

The careful spatial arrangement of the various *huacas* in the Semi-subterranean Temple carried additional symbolic meaning beyond the politico-religious ones outlined above. This sculptural and architectonic assemblage most likely conveyed a public cosmological vision as well, a vision charged with ethnic and political valences, analogous to that described by Wheatley (1971:431–32) for a twelfth-century Southeast Asian state:

> examples of capital cities focusing the supernatural power of a kingdom within their enceintes, and therefore symbolizing whole states, are not difficult to find. . . . One of the most instructive examples is afforded by the ceremonial and administrative complex of Yashodarapura, laid out by Jayavarman II of Cambodia at the end of the 12th century A.D. The centrally situated temple-mountain, known today as the Bayon, consisted essentially of a central quincunx of towers, representing the five peaks of Mount Meru, axis of the world, surrounded by forty-nine smaller towers, each of which represented a province of the empire. According to Paul Mus's elucidation of the symbolism of this structure, the chapels below the smaller towers housed statues of the apotheosized princes and local gods connected with the provinces of the empire, so that the Bayon as a whole constituted a pantheon of the personal and religious cults practised in the various parts of the kingdom. By thus assembling them at the sacred axis. . . , the point where it was possible to

effect an ontological passage between the worlds so that royal power was continually replenished by divine grace from on high, Jayavarman brought these potentially competitive forces under his control.

The Semisubterranean Temple and its sculptural ensemble may very well have functioned as Tiwanaku's Bayon, physically embodying the point of fusion of a centralized imperial ideology with multiple regional and ethnic ideological systems.

We must conceive of the dynamics of Tiwanaku imperial expansion throughout the Titicaca basin, then, in terms of intentional, aggressive policies that balanced force and persuasion, coercion and consent. These policies entailed, mutually implicated, and required the political action of military conquest, the economic action that led to the development of intensive systems of raised field agriculture in optimal lacustrine zones, and the ideological action of co-opting and fusing multiple, complementary belief systems into a pragmatic conceptual armature that both structured and justified the reciprocal social relations between the dominated and dominant classes, the commoner and elite in Tiwanaku society.

THE YUNGAS ZONES: COLONIAL AGRICULTURAL PROVINCES

Tiwanaku imperial expansion, intimately associated with the reclamation of agricultural land, proceeded well beyond the confines of the heartland in the high plateau of the Titicaca basin. There is substantial and growing evidence that Tiwanaku directly colonized and subsequently controlled key economic resources in lower-lying regions, such as the Cochabamba Valley in Bolivia, the Azapa Valley of northern Chile, and the Moquegua Valley of southern Peru, among others, which were ecologically distinct from the *altiplano*.

Perhaps the most interesting element of the interaction between *altiplano* and lowland valley populations during the Tiwanaku regnum were the motivations that each side may have had for fostering and perpetuating this relationship. From the perspective of the Tiwanaku state as a high-plateau polity, establishing agricultural colonies in regions at lower elevations would, of course, have provided access to crops otherwise unavailable in the cold *altiplano*. But what is most significant is the nature of the two principal crops that were grown at lower elevations: maize and coca. If my estimates of the productivity of intensive grain and tuber agriculture in the high plateau are correct within an order of magnitude, there is reason to believe that *altiplano* populations during the Tiwanaku regnum had achieved autarchy. That is, the high plateau under Tiwanaku control would not have required a massive influx of bulk food crops from lower elevations to sustain its urbanized populations: with respect to basic subsistence crops, the *altiplano* was self-sufficient. As Murra (1960) has demonstrated, however, maize and coca were highly valued as ceremonial and prestige crops in the Andes: they were state crops *par excellence* under the Incas and were produced in many areas under the centralized, monopoly control of the government through the labor of forcibly resettled colonists, or *mitmaqkuna* (see, for instance, the remarkable agricultural reorganization of the Cochabamba Valley under the Incas described in Wachtel 1982).

The motive force underlying Tiwanaku agricultural colonization in the *yungas* zones was expansion of the cultivation of prestige crops, particularly maize, which provided the raw material for the production of ritually important commodities, such as maize beer, that were used prodigiously during state-sponsored festivals, which demanded ritual hospitality and the ceremonial display of abundance. Maize and coca as primary products were undoubtedly channeled into the redistributive networks manipulated by the Tiwanaku elite classes as well, providing a storable, high value, state-controlled medium of exchange that could be used by the elites to "purchase" supplementary labor from peasant populations. In short, the agricultural provinces of the Tiwanaku state were essential, not as a source of subsistence goods, but as a source of prestige and ritual commodities that fueled the interpenetrating economic and ideological systems articulated by elite-mediated redistribution.

From the perspective of local populations, in return for a portion of their product and labor, the Tiwanaku state would have provided both a measure of political security and the technological and administrative expertise to develop massive reclamation projects that had been gained through centuries of creating analogous hydraulic works around the edge of Lake Titicaca. Perhaps even more important, through shared participation in a unified economic and ideological system the Tiwanaku state also would have offered indigenous populations incorporation into a broader, more inclusive social universe that mitigated the risks of survival in the harsh natural environment of the Andean world by ensuring the diversity and viability of the means of production. Moreover, in the specific geographical context of the western Andean slopes, Tiwanaku as a state formation was moving in a social environment marked by radically divergent demographic potentials between core and periphery: to be blunt, at the time of initial Tiwanaku colonization, the western *yungas* provinces were relatively unpopulated in comparison with the adjacent high plateau. It would not be surprising, then, even in the absence of overt coercion, that local populations along the western Andean slopes would readily adopt the elite, agrarian-based ideology of the Tiwanaku state.

CARAVANS, CLIENTS, AND THE FAR PERIPHERY

In the far reaches of Tiwanaku cultural influence, such as the area of San Pedro de Atacama, the central Chilean valleys, and the Quebrada de Humahuaca in northwestern Argentina, the nature of the interaction between the *altiplano* polity and local populations was more attenuated than in the core regions of the Lake Titicaca Basin and adjacent *yungas* lands. This attenuation of direct state action is reflected in material culture: here Tiwanaku-related artifacts are concentrated disproportionately in elite domestic and mortuary contexts, and they consist principally of portable art associated with Tiwanaku cult and belief systems (Browman 1981; Kolata 1983). The materials recovered from these specialized contexts include fine textiles, ritual drinking cups wrought of precious metals, featherwork associated with elaborate costumes, and a broad spectrum of elements associated with the ritual consumption of hallucinogenic drugs, including *Anadenanthera* (the source of *wilka* seeds), *Banisteriopsis*, and *Datura* derivatives.

In each of these different areas on the far periphery of the Tiwanaku realm, the precise artifact assemblages and combination of iconographic elements derived from Tiwanaku state art vary, suggesting a selective adoption and local reinterpretation of ideological concepts (Browman 1978). Unlike the standardized, imposed, and pervasive character of Tiwanaku imperial art, architecture, and agricultural construction in the core areas of the state, current evidence from the far peripheries suggests a more fluid, opportunistic, transactional relationship between the state and local populations. Each region seems to have selected those elements of the state belief system that were appropriate to its own cultural setting, generating in the process a multitude of syncretic ritual and religious concepts that were complementary with the ideological system of the *altiplano* state.

Elsewhere (Kolata 1992) I have hypothesized that the regional variability and ideological complementarity in the far peripheries were generated by long-distance exchange between the *altiplano* state and local polities through the medium of organized llama caravans. In this exchange, which was structured along the lines of a clientage relationship, local elites of these distant lands maintained personal relationships with the lords of Tiwanaku and their agents, managing the production and long-distance exchange of desired commodities and simultaneously appropriating emblems of status and authority from their *altiplano* patrons. These personal relationships between *altiplano* patrons and local clients may well have been cast in the metaphor of fictive kinship among elites.

This postulated series of elite, client-patron dyads would account for the specialized context and assemblages of Tiwanaku material culture in the far peripheries, particularly the overwhelming focus on elements of rich personal attire, on rare and precious commodities, and on objects of great value for public display. Unlike in the core regions, the basic patterns of settlement and local subsistence do not seem to have been altered directly by interaction with the *altiplano* state, emphasizing the personalized, transactional quality of the relationship.

The role of Tiwanaku ideology similarly seems quite different in the far peripheries of the realm. Here the state ideology seems to act not as a monolithic, conceptual given, which constructs and justifies cultural identity, but as a fertile source for generating personal or group prestige and authority by establishing an idiom of ritual and conceptual communication between *altiplano* and local lords. Here again state ideology played a central role in structuring the social relations of production, although in a manner quite different from the strategies employed in the heartland of the high plateau.

FORCE AND PERSUASION:
IDEOLOGY, ECONOMY, AND IMPERIALISM

Given the foregoing reconstruction of the political economy of Tiwanaku, we must conceptualize this Andean state formation as a dynamic, heterogeneous mosaic of populations linked (perhaps at times imperfectly) by a mosaic of policies devised by elite interest groups in the core polity of the Lake Titicaca Basin and focused on an economy of extraction. We can most effectively frame the question of the nature of Tiwanaku's political economy in terms of interlocking sets of core-periphery relationships structured around multiple forms of complementary interactions: direct and indirect, centralized and decentralized, administered and autonomous (see Salomon 1985:520 for a comprehensive diagram of institutions of Andean economic complementarity). The Tiwanaku state manipulated various institutional forms of both coercive and consensual economic complementarity (large-scale regional colonization, selective enclaving of population, administered trade, clientage) to intensify production as well as to enhance its own political integration following a principle of context-specific structuring of the relationship between the state and local populations.

It is evident that Tiwanaku was not loath to apply force against competing polities when necessary, particularly in areas that were of prime economic importance, such as the circum-Titicaca basin, which constituted the state's principal source of subsistence crops and camelid herds. It is equally evident that Tiwanaku did not rely solely on coercion to pursue its expansionist economic ends. Tiwanaku ideology, as a paean to social, economic, geographical, and religious complementarity, performed much the same work as military conquest, but at significantly lower cost.

The coercive techniques liberally applied by the Inca state—the calculated military violence, garrisoning of provinces, and uprooting and resettling of populations in alien social settings—were effective but energetically costly and short-term solutions to the problem of political integration. These coercive mechanisms, when applied indiscriminately, inevitably generate instability and hostility in subject populations. They are inherently risky techniques for state building. In this regard, I disagree entirely with Schaedel (1985: 507), who characterizes "shared ideological beliefs and practices" as a "more fragile (if longer lasting) . . . tissue" for "bonding the overarching supra-chiefdom hegemony." It is the shared beliefs and practices of a coherent ideology, and not a preponderance of naked force as Schaedel suggests, that bind pluralistic states into durable political and economic formations.

I would suggest that both the Wari and Inca states were short-lived and inherently fragile Andean political formations precisely because they relied more heavily on coercive rather than ideological techniques of integration. They did not bother to mask, or cast in more favorable terms, the inherently exploitative nature of the imperial enterprise and thereby reduce social tensions between indigenous populations and the alien, state-controlled bureaucracy. Tiwanaku, in sharp contrast, solved the problem of integrating a pluralistic, multiethnic world into a perduring political and economic formation by striking the appropriate balance between force and persuasion, violence and consent. The nearly 1000-year reign of the lords of Tiwanaku in the south-central Andes may be attributed as much to their conceptual understanding and manipulation of the interpenetrating institutions of ideology and economy as to their technological prowess in force-of-arms.

Note

The preliminary results of the research discussed here are based on the research projects entitled "The Technology and Organization of Agricultural Production in the Tiwanaku State" and "Tiwanaku and Its Hinterland." These projects are supported by research and equipment grants from the National Science Foundation (BNS 8607541; BNS 8805490); the National Endowment for the Humanities (RO-21368-86; RO-21806-88); the Pittsburgh Foundation; the University of Chicago, Division of Social Sciences; Tesoro Petroleum Corporation; and the Occidental Oil and Gas Corporation.

5

TOWARD A POLITICAL HISTORY OF TEOTIHUACAN

GEORGE L. COWGILL

In the first millennium A.D. the city of Teotihuacan was extraordinarily large relative to other Mesoamerican settlements. It covered more than 20 square kilometers and had more than a hundred thousand inhabitants. But besides the sheer size of its capital, the Teotihuacan state appears to be unusual in at least three other respects. It seems to have lasted without major disruption for about seven centuries; public celebration of individual rulers or other specific persons appears to have been absent; and temples and other structures connected with religion are, even by Mesoamerican standards, overwhelming in their mass and the scale of their precincts.

One can propose an explanation for all these special features by postulating that religious buildings were so pervasive and constructed on such a grand scale because the Teotihuacan state was exceptionally sacralized; that stress on sacred aspects of rulership made recognition of individual personality and achievements unnecessary or even inappropriate; and that this emphasis on the sacred and on suppression of the individual was also, somehow, the key to the state's remarkable stability.

I do not think it was quite that simple. Even if all available data were consistent with this model, it would have many shortcomings as an explanation. For example, one would still have to explain how and why sacralization should be expected to lead to long-lasting political stability. Furthermore, however great the explanatory value of ideational aspects of Teotihuacan society, one could not simply ignore environmental and economic factors.

In fact, the data themselves are more complex and more equivocal than my opening sketch suggests. The sacred aspects so evident at Teotihuacan must not lead us to underestimate the evidence, now very clear and abundant, for the importance of military elements in the society. Furthermore, recent discoveries make it less certain that named individual rulers were never celebrated or commemorated. Finally, there are hints that there may have been some open struggles between factions and some publicly visible shifts in the ideological bases of rulership during the seven centuries of Teotihuacan's dominance in central Mexico.

One cannot discuss the political role of Teotihuacan ideology without having some idea of the nature and content of that ideology, and knowledge about the ideology in turn requires some grasp of the meanings of Teotihuacan signs, symbols, and glyphs. Our understanding of Teotihuacan signs and symbols is in the midst of dramatic advances. In addition to recent articles on specific topics by various authors, the book by von Winning (1987) summarizes a great deal of knowledge, Langley's (1986) work brings the study of Teotihuacan signs to a new stage, and the contributors to the volume edited by Berrin (1988) discuss paintings of exceptionally rich significance. However, a review of current research on meanings of all signs and symbols of possible political relevance would be too technical, lengthy, and full of uncertainties for the purposes of this book.

Instead, I will limit myself to some rather broad conclusions about political aspects of Teotihuacan ideology that seem justified at this time, and to some conjectures about the political history of Teotihuacan that seem testable in part by reference to data on symbolism and ideology. I have summarized points I still think valid in my earlier publications (especially Cowgill 1983). I have found recent works by Pasztory (1988) and R. Millon (1988a, 1988b) especially valuable because they attempt sketches of the whole range of Teotihuacan history with due attention to ideological aspects, including some of the most recent iconographic and notational discoveries. These articles by Pasztory and Millon are important supplements to this chapter, partly because they sometimes present alternative views (on most things we seem to be in agreement) and partly because they go into greater detail on many matters.

I will organize my discussion in terms of ceramic phases, not because I think that these phases neatly correspond to political or ideological periods but because they are still our best chronological framework for Teotihuacan.

THE CUANALAN PHASE (500–150 B.C.)

Before about 500 B.C. settlements in the northern Basin of Mexico were few and small, and none have been identified in the region that was later to be covered by the city of Teotihuacan (Sanders, Parsons, and Santley 1979). During the Cuanalan phase two settlements appeared in this region. One of them, centered in map square S1W6 (fig. 5.1), although shown as a "small dispersed village" by Sanders, Parsons, and Santley (1979:map 11), is in fact a rather concentrated settlement in which sherd cover is substantial over 15 to 30 hectares, with a population perhaps around 1000 to 2000. A much smaller site in S3E6 (not reported in

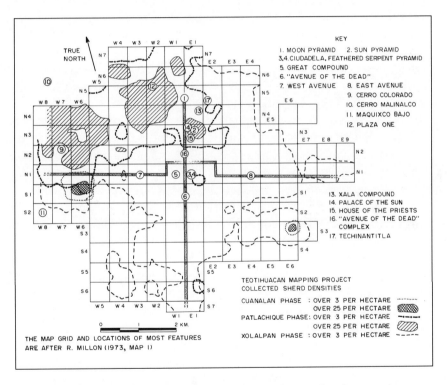

Figure 5.1. Archaeological map of Teotihuacan, showing distributions of ceramics of the Cuanalan, Patlachique, and Xolalpan phases and locations of structures and other features referred to in the text. Each 500-meter square is identified by the combination of its north-south and east-west location— for example, N7W4.

Sanders, Parsons, and Santley 1979) probably had a few hundred people. Toward the western edge of the area surveyed in detail by the Teotihuacan Mapping Project (R. Millon 1973, 1981; Millon, Drewitt, and Cowgill 1973) is a moderately steep and high hill, Cerro Colorado, whose principal summit, in N2W7, is about 100 meters above the valley floor (fig. 5.1, no. 9). A secondary summit separated by a gentle saddle in N3W7 is about 10 meters lower. Another broad saddle connects Cerro Colorado to Cerro Malinalco, a considerably higher hill whose summit, in N5W7 or N5W8, is more than 250 meters above the valley floor (fig. 5.1, no. 10; Sanders, Parsons, and Santley 1979:map 5). During the Cuanalan phase several small settlements were located on the slopes of Malinalco, including a small nucleated village at a site called Tlachinolpan, which was excavated by Blucher (1971). Other "small dispersed villages" shown by Sanders, Parsons, and Santley (1979:map 11) correspond to the low-density scatters of Cuanalan ceramics shown by Cowgill (1974:379) centered in squares N4W7–8, N4W6, N4W5, and N5W2. However, restudy of the ceramics from these sites shows that most if not all of these ceramics date to the following Patlachique phase.

The Cuanalan phase settlements do not foreshadow the later city in any way. There is no evidence for Cuanalan occupation near any of the principal later temples or civil-ceremonial complexes. Nothing suggests ceremonial or civic structures of more than very modest size in any of the Cuanalan settlements near Teotihuacan, or that any unusual sacred, commercial, or military significance was attached to any of these sites. The most obvious explanation for the location of the relatively large Cuanalan settlement centered in S1W6 is that it is on the closest dry land to what is today a small zone (100 hectares or so) of highly productive *chinampa*-like (drained field) cultivation in land that would be swampy if it were not drained. This zone is watered by springs in squares S1W5 and S1W4 that provide a year-round flow for it and also for several thousand hectares of canal-watered land. Given the evidence elsewhere in the northern Basin of Mexico (Nichols 1982; Sanders and Santley 1977), there is little doubt that irrigated agriculture was practiced in the Teotihuacan Valley by Cuanalan times. The localized perennial springs offer a great advantage over rainfall-dependent irrigation because they permit maize to be planted early, which increases the probability that it will mature before the killing frosts of autumn. Since the onset of the summer rainy season is variable and unpredictable, if one has to depend on rain rather than year-round springs one may not be able to plant early enough.

Thus, it seems most likely that the occupants of the Cuanalan settlement in S1W6 were primarily farmers who chose to settle next to exceptionally desirable farmlands. Religious or commercial reasons probably had very little to do with this choice, and military reasons only to the extent that proximity facilitated defense of a prime agricultural resource.

I doubt that either the needs or the opportunities created by the construction and maintenance of small drainage and irrigation canals to handle the placid and dependable flow from the springs or the need for social mechanisms to resolve disputes over water allocation led in any simple or inexorable way to the development of a large, stratified, and politically centralized state. Nevertheless, we should not react too strongly against the excesses of some "hydraulic" models. It is distinctly possible that social arrangements and ideology that arose in connection with canal systems covering a few thousand hectares played a facilitating or "preadaptive" role for later developments. Even if this were the case, however, these later developments are wildly out of proportion to anything that can be explained as a direct consequence of the social impact of canal irrigation.

THE PATLACHIQUE PHASE (150–1 B.C.)

Nothing in the Teotihuacan region before about 150 B.C. leads up to what follows. It suddenly makes sense to speak of Teotihuacan as a city, rather than a piece of countryside that would someday be occupied by a city. However, nearly all our information about the Patlachique phase settlement comes from the surface collections of the Teotihuacan Mapping Project. We still know almost nothing of Patlachique phase structures at Teotihuacan. No paintings or sculpture of this period are known, and decorations on ceramics are limited to abstract designs, although figurines may provide some clues to ideology and conceivably to political aspects of the society. My inferences about Patlachique society are based almost entirely on quantities and spatial patterning of Patlachique ceramics in surface collections. Fortunately, the evidence from early phases that appears on the surface strongly suggests that all important Patlachique occupations are represented by substantial quantities of visible ceramics (Cowgill 1974).

Figure 5.1 shows two major foci. One is on the slopes of Cerros Colorado and Malinalco. The other is centered on square N5W2. Smaller foci occur around the eventual site of the Sun Pyramid (in N3E1), in N6W4, and in N6W1. Lighter sherd cover links all these foci, covers much of what was to become the northern part of the Avenue of the Dead, and extends some distance north and northwest of the area shown in figure 5.1. Other small, isolated, low-density concentrations of Patlachique sherds are in the area where the Ciudadela was later built (N1E1) and near the southern end of the Avenue of the Dead (S6E1). Some Patlachique sherds occur over most of the Cuanalan settlement in S1W6, but the zones of heavy sherd cover for the two phases are separated by several hundred meters.

What does the spatial pattern of Patlachique sherds mean? The fact that many more of them are spread over a much larger area even though they were generated during a shorter time than the Cuanalan ceramics implies a spectacular increase in population. The shift in spatial pattern is also important. The Patlachique settlement foci are close enough to perennially watered land to have made farming that land feasible, but very close proximity to prime farmland was evidently no longer the main consideration. There was ample room for expansion of the principal Cuanalan settlement, if that had been desired. The town could have spread to adjacent land to the west and southwest, where many people live today in the community of Maquixco Bajo (fig. 5.1, no. 11; R. Millon 1973: map 3, no. 26, square S2W8). However, this area shows very little evidence of any Teotihuacan occupation.

The abrupt shift in settlement strongly suggests an abrupt shift in social priorities rather than a gradual development from a Cuanalan nucleus. Possibly the "Patlachique people" were ethnically different, but an abrupt social shift can also be internally generated. My impression is that the kinds and amounts of change in the ceramics of the two periods suggest ethnic continuity somewhat more than replacement, but I do not rule out the latter possibility. Even if an influx of newcomers were demonstrable, however, that fact alone would not *explain* the new priorities that are reflected by the settlement shift.

One of the major Patlachique foci is on the slopes (but not the tops) of Cerros Colorado and Malinalco. The Tezoyuca ceramic complex, which is still enigmatic, perhaps dates to about the end of Cuanalan times and the beginning of the Patlachique period. It is associated with hilltop sites in the Teotihuacan Valley (Sanders, Parsons, and Santley 1979: 104–105). However, architectural remains atop Cerros Colorado and Malinalco are very modest, do not suggest Tezoyuca occupations, and date mostly to Tlamimilolpa (A.D. 200–400) or later times.

The first major occupation of a prominent hill in the Valley of Oaxaca occurred with the founding of Monte Albán around 500 B.C. (Feinman et al. 1985: 345–48). Is it possible that the Patlachique phase people of

Teotihuacan were emulating this model? If one wanted to build something like Monte Albán in the Teotihuacan Valley, Cerros Colorado and Malinalco offer the least unsuitable setting, since other hills are too remote. The saddles between the summits of these hills provide some level space, but less than the area of the monumental center of Monte Albán. However, a ceremonial center atop these two hills would not dominate the Teotihuacan Valley in anything like the way that Monte Albán overlooks the Valley of Oaxaca. It seems unlikely that the Patlachique occupation of the slopes below the summits of these hills was a short-lived gesture toward a "sacred mountain" syndrome, although it remains a possibility.

Conceivably people moved to the hill slopes for better defense. No signs of Patlachique phase fortifications have ever been recognized, but absence of fortifications need not mean that the defensive advantages of the location were unimportant.

The other principal Patlachique phase settlement focus, in and around N5W2, is in an area that is generally flat, although broken by some caves and collapsed lava tubes, and it has no obvious defensive or agricultural advantages. It is, however, a region with some important pyramid complexes. Excavations in one (Plaza One, fig. 5.1, no. 12) found Tzacualli phase earth floors underlying extensive later construction (Millon and Bennyhoff 1961; Millon, Drewitt, and Bennyhoff 1965:6). René Millon (personal communication, 1989) says that the principal temple (1B:N5W2) may contain elements dating to the Patlachique phase. We have virtually no relevant excavation data from other pyramids in this broad region, some distance west and northwest of the Avenue of the Dead. However, I have made a site-by-site review of the Teotihuacan Mapping Project computer files and other data bearing on the question of whether the vicinities of any of these pyramid complexes may have already been concentrations of occupation in the Patlachique phase. I looked for places where Patlachique sherds form an unusually high proportion of all sherds of the Patlachique through Metepec phases (ca. 150 B.C. to ca. A.D. 750). Of twelve of the major "three-pyramid" complexes in or very near the zone of heavy Patlachique sherd cover, four have decidedly higher proportions of Patlachique ceramics than other nearby sites. Another three do not have especially high proportions of Patlachique sherds but have immediately contiguous sites with above-average proportions. Three others have so little Patlachique pottery nearby that it seems unlikely they were of any significance at that time. Evidence about the remaining two complexes is ambiguous.

Excavations are needed to test the inferences suggested by these data from surface collections. However, the surface data suggest that many, though not all, of the larger three-pyramid complexes in the northern and northwestern parts of Teotihuacan, including some near the Avenue of the Dead and others more than a kilometer and a half away, were already places of special importance in the Patlachique phase.

The vast bulk of the Sun Pyramid dates to the following Tzacualli phase (A.D. 1–150), but some of the small structures found in the lower tunnels dug within it by archaeologists may be earlier. Millon (1981:231) says that the cave underneath the pyramid (not to be confused with the tunnels) was extensively used throughout the Tzacualli phase but does not say whether any Patlachique ceramics were found. The earliest stages of the Moon Pyramid are unknown. The possibility of a minor Patlachique occupation in the area of the later Ciudadela requires further study. Nothing clearly suggests that the Avenue of the Dead existed in Patlachique times.

In sum, the evidence hints that temples were already important in Patlachique Teotihuacan. One important reason for the settlement focus in flat land west of the Avenue of the Dead may have been a desire for proximity to sacred places. However, there is no indication that the vicinity of the later Sun Pyramid and the cave beneath it were markedly more important than several other locations to the west and northwest.

Another significant aspect of the Patlachique city is its sheer size and the rapidity of its growth. It seems hard to dispel the notion that the Patlachique phase was notable mainly as a prelude to the "explosive" growth of the city in the Tzacualli phase. By late in the Patlachique phase, however, Teotihuacan was already a city of at least 20,000 and perhaps more than 40,000 people. A settlement of this size cannot be called a village or even a town. The Patlachique city looks small only in comparison with what was to come. Relative to almost all other pre-Columbian settlements at any time anywhere else in the New World, it was quite large. Surely it was fully urban, and it so greatly exceeded other settlements in the Basin of Mexico, except for Cuicuilco far to the south, that it should probably be thought of as a "primate" city.

Furthermore, its rate of growth was, for a nonindustrialized city, extremely rapid. Between 150 and 1 B.C. the population increased by at least tenfold, more likely by twentyfold, and perhaps by fortyfold. A tenfold increase, if spread as evenly as possible over 150 years, is an annual rate of 1.5 percent (doubling in less than 50 years); a twentyfold increase corresponds to 2 percent (doubling about every 35 years); and fortyfold, to 2.5 percent (doubling in 28 years). Part of the reason that the *rate* of increase was so high is that the starting population was so low. Nevertheless, the absolute *amount* of the increase was probably more than 30,000 people.

It is unlikely that there was any great excess of births over deaths, so most of the increase was probably due to in-migration, though the newcomers were not necessarily ethnically very different from the native-born. Furthermore, much of the increase may well have occurred in abrupt surges, rather than gradually. Thus, accommodation of large numbers of newcomers was not altogether a novelty for the Tzacualli city. The Patlachique phase society had already had to deal to some extent with the same problem, although if the influx was in fact gradual, it would have amounted to no more than a few hundred per year. In contrast, an abrupt doubling (or more) of the city's population at the onset of the Tzacualli phase is postulated by Sanders, Parsons, and Santley (1979), who believe that very nearly the entire population of the Basin of Mexico was suddenly moved to Teotihuacan at that time.

Any model of Patlachique society has to include some explanation for why so many people were, in Childe's classic phrase, "persuaded or compelled" to move to the city, what impact the influx of newcomers had, and what institutions were employed to deal with them. It is reasonable to think that whatever explains the shift from the Cuanalan village to new settlement foci will also explain the dramatic growth of the Patlachique city.

We can specify some of the phenomena that models of Patlachique society must take into account, but we have little else to go on. It is possible that obsidian working was already a major industry that contributed to the city's growth. Spence (1984:95–96) has identified nine sites with good evidence of obsidian working and abundant Patlachique ceramics but little pottery of later phases. Many other sites with good evidence of obsidian working also have abundant Patlachique ceramics but a great deal of later pottery as well. Without excavations, we cannot say how important obsidian working was in the Patlachique city. We know even less of other possible industries.

If the suspicion that there were already several important temples in the Patlachique city is confirmed by excavations, one could still ask whether these temples were more a consequence than a cause of the growth of the city. It would have been strange if the people of a thriving city anywhere in Mesoamerica had not put some of their wealth into temples. However, possibly some of the sacred places at Teotihuacan were already of more than local significance and were attracting outsiders.

Perhaps special features of Teotihuacan ideology already differentiated the society from its neighbors and made it in some ways better or more effectively organized. It is unlikely that the characteristics of Tzacualli phase society sprang up all at once, without antecedents. Also, the existence of exceptionally important sacred places would explain one of the two new foci of settlement.

We can speculate that the explosive growth of the Patlachique city was due to some combination of commercial success, military prowess, strong leadership, a good location, luck, and some special religious appeal. This is only a "laundry list," but we cannot be less vague until we have more information from problem-oriented excavations. I discuss some of these matters in the next section. For the present, the sheer size of the city and the rapidity of its growth are our most important data. These facts alone suggest that Patlachique society was complex and differentiated and almost surely had a strong leadership of some sort.

THE TZACUALLI PHASE (A.D. 1–150)

Sanders, Parsons, and Santley (1979) argue that at the beginning of the Tzacualli phase nearly the entire population of the Basin of Mexico was abruptly shifted to Teotihuacan, since they rarely find Tzacualli phase materials elsewhere in the basin. Teotihuacan expanded from about eight square kilometers to about twenty, and its population to perhaps 60,000 to 80,000 (R. Millon 1981:221). This implies that something like 30,000 to 50,000 people were added suddenly. In a very short time, apparently, the population of the city doubled or tripled. It is hard to believe that this movement was entirely voluntary, and surely Teothihuacan politically dominated at least most of the Basin of Mexico. The size of the city suggests political control or at least strong influence over a much larger area than the basin, but there seems to be little evidence in support of this suggestion, although Tzacualli-like pottery certainly occurs in northern Puebla. The Teotihuacan Mapping Project collected a few sherds of exotic redware with lowland Maya affinities, tentatively identified as Preclassic Sierra Red. If this identification is substantiated it would imply participation in exchange networks that reached to the Maya lowlands, probably in Tzacualli times and certainly no later than Miccaotli times.

In contrast to the discontinuity between the Cuanalan and Patlachique settlements, the Tzacualli settlement is a logical expansion of the Patlachique city. The focus centered on N5W2 expands in all directions, especially to the east and south. The western focus on the slopes of the hills

continues, but the intensity of occupation decreases. The differences between Patlachique and Tzacualli ceramics are not great and strongly suggest ethnic continuity. In many respects the Tzacualli city seems to be the
continuation and intensification of trends already well developed during
Patlachique times.

In contrast, the virtual depopulation of most of the Basin of Mexico is
more than an "intensification" of the Patlachique in-migration. It is conceivable that lands throughout most of the basin continued to be worked
by an archaeologically almost invisible population living in scattered in-
substantial structures, perhaps for only parts of the year. It is inconceiv-
able, however, that many Tzacualli settlements larger than tiny hamlets
could have been missed by the Basin of Mexico surveys. Tzacualli phase
Teotihuacan must have been a kind of "super-primate" city for a region
in which intermediate levels of a settlement hierarchy were missing.

The implication is that the rulers at Teotihuacan had extraordinary
power to affect people's behavior in much of the basin, presumably by
means of some combination of coercion, ideological appeal, and economic inducements. In a sense, the central authority must have had extremely strong power in order to be able to see to it that no secondary or
tertiary centers existed for many kilometers around. In another sense,
however, intolerance of subsidiary centers may be a sign of weakness or
poorly developed statecraft. Perhaps the central authority felt it could not
keep control if it delegated any authority to representatives of lower levels
of the political hierarchy who were not located immediately at hand
within the city itself.

Another Tzacualli manifestation that was more than a simple intensification of Patlachique trends was the astonishing Sun Pyramid (fig. 5.1,
no. 2). Nothing of any great size existed on the spot before Tzacualli
times, but by the end of that period it had already reached nearly its
present height and volume.[1] It covered about the same area as the Great
Pyramid of Cheops and was about half as high, with a volume of nearly
a million cubic meters. Furthermore, more than twenty other pyramid
complexes, some of them perhaps begun in the Patlachique phase (as
discussed above), were in existence by this time (R. Millon 1981). Many
of them were "three-temple" complexes, in which pyramids face inward
on three sides of a plaza. Often the fourth side of the plaza is bordered by
a low transverse platform. Some of the complexes form symmetrical pairs
along the Avenue of the Dead, the west member facing east and the east
member facing west. Others, less closely associated with the Avenue of
the Dead or at some distance from it, especially in the northwest quadrant

of the city, face south. According to Millon (1981) at least the northern part of the Avenue of the Dead must have been laid out by this time, although the structures then in existence may not have looked much like those now visible. The Sun Pyramid was therefore only the largest element in a vast area of monumental construction that, as Millon (1981:212) says, seems designed to overwhelm the viewer by sheer size, scale, and number. "The bold self-confidence manifest in the planning and execution of the grand design points to an authority, be it individual or collective, that had unchallenged prestige, with an ability to motivate masses of people and the power to mobilize and direct workers and resources on a scale that until then was without precedent in Middle America" (R. Millon 1981:212).

We know scarcely more of Tzacualli than of Patlachique iconography. Designs on pottery remain abstract. A vessel from Plaza One, a three-temple complex in N5W2 (fig. 5.2, no. 12), shows what may be the "feathered eye" sign (Millon, Drewitt, and Bennyhoff 1965:70, fig. 96). Langley (1986:249–51) notes that Caso (1967) suggests an equation with a Zapotec year-bearer day sign, but Langley also notes that von Winning suggests it may represent a spring, and Langley himself considers the interpretation of the vessel sign as the feathered eye sign problematical. In their Sun Pyramid investigation Millon, Drewitt, and Bennyhoff (1965:69, fig. 93) found an effigy vessel of the storm god (a so-called Tlaloc jar) that may date to the Tzacualli phase. Tzacualli figurines have headdresses and sometimes other attributes of probable symbolic meaning (e.g., Barbour 1975). However, the political relevance of all these bits is anything but clear.

Many large carved stones, no longer in situ, were found near the front of the Sun Pyramid. These large stones were surely part of elite or state-related symbolism. Many or all probably belonged to the later platform built up against the front of the pyramid or to structures in the Sun Plaza, and they are probably post-Tzacualli. Nevertheless, unless there were significant changes in the meaning of the Sun Pyramid, these carvings must be consistent with the cults associated with that pyramid in Tzacualli times. Among these carvings are some great stone skulls (Beyer 1979:170–71, pl. 82; R. Millon 1973:fig. 23b). They probably do not represent the principal deities, and surely not the only aspects of the deities worshipped at the pyramid. Other carved stones found there represent other subjects, as do the paintings in the Sun Palace (Miller 1973). Some are plausibly associated with fertility, and felines are possibly connected with political authority.

Nevertheless, it is clear that cults associated with death and sacrifice were among those celebrated in structures near the Sun Pyramid, at least at certain times in Teotihuacan's history. In addition to the great stone skulls, which are undated, very late (Metepec phase) murals in the Sun Palace show celebrants in bird costumes with bloody hearts impaled on sacrificial knives (Miller 1973: fig. 85). These murals could represent a marked change in cults associated with the Sun Pyramid over the five centuries that separate Tzacualli from Metepec. More likely, however, death and sacrifice were aspects of Sun Pyramid cults from the beginning, though complemented by other aspects emphasizing creation and probably abundance and fertility.

The vicinity of the Sun Pyramid was probably the political as well as the sacred center of the Tzacualli city. The highest political authority was probably closely associated with the principal cult or cults celebrated at the Sun Pyramid. The politically most important people probably lived nearby, perhaps in the House of the Priests on the platform south of the pyramid (fig. 5.1, no. 15), at the site of the later Sun Palace in the plaza west of the pyramid (fig. 5.1, no. 14), or possibly in the Xala complex a short distance to the northeast (fig. 5.1, no. 13).

The neighborhood of the Ciudadela (fig. 5.1, no. 3) was surely occupied in Tzacualli times, and it may already have been a place of special importance. Cut stones are found in the fill of the later Feathered Serpent Pyramid (fig. 5.1, no. 4), and one of the feathered serpent heads is a reused block with earlier carving on the rear (Cabrera and Sugiyama 1982: 167 and photo 6). In a test pit dug in 1988 the author encountered a concentration of relatively large Tzacualli polychrome and resist-decorated sherds. A recent tunnel into the pyramid (Cabrera et al. 1989) shows that it was built in a single operation, probably quite early in the Tlamimilolpa phase. Traces of earlier structures are evident on the spot where the pyramid was built, however, and one badly looted burial pit is probably also earlier (S. Sugiyama, personal communication 1990). Little is known of these earlier features, and they are probably not much earlier than the pyramid.

Even if the vicinity of the Ciudadela was already special, it must have been vastly overshadowed by the Sun Pyramid, because whatever was there in Tzacualli times was not large enough to be easily detected archaeologically under later structures.

The Moon Pyramid (fig. 5.1, no. 1), a monumental structure at the north end of the Avenue of the Dead (fig. 5.1, no. 6), also offers us puzzles. I know of no evidence as to whether there was already a major pyramid here in Tzacualli times. However, the abundance of Tzacualli pottery in the vicinity is consistent with this possibility, and the evidence that the Avenue of the Dead was already in existence suggests that an important structure already marked its northern terminus.

Beyond doubt Teotihuacan was seen by its inhabitants as a place of unparalleled cosmic significance. The cave underneath the Sun Pyramid was probably a place of ancestral emergence, a place with critical connections to the underworld (Heyden 1975; Millon 1981). It may have been regarded as the place where time began (Millon 1981); conceivably something like the Aztec myth that located the events leading to the creation of the Fifth Sun at Teotihuacan was already in existence and influential. Furthermore, Teotihuacan may have been seen by its inhabitants as the place where cosmic axes converged.

Even very small settlements can be fraught with sacred significance deeply felt by their inhabitants. Gossen (1974) describes how the people of Chamula, a highland Maya municipality in Chiapas, are convinced that they live at the center of the world and can point to the spots within their territory where the key events of creation took place. Teotihuacan would not have been unusual among Mesoamerican centers simply by virtue of similar beliefs. However, the monumentality of Tzacualli phase sacred architecture is exceptional. Once the Sun Pyramid and spacious configurations of other pyramid complexes had been built, it is easy to imagine that they proclaimed, and by their very existence helped to authenticate, significance for other societies far beyond the local scene. With the near disappearance of other population centers in the Basin of Mexico, probably most beliefs that attributed special significance to these places died out. In addition, although more distant centers that remained well populated did not necessarily relinquish local myths and ceremonies celebrating their own sacred importance, they could very well have added beliefs about Teotihuacan as a sacred city, untroubled by anything we might perceive as logical inconsistency. Every community might equally be a place of cosmic significance, but Teotihuacan was doubtless a great deal more equal than others.

Possibly in Patlachique times Teotihuacan had already somehow acquired extraordinary sacred significance that had strong attraction for many outsiders, and this attraction alone might account for the city's rise to dominance. Some evidence, such as the enormous proportion of resources devoted to creating sacred buildings and the absence of fortifications and of explicit celebration of military victories in Teotihuacan art (in marked contrast to Monte Albán and the lowland Maya) might seem to support this possibility. However, I am extremely skeptical of casting the leaders of Teotihuacan in the role of the gentle unworldly priests that was assigned to Maya hierarchies a few decades ago. Furthermore, at least in later periods there are many armed figures in Teotihuacan art and references to human sacrifice. The key difference between Teotihuacan and the lowland Maya is not that the Teotihuacanos were unwarlike or never referred to war in their art. It is, rather, that their rulers do not seem to have publicly celebrated their individual exploits or their ancestry.

It seems that being able to claim personal credit for military victories or descent from the right individuals was not very important for legitimizing rulership, or, at any rate, it was not important to memorialize this prowess or descent in stone. Furthermore, the Teotihuacan state does not seem to have celebrated defeat of individualized enemies or control over distant places to anywhere near the extent that Monte Albán did (Marcus 1984).

Another possibility is that the sacred qualities of Teotihuacan actually had little to do with the city's dramatic growth during the Patlachique phase. Perhaps Teotihuacan first acquired control over vast resources and large numbers of people through some combination of successful warfare and commercial enterprise and only subsequently, during the Tzacualli phase, "invested" in monumental temple complexes that could be used to legitimize and stabilize the city's control by endowing it with exceptional sacred significance.

This last suggestion seems improbable, although the odds in its favor would increase if excavations in the places most likely to have been sites of Patlachique temples persistently fail to find evidence for anything but minor structures before Tzacualli times. Evidence for sizable Patlachique temples would, on the other hand, support the view that religion contributed much to the development of the Patlachique city.

In the absence at present of this or other evidence bearing on these issues, a plausible speculation is that Patlachique growth was based on *both* military effectiveness and unusual religious appeal, and that commercial factors were perhaps already important. The Tzacualli developments might then reflect a growing emphasis on religion, although it is highly unlikely that military effectiveness would have become unimportant. Millon (1981, 1988a, 1988b) stresses the importance of military elements at Teotihuacan, even if they are underplayed in the imagery, but he is also convinced that the religious appeal of Teotihuacan was extremely strong to outsiders as well as to Teotihuacanos. Pasztory (1988) notes how awed visitors must have been by the monumentality of the city and its temples and other structures, but she still finds it difficult to say whether Teotihuacan's religion was intended to appeal strongly to outsiders.

THE MICCAOTLI AND
EARLY TLAMIMILOLPA PHASES (A.D. 150–300)

Excavations in 1988 and 1989, within and adjacent to the Feathered Serpent Pyramid (also known as the Temple of Quetzalcoatl), were directed by Rubén Cabrera, Saburo Sugiyama, and the author (1991). These excavations pertain mainly to the Miccaotli and Early Tlamimilolpa phases. Both ceramic chronology and stratigraphic evidence enable us to distinguish a sequence of events, but it seems best to discuss the period as a unit, rather than breaking it into subphases.

Population of the city may have increased somewhat, but not dramatically; the period of rapid urban growth was over. Given the size of the city, evidence of Teotihuacan influences of any kind elsewhere in Mesoamerica at this time is curiously scarce. Perhaps this scarcity of evidence is more apparent than real, because the ceramics of the period are not well known, a situation that will be remedied by publication of Rattray's monograph on Teotihuacan ceramics (Rattray 1981).

The most striking development of this period was the construction of the monumental Ciudadela complex, a great enclosure about 400 meters on a side, about a kilometer south of the Sun Pyramid (fig. 5.1, no. 3). Evidence from Teotihuacan Mapping Project Test Excavation 19 and from recent work of the Proyecto Arqueológico Teotihuacán (Cabrera, Rodríguez, and Morelos 1982a, 1982b) indicates that its monumental surrounding platforms, about 80 meters wide on the north, east, and south, were built to within a meter of their present height (about eight meters) in a single immense operation in the Miccaotli phase, a short time after the major period of construction on the Sun Pyramid. It has long been believed (e.g., Armillas 1964:307; R. Millon 1973:55) that the Ciudadela housed the heads of the Teotihuacan state.

Teotihuacan architectural layouts are often characterized by symmetries that are not especially subtle and often use approximately balanced pairs. Most of the major structural complexes on the east side of the Avenue of the Dead have an approximate counterpart on the west side (e.g., the Ciudadela is roughly balanced by the Great Compound [fig. 5.1, no. 5], although the two complexes differ considerably from one another). The Sun Pyramid is a major exception. The region west of the Avenue of the Dead opposite the Sun Pyramid has nothing that is even approximately a counterpart. Perhaps the explanation is that two Sun Pyramids were too much even for the Teotihuacanos, and they may have felt that no counterpart at all would be better than some pale reflection of their most colossal monument.

Even so, I am troubled by the absence of an extremely simple and obvious connection between the Sun Pyramid and the Avenue of the Dead. The Moon Pyramid's location at the avenue's northern terminus provides such a connection. It seems logical to me that a great ceremonial way should have run west from the Sun Pyramid, but it is very unlikely that such an avenue ever existed. It cannot have been marked by very large structures unless they were quite thoroughly razed later, and apartment compounds of the Xolalpan and Metepec phases seem to have been built without regard for any such hypothetical avenue.

In fact, the only known major east-west axis, defined by "East" and "West" avenues (fig. 5.1, nos. 7 and 8), passes through the Ciudadela and the Great Compound, more than a kilometer south of the Sun Pyramid. These avenues may not have existed in the Tzacualli phase, but the Avenue of the Dead, which probably did exist then, runs *past* the Sun Pyramid and does not have an obvious connection with it. Either the kind of planning involved was unusually subtle for Teotihuacan or, as I think more likely, the locations of the Sun Pyramid and the Avenue of the Dead (and its numerous associated structures, including the Moon Pyramid, the Ciudadela, and the Great Compound) were determined by different considerations.

Nothing about the Sun Pyramid seems to require the Avenue of the Dead to be where it is, and nothing about the Avenue of the Dead calls for the Sun Pyramid to be where it is. The location of the pyramid is surely determined by the location of the sacred cave underneath it. It seems that some other principles or considerations governed the locations of the Avenue of the Dead, East and West avenues, and their associated structures. These different principles need not have been in conflict or have reflected cleavages in Teotihuacan society, but they at least suggest something other than a single-minded focus on one overriding theme. Also, several sizable temple complexes in various parts of the city, especially the northwest, share the Teotihuacan orientation but have locations that do not seem closely related to either the Avenue of the Dead or the Sun Pyramid.

The *orientations* of all monumental Teotihuacan structures are very similar. The only question is whether all have a deliberate skewing of about a degree between their north-south and east-west axes (very clearly present in the Ciudadela) or whether some (such as probably the Sun Pyramid) are rectangular to within a small fraction of a degree.

It is tempting to suggest that the principle represented by the Avenue of the Dead, East and West avenues, and associated structures, including the Ciudadela, did not gain prominence until the Miccaotli phase. Nevertheless, at least the northern part of the Avenue of the Dead seems to have existed before the Miccaotli phase, so perhaps both principles already coexisted in the Tzacualli phase.

The Feathered Serpent Pyramid is the principal pyramid of the Ciudadela. It was the third largest pyramid in the city, about 20 meters high and 65 by 65 meters at the base (Cabrera and Sugiyama 1982:167). We still have little evidence about what was present in the Ciudadela before the pyramid was built. The palatial apartment compounds just north and south of the pyramid are slightly later, and only traces of earlier structures have been found (e.g., Sugiyama 1989a).

The most striking feature of the Feathered Serpent Pyramid is the massive stone carvings that constitute its talud-tablero facades. The carvings on the west side were discovered in relatively good condition by Gamio and Marquina about 1920 (Gamio 1979). More recent work (Cabrera and Sugiyama 1982; Cabrera, Sugiyama, and Cowgill 1991; Cabrera et al. 1989) has demonstrated that similar sculptures covered the other three sides. The several hundred carved heads, plus the stones of the panels and sloping aprons, amount to thousands of stones, of which hundreds weigh several tons each. A number of carved stones this large or larger are known from elsewhere at Teotihuacan, but at no other place in the city is a whole pyramid faced with blocks of comparable size and weight. Most monumental structures at Teotihuacan were achieved by accumulations of stones, adobes, or other individual objects that could be carried by a single person.

The facades of the Feathered Serpent Pyramid provide the earliest securely dated and in situ iconography at Teotihuacan that is clearly related to very high status. One of the two entities that occurs repeatedly is a rattlesnake with feathered body, a somewhat feline nose, and fringed eyes with fringed curls behind the eyes. It would be unwise to connect the meanings of this feathered snake too closely with those of the sixteenth-century Quetzalcoatl. At Teotihuacan, feathered serpents probably had multiple meanings. Grove (1987c) suggests that serpents in Mesoamerica already symbolized rulership in pre-Teotihuacan times. It is tempting to think that rulership was one of the meanings of the feathered rattlesnakes on the Feathered Serpent Pyramid (cf. Taube 1991).

The other major figure that alternates with the serpent heads on the panels of this pyramid has often been called "Tlaloc" because it carries paired rings suggestive of the Teotihuacan storm god. In fact, the rings are above the eyes, not around the eyes, and there is little else to link this figure with any varieties of the storm god. Sugiyama (1989b) argues convincingly that it is not a head at all, but a headdress, comparable to those found on a number of other Teotihuacan representations, often in association with serpents, as in the borders of some Tepantitla murals. R. Millon (personal communication, 1989) notes that Pedro Armillas also identified this representation in the Tepantitla border, as well as on the famous stucco painted shell trumpets with bar-and-dot numerals (Gamio 1979). Taube (1991) also interprets this entity as the headdress of the solar fire serpent, with war and military associations.

The facades of the Feathered Serpent Pyramid are also decorated with numerous representations of conches, scallops, and other marine shells. Similar shells also appear in many later murals and are found in offerings at the Feathered Serpent Pyramid and elsewhere.

Michael Coe has suggested that the facades "represent the initial creation of the universe through a series of dual oppositions" (1981a: 161). He suggests that the rulers of Teotihuacan "established for themselves an identity with the dual creator divinity and the power emanating from him/her." This idea is perhaps not inconsistent with the more recent interpretations of Sugiyama and Taube, and it should also be taken into consideration.

Others, including Coggins (1983b) and Drucker (1974), have suggested that the pyramid facades, as well as other Ciudadela features, may have calendrical significance. Undoubtedly Teotihuacan used at least some aspects of Mesoamerican ritual calendars (Caso 1937, 1967; Langley 1986: 143–53), but I am hesitant to postulate connections between Ciudadela symbolism and calendrical notation or ritual.

Why was the Ciudadela, a monumental structure very different from the Sun Pyramid, built a few decades after the major construction episode of the latter structure? Possibly it represents the orderly unfolding of a long-range plan. Teotihuacan society probably would not sustain the simultaneous construction of two structures as massive as these, and the Ciudadela, even if it were part of the same master plan as the Sun Pyramid, would have had to wait until the Sun Pyramid was finished. I think it more likely, however, that the planners of the Sun Pyramid did not foresee the Ciudadela, and the Ciudadela probably represents new ideas about the symbolism of monumental architecture. It may also represent a new direction in political organization and the ideology underwriting the highest political authority.

The Feathered Serpent Pyramid is also notable for the number of sacrificial burials associated with it (Cabrera, Sugiyima, and Cowgill 1991; Cabrera et al. 1989; Sugiyama 1989a). Single burials that are probably sacrificial are reported from the corners of the several levels of the Sun Pyramid, but as yet we have no evidence of burials on a large scale there. In contrast, multiple burials on both the south and north sides of the Feathered Serpent Pyramid each contained 18 individuals, many with evidence that their hands had been tied behind their backs. They were accompanied by items of military attire, such as slate disks (probably bases for pyrite mirrors); numerous obsidian spearpoints (more than a hundred in the southern multiple burial alone); both real human maxillae and shell imitation maxillae; and thousands of imitation teeth carved from shell. Several individual sacrificial burials have also been found on the south and north sides of the temple. In the most recent work (Cabrera, Sugiyama, and Cowgill 1991; Cabrera et al. 1989), similar multiple burials have been found on the east side of the pyramid and also (in shallow pits) in its interior. An undisturbed multiple burial at ground level at the exact center of the pyramid contained another 20 individuals with different and richer grave goods, including many jade and greenstone ornaments. A very large burial pit a few meters to the west, on the central axis of the pyramid, had been almost completely looted in antiquity, although remnants of rich offerings were found. This pit, as well as another large looted pit found just west of the stairway of the pyramid, might (or might not) have held the remains of one or more exalted rulers. The residue left by the looters is being closely examined for decisive evidence, but at present the question is tantalizingly open. It is *possible* that all the offerings and sacrifices were dedicated solely to the deities associated with the pyramid. I think it much more likely, however, that one or more rulers were buried there.

Much of the pyramid remains unexplored. In all, around two hundred persons were sacrificed there in one episode. This number is low compared to some of the Aztec mass sacrifices, but it is high compared to anything else we know for Teotihuacan. At present the identity of the victims is unknown. They may be captives, and it has even been conjectured that they might be Maya (e.g., Mercado 1987). A number of them have "mutilated" teeth (teeth that were filed or inlaid, or both, for decoration), but these practices are known from the central Mexican highlands as well as the Maya area. The fact that the spearpoints and surviving items of attire are typical of Teotihuacan suggests that the victims may have been retainers of a Teotihuacan ruler rather than captured enemies. Physical anthropological analyses in progress may establish whether the victims were from central Mexican populations or from farther away.

A few years ago I suggested, largely on the basis of its architectural form, that the Ciudadela may have been "the physical realization of the vision of an extremely powerful ruler" (Cowgill 1983:335), although I added that political authority at Teotihuacan had already been strong for some time. I said that although the Ciudadela might reflect important political and perhaps ideological changes, it was also possible that it merely reflected the "orderly intensification of long-term trends" (Cowgill 1983:336) already present at Teotihuacan.

Both Pasztory (1988) and R. Millon (1988b) have carried somewhat further the idea that the Ciudadela represents an exceptional political episode. Pasztory says that construction of the Ciudadela, so different from the earlier three-temple complexes, suggests a change in the nature of political leadership at this time. She sees it as a time of maximum centralization, although she also stresses that "the images on the Quetzalcoatl Pyramid avoid any references to personality or to military conquest. Clearly the state wanted to emphasize cosmic values" (Pasztory 1988). Millon (1988b:112) suggests that "perhaps a successor to the early great leader probably buried in the center of the Sun Pyramid established despotic rule and so tyrannized those in the upper strata of Teotihuacan society that when the opportunity arose, it provoked a reaction strong enough ultimately to lead to an abiding limitation on the power of the ruler."

According to Millon, the rule of this postulated despot was enhanced by the sacralized aura of rulership at Teotihuacan, but I believe he thinks the despot simply manipulated preexisting ideology and did not attempt to create something new. For Millon, the Feathered Serpent Pyramic episode is perhaps less important than the reaction to it, which he suggests set the tone and also the limits of political authority at Teotihuacan for the next five centuries. To me, however, the novelty of the Ciudadela and its monumentality suggest a distinct and intentional break with an earlier ideology whose central focus was the Sun Pyramid. Moreover, we have no evidence elsewhere in Teotihuacan for large-scale dedicatory human sacrifices, although it is possible that others will be found. There is abundant reference to sacrifice in later murals, but no evidence that it was either on a large scale or dedicatory.

In Early Tlamimilolpa times the extensive construction in the apartment compounds that flank the Feathered Serpent Pyramid on its north and south sides included at least one major change in room plans (Cabrera and Sugiyama 1982; Drucker 1974:113–14). There is little doubt that these compounds housed the rulers of Teotihuacan at this time. It is not clear what meanings were initially attached to each compound. The evidence suggests that they began as highly symmetrical units, and through time the northern one was modified to become less accessible and have a stronger managerial emphasis, while the southern one may have had stronger ritual associations (Cabrera, Rodríguez, and Morelos 1982b; Millon 1988a). The paired compounds suggest dual rulership (one should not confound this duality with a moiety system [as does Becker 1975–76] or with the existence of very important subordinate offices), but I know of nothing else at Teotihuacan that suggests a concept of dual rulership was important.

THE LATE TLAMIMILOLPA PHASE (A.D. 300–400)

During the Late Tlamimilolpa phase there may have been a reaction against the earlier regime. One piece of supporting evidence is a quite large, stepped platform that obscures most of the stairway and western facade of the Feathered Serpent Pyramid, the side that faced the main plaza of the Ciudadela. It does not conceal all the west side, and the other three sides were not covered. Nevertheless, the effect would have been to deemphasize the Feathered Serpent Pyramid considerably, and the new platform would have become the object most prominently visible to persons entering the Ciudadela. The platform was built in the style that had become standard for Teotihuacan pyramids: multiple talud-tablero stages in which the moldings of the tablero panels are supported by thin flat tabular stone slabs, whereas the rest is composed of uncut stones and rubble faced with a thick layer of hard concrete and covered with stucco. The final form is very similar to that of the Feathered Serpent Pyramid, but the building blocks are much smaller.

It has been thought that this platform obscured the Feathered Serpent Pyramid very soon after the latter's completion, perhaps no more than 50 years later. Preliminary studies of ceramics from 1988 test pits in the platform, however, suggest that it may have been as much as two centuries later (Cabrera, Sugiyama, and Cowgill 1991).

Construction of the platform suggests a reaction against, or at least a considerable decrease in emphasis on, the things the Feathered Serpent Pyramid stood for. If the platform was built soon after the pyramid it could represent part of a rather direct reaction to the persons, ideology, or both responsible for the pyramid and its accompanying sacrifices. If a period of two centuries elapsed before the platform was built, then reaction to the Feathered Serpent Pyramid and what it meant was either expressed differently or was delayed. For these reasons, a firm date for the platform is urgently needed.

What we now know of the platform tells us little of the new ideology it may have proclaimed. Presumably this new ideology, in general terms, characterized Teotihuacan throughout the rest of its history. Traces of mural painting can be seen on the facade of the platform, including a clear example of a red trilobe sign. The trilobe may have several meanings, but sometimes, especially when red, it indicates sacrificial blood (Langley 1986:296).

Besides the new platform, there are other signs of possible trouble in connection with the Feathered Serpent Pyramid. The details on the left side of at least two of the serpent heads were never completed, although they were covered with red stucco, like the others (Marquina [in Gamio 1979:154 and pl. 69a, b] notes one of these). This could suggest haste in completion of the structure. Moreover, the end of a large fallen stone of the type used for the serpent heads has been quite thoroughly battered and then covered with red stucco (Sugiyama, personal communication 1988). Perhaps in an iconoclastic episode some of the heads, while still in place, were severely damaged and then later covered again with stucco. Finally, there is evidence of an intense fire at the base of the stairway of the Feathered Serpent Pyramid, before it was covered by the new platform. This fire undoubtedly represents ritual destruction, but nevertheless it also suggests that a sharp break was intended.

Both Pasztory (1988) and Millon (1988b) suggest that an institutionalization of an effective restraint on despotic rule occurred at this time, which may have been at least in part a reaction to the postulated tyranny of the preceding era. This new emphasis is, they believe, reflected in the impersonality of later Teotihuacan art, as represented especially by mural paintings, and perhaps by the great proliferation of housing in substantial apartment compounds. Pasztory speaks of a "corporate" ideology, but at least some senses of this term imply something quite different than what Millon (and I think Pasztory herself) has in mind, and some other word would be preferable.

THE XOLALPAN THROUGH
METEPEC PHASES (A.D. 400–750)

The long period spanning the Xolalpan and Metepec phases is by far the best represented in Teotihuacan mural painting and decorated ceramics (and probably in stone carvings other than those on the Feathered Serpent Pyramid). This time, especially the century or two after A.D. 350, is also when Teotihuacan-related symbols and sometimes objects imported from Teotihuacan are most widely recognized, notably on the Gulf coast, at Kaminaljuyu, and at Tikal and other lowland Maya sites. Nevertheless, the area actually administered by Teotihuacan was probably rather small. Millon (1988a) suggests that the "core area" may have covered no more than 25,000 square kilometers, with a population on the order of a third to a half million. I consider these estimates to be minimal; the actual territory and population ruled from the city may have been significantly larger. Surely, however, Teotihuacan never ruled anywhere near the number of people incorporated in the Aztec empire, and it is extremely unlikely that Teotihuacan's political control extended to anything like the number of places controlled by the Aztecs. Nevertheless, Teotihuacan seems to have created a situation in which, for several centuries, it was not threatened by any serious rival. It probably directly administered a fairly small area and perhaps did not even exact tribute or formal acknowledgment of subordination from a very large area, but it was apparently able to discourage the growth of strong competing centers throughout much of central Mexico.

In general, the ideology that was probably institutionalized by Late Tlamimilolpa times seems to have continued, although Pasztory (1988) feels that it may have given way to a more individualistic emphasis and a weakened central authority during the final century or so. Effort seems to have been focused less on monumental architecture than on the more than two thousand large substantial apartment compounds, most of which were first built during the Late Tlamimilolpa subphase and continued into Late Xolalpan or Metepec times. This picture of a society that concentrated on massive areas of rather standardized housing is, however, potentially misleading in two ways. First, great areas of temples and platforms were very significantly enlarged and reworked during this period, and the total volume of this construction was very great (the Ciudadela palaces are one conspicuous exception; after Early Tlamimilolpa times they do not seem to have been rebuilt until the Metepec period). Second, an exaggerated impression of the uniformity of Teotihuacan apartment compounds prevails. Although the *average* size is around 60 by 60 meters, the variation about this average is great, and a high proportion of compounds are considerably smaller or considerably larger. Moreover, the internal layouts of the few compounds thus far excavated have differed strikingly from one another.

Nevertheless, the renovations and expansions of ceremonial and civic architecture during these centuries seem better characterized by the term *substantial* rather than the superlatives used for the awe-inspiring earlier accomplishments, such as the Sun Pyramid, the Ciudadela, and the Avenue of the Dead. As for the apartment compounds, what may be more significant than their variability is their pervasiveness—the fact that an extremely high proportion of the population lived in these substantial structures rather than in the far flimsier or smaller dwellings that sufficed or still suffice for so many people in other nonindustrialized (and industrialized) cities. I do not know what this finding means, but it is surely consistent with Millon and Pasztory's impressions of the ideological changes that characterized Late Tlamimilolpa Teotihuacan.

All these interpretations are plausible, but still provisional. Our understanding of Teotihuacan signs and symbols, including those of political significance, is rapidly increasing. Soon we should know a great deal more about the political ideology of Teotihuacan, and perhaps it will look a little less impersonal than it now seems.

The apparent lack of intense building activity in the Ciudadela until the last century of this period suggests that although it continued to be of high symbolic political importance, it may not have continued to be the central focus of administrative activities (Cowgill 1983). The focus may have shifted to the Avenue of the Dead Complex, a large, mostly walled complex of compounds, pyramids, and spaces that straddles the Avenue of the Dead north of the Ciudadela and south of the Sun Pyramid (fig. 5.1, no. 16). A relief from one of the principal plazas of this complex (Cabrera, Rodríguez, and Morelos 1982b: 312) is accepted by many authorities as a representation of the Teotihuacan "Great Goddess," a principal deity at Teotihuacan. However, I will venture a different interpretation. In both hands, in addition to buds (probably of waterlilies), the figure holds what I think are flaming bundle torches marked with a variant of the trapeze-and-ray "year sign." The nose pendant with fangs worn by this figure is an attribute of the Great Goddess, but it is also rather similar to the nose pendants that occur inside the jaws of the problematic figures with paired rings on the Feathered Serpent Pyramid. Two somewhat similar nose pendants were found in the large looted pit under the

Feathered Serpent Pyramid. Grove (1987e) discusses bundle torches as symbols of rulership in Mesoamerica. The relief from the Avenue of the Dead Complex may represent a ruler, or possibly a deity closely connected with rulership, rather than the Great Goddess.

A Teotihuacan object closely connected with very high position, and perhaps rulership, is the "tassel headdress" discussed in a brilliant paper by Clara Millon (1973). It occurs in Teotihuacan-related contexts at Monte Albán, Tikal, and elsewhere. Many Teotihuacan examples are on looted murals traced by René Millon to a group of adjoining structures in the southwest corner of Teotihuacan map square N5E2. Millon (1988b) has named this barrio Amanalco, and the principal source of murals, apparently an apartment compound of exceptional size (at least 75 by 95 meters), is called Techinantitla (fig. 5.1, no. 17). Here I can only touch on a few of the most relevant aspects of these murals (C. Millon 1988; R. Millon 1988b; Pasztory 1988).

A number of clear glyphs, not merely conventionalized signs, appear on these murals. Only very fragmentary bits of glyphs have previously been known, from the Tetitla apartment compound (Foncerrada de Molina 1980; C. Millon 1973; Villagra 1956–57), where possible foreign associations have made their relation to Teotihuacan problematic. The glyphs from Techinantitla now offer greatly improved prospects for decipherment and perhaps for discovery of the principal language of Teotihuacan. Notable in the Techinantitla murals are unmistakable references to sacrifice, strong military associations (both features also prominent in the murals of the Atetelco apartment compound), and the association of compound glyphs with the figures wearing the tassel headdress (C. Millon 1988).

At least nine of these figures are now known. The figures themselves exhibit no detectable individuality, but a different glyph compound is associated with each. At the very least, this variation represents some sort of differentiation and individualization. The glyphs could stand for places or organizations with which the figures were associated, lineages to which they belonged, or conceivably offices they held. They very possibly represent individual names or titles. Most cannot yet be connected with rulership; however, one of the glyphs shows a serpent head on a mat. The mat is a well-established symbol of rulership among the Maya, Zapotec, and Aztec. Mats are fairly common in Teotihuacan imagery, and they may be associated with rulership there as well (Langley 1986:273). The combination of serpent head on mat is rare, but in addition to the Techinantitla example it is found on a red-on-buff sherd illustrated by Séjourné (1966: 18–19, fig. 1).

Various interpretations of the figures with tassel headdresses at Techinantitla are possible. René Millon (1988b) suggests they may represent celebrated generals. Another possibility is that they are rulers. It seems unlikely that Techinantitla was a royal residence, even though it is exceptionally large; however, rulers might be celebrated in nonroyal structures.

The associated ceramics indicate that the Techinantitla murals are probably quite late. Whether the persons with the tassel headdresses are generals, rulers, or something else, they were probably deceased persons who figured prominently in Teotihuacan traditions. Thus, it seems that important persons at Teotihuacan were not always truly anonymous and uncelebrated. Nevertheless, what we see at Techinantitla is a far cry from the self-celebration that was a vital part of the political game for Maya, Zapotec, and Aztec rulers.

We know enough of the iconography of Xolalpan and Metepec Teotihuacan to be certain that human sacrifice, if it was ever depicted explicitly at all, was not shown often. Yet the art is replete with figures brandishing impaled and bloody hearts and other indirect references to sacrifice, and armed figures in military regalia are well represented. Clara Millon (1988) argues very persuasively that military units (e.g., one associated with coyotes) are celebrated in murals at Techinantitla and Atetelco. It may be that celebration of military persons and units is a late development, but we know so little of earlier art that we cannot be sure.

Nevertheless, everything we now know suggests that Teotihuacan rulers represented themselves as free of any need to be deeply concerned with any human rivals, and that the depiction in public art of success in warfare or of a divine pedigree was not important to legitimize high office. Many people have suggested that Teotihuacan's rulers may have been selected from among some sizable category of eligibles, which would explain the lack of emphasis on ancestry. The absence of victory celebrations may be because Teotihuacan had long since won all the important wars in the core area that it controlled and had no wish to create a larger empire. If they were able to suppress the development of foreign rivals for many centuries without costly struggles, this situation would go far to explain the long duration of Teotihuacan's dominance in central Mexico.

At the same time, a long period without major wars may provide a key to the lengthy persistence of a highly sacralized rulership, and the eventual weakness of that rulership. Eisenstadt (1963) emphasizes the struggle of rulers of early empires for "free-floating resources," that is, for resources that rulers can control or dispose of directly, without being accountable to other individuals or institutions. One highly effective way of acquiring these resources is through conquest; rulers can take personal possession of great quantities of loot and they can rule over subjugated peoples without the inherited institutional constraints that limit their powers over their own people. Another effective way of gaining a higher degree of autocratic power is to assume special emergency powers during some crisis, such as invasion by outsiders, and then refuse to relinquish the powers after the crisis passes.

If Teotihuacan went for several centuries without imperial ambitions and without serious external threats, its rulers may have found it extremely hard to become more autocratic. This lengthy period of peace following on the institutional reaction to an earlier despot postulated by Millon, might explain the persisting sacralized and impersonal appearance of the Teotihuacan state. This model is consistent with the apparent trend toward stronger and more visible military elements. With weak central authority, military units could become strong and self-celebratory, even without much need for serious fighting.

The causes for the violent collapse of Teotihuacan around A.D. 750 remain poorly understood. If one accepts the model I have just sketched, of rather weak rulership that was never able to free itself of traditional constraints, one can easily imagine the society eventually being torn apart by increasingly strong internal factions. But it is at least equally easy to imagine a tradition-bound leadership that was unable to respond effectively when, eventually, other serious rivals, probably less bound by tradition, did arise in Mesoamerica. And, of course, the two possibilities are not mutually exclusive—both may be a significant part of what happened toward the end.

-------- Notes --------

This chapter has profited from the editorial hand of June-el Piper and from comments on earlier drafts by Joyce Marcus, Barbara Stark, Lillian B. Thomas, Robert Zeitlin, and, especially, René Millon. I have not followed all their suggestions, and I take full responsibility for the final version. Writing was aided by a National Endowment for the Humanities Fellowship for University Teachers.

1. Smith (1987) suggests that construction of the Sun Pyramid extended well into Tlamimilolpa times; however, a Teotihuacan Mapping Project excavation in the archaeological tunnel in the uppermost part of this pyramid found no ceramics later than Late Tzacualli.

6

THE TREES OF LIFE

AHAU *AS IDEA AND ARTIFACT IN CLASSIC LOWLAND MAYA CIVILIZATION*

DAVID A. FREIDEL

The discussion of this paper at the advanced seminar in Santa Fe revealed a certain perplexity concerning the Maya field. The new insight we are gaining from the translation of hieroglyphic texts, and the concomitant interpretation of the rich material symbolism of this civilization, is warmly welcomed as a major step in the direction of an anthropological archaeology. Yet the other seminar participants repeatedly challenged me with the slogan, "How do you know?" The problem for Mayanists who are working on the highly volatile and dynamic revisions of our interpretations of ancient lowland Maya civilization is where to begin and what to cover in our status reports from a field that is witnessing discovery at every level of analysis.[1] Technical analyses detailing how we know what we know from epigraphy and iconography are just as dull and opaque to the uninitiated as technical analyses of any other kind in archaeology. So I will boldly assert what I believe we can know, pass over the grim details lightly, and let the skeptical but still interested reader go to the endnotes and the citations. I make no claims to new interpretations or new data here. This chapter presents my armchair view of what I think is going on in the study of Maya ideology.

I intend to cover some of the basic building blocks of Maya civilization. Quite literally, these are the stone buildings, monolithic stelae, and related materials registering power over collective labor and pertaining to the Maya definition of central authority, the *k'ul ahau*, holy lord or spirit master.[2] Before getting into the esoterica of Maya elite material culture, however, let me address some of the problems raised by the seminar. First, the term *ideology* carries a lot of intellectual baggage; I am less interested in the design of the bags than in their cultural contents. Nevertheless, some opening definitions are in order.[3]

I conceive of ancient Maya ideology as the interconnected, fundamental ideas held by elite and commoners alike about the order of the cosmos and everything it contains. Through these ideas, Mayas explained to each other existing patterns and dynamics in the natural and supernatural worlds by means of causal relationships between phenomena. Maya ideology was further a guide to ritual practice, in which people participated in these causal relationships between phenomena—people, things, spiritual forces, natural forces—to achieve certain ends.

Maya ideology, then, was a collective enterprise involving nobility, craftspeople, peasants, the spectrum of society. The reason for this commonality and the redundant, replicative nature of ideological action at different levels of the Maya hierarchy (see Demarest, chapter 7, this volume) is that the ideology was (and essentially remains) shamanic.[4] In shamanism, the material, prosaic world is paralleled by a supernatural world in which the gods, spirits, and ancestors live.[5] Shamans capable of passing between this world and the supernatural one are able to bring to bear the power of gods, spirits, and ancestors to accomplish specific objectives in the prosaic world. The relationship between the natural and supernatural Maya worlds may be to some degree symmetrical, the source of causation in the one resting in the other (certainly ancestors come into this world and end up in the other one.)[6] If the Maya king was at the social and ritual apex, it follows that Maya kingship must have been essentially a shamanic role. Logic aside, ongoing analyses of Maya iconography and epigraphy suggest that Maya royal ritual was indeed shamanic.[7]

Idealism comes in here, in the attempt to engage the forces of the world correctly and effectively. Differential access to the ideal instruments and facilities for implementing ideology in the manufacture of power—temples, jewels, carved stone stelae—reflects the social inequality and hierarchy of the ancient Mayas. This point is an important one, for if Maya ideology was shamanic, then, by analogy with the post-Columbian Mayas, these people widely shared access to its premises and general content. Further, this sharing would have undergirded the integrating effects of ritual performance by kings and other central authorities. If the same kinds of ritual performance were carried out with less effective, less far-reaching instruments and facilities at every level of Maya society, we have a potential explanation for voluntary participation in the construction of the great facilities.

Maya social segmentation was certainly not all sweetness and otherworldly light. We have known all along from contact period documents and descriptions that the Mayas included both rich and poor, that the elites enjoyed the best of everything, and that some Maya commoners in some circumstances suffered privation as a result of inequality. Knowing that the Mayas experienced the dark side of inequality is hardly news: it is virtually an intrinsic feature of social complexity. What is newsworthy is the mounting evidence that we can discern the ideological rationales for inequality, even as we empirically pursue its material expressions through field archaeology.

The broader, institutional expression of the shamanic premises is a complicated matter, especially since it encompasses more than two thousand years of history. Prophets, priests, and sorcerers abound in the contact period literature, along with kings, governors, and warriors.[8] All these people participated in direct communion with supernatural beings and forces to accomplish goals in this world. In the Classic period, the literate elite included scribes, artisans, and second-rank nobility, who, along with the king and his immediate relatives, participated in shamanic rituals. There are many more titled roles and possibilities for interpreting the institutional arrangements of the Classic period courts, but these titles are also expressed in the context of the shamanic rituals.

The institutional arrangements of modern Maya political and ritual life are also variable and complicated; they involve such principles as the cargo hierarchy and the cofradía, and they are characterized by significant syncretism. (Cargo hierarchies are the modern institutions composed of officials responsible for the religious festivals and civic affairs of some highland Maya communities. Cofradías are brotherhoods responsible for major religious festivals in other highland Maya communities.) Still, all of them include a belief in the existence of a supernatural world that is directly accessible by shamans. Peasant Maya spatial and temporal cosmologies are shamanic; they continue to believe in the animal-spirit companions of the shamanism. Shamanism was and remains the foundation of Maya ideology (Vogt 1976), not just for the elites but for all Mayas. My working hypothesis as an archaeologist is that the commoner analogs of elite ritual action can and will be found through the identification and analysis of analogical instruments and facilities (Freidel and Schele 1988a).

Theoretically, ideology can be qualified as political, religious, economic, and so forth. These arbitrary divisions pertain to our own outside viewpoint. For peoples with an integrated world view and ethos, such as the Mayas, ideology was unitary. It is important for us to aim at discovering this unified understanding of the world, for only by passing through it can we usefully isolate these imposed domains for our own purposes. The categorical assertion, for example, that Maya ideology as expressed in ancient texts was religious blinded us to the fact that the Maya clearly also declared political dimensions of their world order in this symbolic material (see Demarest, this volume, chapter 7).[9] The same blindness currently applies to the notion that Maya texts do not contain an economic frame of reference.[10] Unbundling the concept of kingship, then, is an effort to expose the central and unitary ideas. The kingship was the mainpost of Maya ideology; not only did it rationalize central authority, it also guided rational religious, political, economic, and social behavior generally.

In recent work, Linda Schele and I have tried to place a framework around the history of the Maya civilization.[11] In those efforts, we identify what we regard as revolutionary episodes punctuating periods of consolidation and the gradual build-up of new destabilizing social contradictions. These episodes signal the "reinvention" of Maya ideology to cope with pervasive and debilitating social crises. We call these episodes of reinvention *structural transformations* because they involve the redefinition of basic structural building blocks in Maya ideology, which conveniently take such forms as dualities mediated by triadic principles and concentric dualism.[12] Shamanism undergirds these disjunctions and prevails as an enduring and continual frame of reference from the earliest evidence of Maya culture to the present day. The organizing principles of contrast and substitution lend themselves to the manipulations of both ancient leaders and modern structuralists. Our struggle for a cultural evolution of the Mayas draws unabashedly on such diverse theorists as Levi-Strauss, Rappaport, Flannery, and the French Marxists, but I refer the reader to other publications for further consideration of the big picture.[13]

This grand view of the ancient Mayas, "the forest," must be evaluated in light of our understanding of "the trees." The trees, in both modern and ancient metaphors, are the kings of the Mayas, for the institution of k'ul ahau embraces that metaphor among many others, and the kingship is the key to the main span of Maya civilization from the first century B.C. through the ninth century A.D.

Mayanists are confronted with an extraordinary and novel problem as scholars of a pre-Columbian society; our epistemology can no longer be based on material, or materialist, generalities that depend on a silent record. The ancient Mayas may not be talking to us as informants might, but they surely spoke to each other. With text translation we enter the world

of Maya thought and we must contend with their words, their explanations, their frames for the material world. To return to the challenge mentioned above ("How do we know?"), first we must figure out what *they*
knew. Then we have to figure out how to extend that knowledge to the
archaeological record they created, often quite deliberately.

What follows, then, is a status report on some "local knowledge"
(Geertz 1983: 4), Maya ideology as expressed in the central Maya institution of *k'ul ahau*, and some thoughts on how that institution relates to
the largest artifacts left to us by the Mayas, public buildings. We face a
formidable task in translating that local knowledge of the Mayas into comparative terms that do it justice and yet also make it amenable to an
analysis of the cultural evolution of ancient complex society. We are well
on our way, and we are equipped with methodological principles that
work. How do we know? We know because the correlation of text translation, analysis of material symbols, and the identification of intentional
behavior in the context of the archaeological record decisively incorporates more of Maya history, and more Mayanists, all the time. Back in the
good old days of the New Archaeology, my teachers and mentors spoke
of paradigm shift and scientific revolution. Now I know what they were
talking about.

AHAU AS ARTIFACT

By A.D. 199, the lowland Maya had firmly established their definition of
central power, *k'ul ahau*, as both idea and artifact. This idea emerged
during the previous three centuries of the Late Preclassic period. During
this period, the institution of kingship was materially manifested in the
artifacts used by kings in displays of supernatural power: objects to be
worn or grasped in ritual action and architectonic frames on which these
rituals were carried out. Although fragmentary examples of carved stone
stelae occur in contexts predating A.D. 199, and a plain stela is reported
from a Late Preclassic context at Cuello (Hammond 1982), A.D. 199 marks
the first clear display of a Maya king performing shamanic rituals of his
office (Bac-Tul, "rabbit-bone," on the Hauberg Stela; Freidel and Schele
1988a; Schele 1985). The king is conjuring up a Vision Serpent named
Wac Chan (hoisted up, established sky) from whose gaping mouth a god
peers down.

The title of this essay is more than metaphor, for the carved portraits
of kings in ritual action express their supernatural personae in material
form. A central icon of shamanism is the World Tree of the Center, also

called the *axis mundi*. Linda Schele and David Stuart have recently reported discovery of the glyph for stela, *te tun* (stone tree), at Copan
(Schele 1987; Schele and Stuart 1986b). Indeed the Classic Maya king is
routinely portrayed as the World Tree (*yax te* [*che*], green/central/first
tree) by wearing the square-snouted polymorph of lineage (glyph interpreted in Schele and Stuart 1986a) and the god C icon of lineage blood
(Schele and Miller 1986: 77; Stuart 1984a), the principal diagnostics of
the World Tree. In the case of king Bac-Tul, Schele (1985) has documented iconographically that a tree is growing from the vicinity of his
face down over his outstretched hand. As we shall see, the *k'ul ahau* is
not only portrayed as the World Tree, he also raises the sky by means of
the tree as an object (Schele 1987; Schele and Stuart 1986a).[14] He is the
axis mundi facilitating communion between the supernatural and natural
worlds.

HOLY BUILDINGS AND CENTERS

To understand the role of *k'ul ahau* in Maya civilization, we must begin
by dismantling and reconstituting the empirical artifact categories associated with this institution. A very substantial amount of the physical action
producing the germane record of this institution was ritualized, intentional, and systematically interrelated behavior. One of the larger general
categories of artifacts associated with kings is the public buildings of major centers. Where we now have adequate information, we can demonstrate that these buildings were constructed under the aegis of particular
rulers for particular ritual and political functions in the context of particular historical situations.

If ideology is to be explanatory in archaeology, surely this role will be
manifest in the interpretation of "power" as congealed and revealed in
public labor projects. Much has been written on the theoretical implications of Maya public monumental architecture from an etic point of view
(e.g., Flannery 1972; Rathje 1975; Turner, Turner, and Adams 1981).
Although worthwhile, these attempts cannot generate useful hypotheses
for further work on Maya civilization because they are anchored in igno-
rance of the rationales that drove the Mayas to raise these structures. We
are now in a position to approach comparative, etic analysis from a much
more lucid vantage. Maya public buildings were the declared and commissioned work of kings and lesser rulers of the hereditary elite designed
to express the power of their governments and their relationships within
and between realms. Maya kingship was predicated on an official super-

natural charisma that can be usefully compared to the legitimating ideologies of other kingships elsewhere. Maya kingship was dynastic; the
dynasties were predicated on a norm of patrilineal succession reckoned
from founding royal ancestors. This principle of ranking embraces the
Mayas in a large etic category of known institutions of kingship world-
wide. Maya rulers practiced patron-client relationships with lesser elite of
their courts and realms. Again, this common feature of preindustrial complex society is amenable to comparative analysis.

Maya monuments, and elite culture generally, have proven a perplex-
ing problem for archaeologists (e.g., Sanders and Price 1968; Sanders and
Webster 1989) who regard Maya civilization as having sustained a limited
vertical political order that was of minimal economic utility to the larger
society. Maya monumental architecture is indeed a problem because, no
matter how one thinks about it, every year adds to the inventory of
known sites of large scale. The atlas produced by the Yucatan project
(Garza and Kurjack 1980) alone has added hundreds of sites to that single
section of the lowlands. Some of these sites, such as Chunchicmil (Vlcek,
Garza T., and Kurjack 1978), are staggering in their size and structure
density. Similarly, the research at El Mirador in Guatemala (Matheny 1987)
and nearby Nakbe (Hansen 1989) displays the vast size of individual
monuments that Maya governments were capable of building even at
the outset of the civilization in the Middle and Late Preclassic periods
(600 B.C.–A.D. 100). To regard this level of construction as a peculiar
aberration of a basically simple and rural economy is ludicrous.

The failure of Maya archaeology to integrate its most overt expressions
of human behavior, elite material culture and central architecture, has
fostered the characterization of Maya social hierarchy as especially parasitic and ultimately dysfunctional (see Demarest, chapter 7, this volume)
when, in fact, it has been merely confounding. Simultaneously, this failure
to integrate the data has encouraged a focus on the archaeological remains
of simpler Maya residences and communities (Rathje 1983). The notion
that an understanding of village life in the Maya region will reveal an
understanding of the larger society is certainly reasonable. What is not
reasonable is the idea that elite activity is somehow epiphenomenal to the
adaptive forces operating through the common folk. It is not reasonable,
at least, as a defining premise for interpretation. It is a workable hypothesis, if—and only if—the connections between elite activity and the living
conditions of the common folk are elucidated. We can only approach this
hypothesis through effective work on both ends of the social spectrum.

THE PALENQUE POLITICAL LANDSCAPE

Presently, archaeologists classify relatively small, elevated masonry structures with limited interior space as "temples," which suggests that they served as places of worship. We further classify larger, lower masonry structures with extensive interior space as "palaces" or "range structures," which implies that they served as elite residences and administrative facilities. Where we now have substantial epigraphic and iconographic evidence of function, and even named categories, we can demonstrate that these etic categories can obscure rather than clarify the behavior associated with the function and use of these buildings.

For example, House E of the palace at Palenque, the core of an elaborate complex of buildings, is named the *zac tun na* (white stone house) on the Tablet of the 96 Glyphs and is the location of "seating" or accession of the dynasts of this center, who descended from the builder of the complex, Pacal the Great (as declared by the monument's patron, King Bahlum-Kuk II; see Schele 1985 for a gloss of this text). This beautifully carved monument was found near House E in the southwestern court of the palace. It was probably set in a niche in the south stairway of the tower, which in turn was designed to enable observation of the sun setting above Pacal the Great's funeral monument, the Temple of the Inscriptions.

The white stone house was commissioned by Pacal the Great, who placed within it a throne and behind the throne the Oval Palace Tablet, a relief monument showing his mother, Lady Zac Kuk, Resplendent Quetzal, handing him the crown of kingship. Schele (1986) has explicated the iconography of the stucco masks and mouths around the doorways of House E to demonstrate that these artifacts are portals connecting the room to the spiritual Otherworld. Not only does the iconography declare this function, but the room is literally connected to the physical underworld of subterranean chambers below the palace. The *zac tun na* is thus also a place for the king to perform his functions as shaman, to commune with the Otherworld beings.

House B of the palace carries an architectonic image identified by Schele and Stuart (1986a; Schele 1987; Stuart 1987) from their work at Copan to mean *witz*, "mountain," with the connotation of the living mountain. Iconographic analysis shows that the living mountain is an architectonic portal connecting this world to the supernatural, and it is through this portal that the Vision Serpent emerges when elicited by the autosacrifice of the royal person and his immediate family (Schele and Miller 1986: 308).

More than a place of coronation, the North Palace at Palenque is the place of communion that perpetuates the power of *ahau*. Each king of Palenque after Pacal the Great—with the notable exception of Chan-Bahlum, his first son—was crowned here. More than a facility, the palace is the instrument through which *ahau* accesses this power. But the category of *witz* is not confined to palaces: Structure 5D-33-2nd, the pivotal Early Classic royal temple pyramid in the North Acropolis at Tikal (Miller 1986: fig. 15) is also demonstrably a *witz* (Schele and Freidel 1990). Not only is it decorated with the appropriate image, but it has images of humans giving sacrificial offerings in the maw of this creature—the act of which elicits the Vision Serpent from its bowels.

The crosscutting of imposed categories is further illustrated by consideration of the Temple of the Cross group at Palenque. These buildings are ostensible "temples," and in the aggregate they are called the *kuk na* (the House of Kuk or quetzal bird, the historical founder of the dynasty of Palenque after whom the patron of the Tablet of the 96 Glyphs was named: Schele 1987; Schele and Stuart 1986b). *Witz* monsters decorated the outer facades, declaring these buildings to be sacred living mountains. Within the sanctuaries of these buildings, King Chan-Bahlum is portrayed with his dead father, Pacal, from whom he is receiving the objects and prerogatives of the kingship (Schele and Freidel 1990). To underscore the shamanic qualities of the king, he is entitled "way, trancer, co-essence of the Sun." Within the Temple of the Cross, which reiterates the original raising of the sky by First Father, the creation of the house of the Mayas, is a list of Palenque kings that extends back to the gods and commemorates the kings' coronations.

Like House E, then, the Temple of the Cross group is a dynastic monument of the Palenque kings and a place of accession. It is also a place where the king communes with gods and ancestors as a shaman. Architecturally, House E of the palace and the Temple of the Cross could not be more different; functionally, they are demonstrably the same kind of facility. Indeed, they were regarded as such by the kings of Palenque, who understood the one major difference between them: House E was regarded as the place of the dynasty descended from Pacal, whereas the Temple of the Cross was the place of Chan-Bahlum.

The temple group in its final form was commissioned by Chan-Bahlum, first-born son of Pacal, as the monument to his personal accession to the throne (Mathews and Schele 1974; Schele 1976). Accordingly, Chan-Bahlum is not included in the list of dynasts who were "seated" in the *zac tun na*; the list moves directly from Pacal to his second-born son, Kan-Xul, as given by Bahlum-Kuk II on the Tablet of the 96 Glyphs. This empirical pattern confirms the fact that these very different building complexes are functionally identical in this central aspect.

The text and images in the Temple of the Cross group further show that Chan-Bahlum celebrated his accession to the status of *k'ul ahau* in an elaborate discussion of the sequential ritual events and historical actions that declared his divine status. Upon his death, the temple group was replaced as the religious and political focus of the dynasty by the construction of Temple XIV. This temple contains a wall plaque that shows Chan-Bahlum dancing out of the underworld and heading off to the northern sky to join his ancestors (Schele 1988a). The temple group, then, functionally replicates House E but served this purpose only during the lifetime of one king.

Although the Temple of the Cross at Palenque was commissioned by Chan-Bahlum, it probably occupies a traditional site of a royal lineage house of this polity. First, antecedent construction underlies the temple, and Chan-Bahlum's building was merely the last in a series of unknown antiquity—this kind of stratigraphy is a common occurrence in the Maya archaeological record. Second, the tripartite design of this group is the most ancient expression of public architecture in the civilization. One way to test this hypothesis about the placement of the temple group would be to determine whether the House of Kuk is directly underneath the lineage house of Chan-Bahlum in the Temple of the Cross (Schele 1987). Perhaps Pacal did not build his lineage house directly on this ancestral site because his claim was through his royal mother, Lady Zac-Kuk, rather than through his father, Kan-Bahlum-Mo' (Schele 1976). Pacal's oldest son evidently felt the necessity of asserting his legitimate dynastic claim by re-dedicating the ancient lineage house site. Why Chan-Bahlum felt this necessity, whereas his brother Kan-Xul and the subsequent rulers did not, remains a puzzle in the history of this polity.

The Mayas created other architectural categories that we could not see without epigraphic and iconographic control. Grand stairways on buildings, usually accessways to the summits for practical purposes, could be perceived as ballcourts and edges of the Great Abyss, prime portal to the Otherworld (Miller and Houston 1987; Schele and Freidel 1991). Even at Palenque, where the actual masonry court is a modest affair, Chan-

Bahlum proclaims himself a ballplayer in his most important texts in the Temple of the Cross group. His younger brother Kan-Xul designed as his most important monument a grand stairway on the north face of the palace group—a stairway that ended in a single summit facade and did not give access to the palace.

However the historical dynamics play out at Palenque, we now have substantive and testable hypotheses for why Maya governments rebuilt central architecture to create the massed complexes we find. The general trend of the combined textual, artistic, and archaeological evidence shows that Maya rulers rebuilt, refurbished, and rededicated lineage houses of their founding ancestors. Periodically, great kings or great political crises would demand innovative localities and designs, such as Pacal's funerary Temple of the Inscriptions at Palenque. How they redesigned their ceremonial architecture may have much to tell us about their particular strategies of proclaiming and maintaining political power.

THE HISTORICAL ANALYSIS OF MAYA CENTERS

There are many other examples of intentional strategies in the construction of public architecture in Maya centers (Schele and Freidel 1990). Each center for which we have sufficient epigraphic and iconographic control consists of the historical accumulation of similar royal instruments and statements. The emic category of lineage house, named for an anchoring ancestor or signaled as the reiteration of the primordial act of building the home of the Mayas between earth and sky, is just one of many that challenge Mayanists. The funeral monuments, ballcourts, and grand stairways, for example, have been mentioned in passing. In epistemological terms, we can no longer assume that form is a useful guide to function, or that the scale and elaborateness of individual centers are useful guides to their importance in Maya geopolitics—the Temple of the Cross group was, for all intents and purposes, virtually nonexistent within the context of the ongoing ritual activity of the center following the death of Chan-Bahlum.

What is true of this most overt of material categories also holds for the rest of the archaeological record of the Maya. Before we can usefully assess the determinate role of ideology in the evolution of this civilization, we must systematically rearrange the material record into categories of analysis that are germane to this type of inquiry. We will not be able to identify the conditions and dynamics that undoubtedly stand behind the intentional command of the *ahau* until we have mapped out the remains of intentional behavior. These remains constitute a very substantial fraction of the total record.

As if to confirm the urgency of rethinking our understanding of Maya public architecture, Sanders and Webster (1988) have recently discussed the city of Copan in an important article on urbanism in Mesoamerica. Because these scholars have spent many years working with the archaeological record of this community, one might reasonably expect their command of the royal history to register the knowledge of the epigraphers and iconographers who have also been working at the site in recent years.[15] Central to Sanders and Webster's interpretation is the identification of Temple 22 as the residence of King Yax-Pac, and of the nearby courtyard as his residence group (Sanders and Webster 1988: 530). This identification leads them to propose that the Copan acropolis conforms to the expectations of a particular type of city, the "regal-ritual city" (Fox 1977):

> A number of specialized features, such as the . . . greatly enlarged royal household [the eastern courtyard focused on Temple 22], emerged out of earlier institutions . . . but seem to have appeared very late in Copán's evolutionary history, perhaps only during the reign of its last powerful king [Yax-Pac]. The evidence of unusually massive architectural efforts during this reign, along with the appearance of a distinctive ideology based on a syncretism of warfare and solar cults that complemented the old ancestral cults, suggests the rapid crystallization of a true state, as opposed to a ranked or chiefdom form of political integration (Sanders and Webster 1988: 534).

Because Sanders and Webster do not cite any epigraphic or iconographic studies in their analysis of Copan, it is difficult to know how they arrived at their posited ideological syncretism and the bold assertion of state formation under Yax-Pac. What is clear is that their analysis of the city organization of Copan is fatally flawed by misidentification of architectural function. They entirely neglect Yax-Pac's major contribution to the acropolis, his accession monument, Temple 11; in addition, Temple 22 was dedicated by an earlier king, Uaxaclahun-u-Ba-Kawil (18-Rabbit) and functioned as a sacred mountain and a portal to the Otherworld, a place of royal ritual and not a residence.[16] One need only compare the interpretations of Sanders and Webster to those of William Fash (1988), who is conjoining archaeology and history at Copan, to judge the value of a secure command of epigraphic and iconographic evidence. On the positive side, Sanders and Webster are willing to consider history and ideology in the comparative analysis of urbanism in Mesoamerica. We hope that in the future they will pursue this interest armed with the evidence now available to them.

AHAU AS CONCEPT

The title of this chapter looks beyond the epistemological challenge to the theological, philosophical, and political definitions of power inherent in the institution of *ahau*. These meanings are becoming increasingly accessible with text translation and iconographic analysis. The notion of *ahau* as tree, for example, is epigraphically and iconographically demonstrable as a metaphor (Schele and Miller 1986) used by the Mayas to correlate the commonsense dynamics of natural reproduction with the social reproduction of hierarchy and the metaphysical reproduction of sacred power. It is worth contemplating the Maya view of trees and tropical forests as the modern world destroys their forests—along with the rest of the tropical forests of the world—with uncaring abandon.

Trees, for the Mayas, always constituted not only the ambient quality of nature as forest, but also a central means of imposing the qualities of property and human definition on the landscape. Fruit trees and other planted or selected trees are regularly owned, whereas land is usually not owned but rather is temporarily used. Wood is the pervasive medium of life, the source of ash in swidden fields and of the anchoring roots of drained fields, the source of foods and raw materials, and the definition of home, both in the posts of the house and in the surrounding forest. One of the known titles of *ahau*, in addition to *ahau-te*, "Lord Tree," is *chac-te*, "great or red tree." *Chac-te*, in Yucatec, is one of the most common woods used for house posts. Stela 19 at Copan, one of a set of stelae used by Smoke-Imix-God K to delimit the valley as his province, is an *am-te* (Grube and Schele 1988), a tree set up to define the sacred space of ritual (Freidel and Schele 1988a). It should hardly be surprising to learn that a forest-dwelling people used trees for central connecting metaphors in their understanding of the relationship between common experience and sacred experience. Any self-respecting group of Maya farmers can, and could in antiquity, build a house of *chac-te*, but only a worthy polity could build a *ch-ul na*, "holy god house," under the tutelage of a lord inspired by the divine. Any farmer can, and could in antiquity, grow a tree but only an act of divine inspiration could bring forth an *ahau-te*, a "Lord Tree," and the raising of the sky.

We see a world of natural wood and human-made stone in the Maya lowlands, but the Mayas saw a world of human-made wood as well: an organic world of orchards, cultivated jungle, and—as David Stuart has put it—forests of stelae. Whether the Maya farmer of the Classic period regarded his royal dynasty as a natural entity, like the wild fruit tree he chose not to cut when he was preparing cornfields, or as something he himself created and owned, like a planted fruit tree, is perhaps moot. It seems likely, however, that the farmer regarded the nearby center and its king as creations in which his participation was integral. This personal identification is seen in the technology of monument construction. The internal lattice design of Maya substructures is not only a means of encouraging vertical and horizontal stability, it is also a handy, small, and relatively standard unit of effort by which the contributions to public work by different factions of a community can be measured (Freidel 1986c).

The most salient feature of the "ideology" of Maya power is that there is no clear break between the perceptions of the culture held by the population as a whole and the perceptions of the elite. Only a few examples have been given here, but many more are now under investigation (e.g., Taube 1985). Maya kings were regarded as the instruments, objects, and sacrifices of their constituencies. They were the human stuff of power, and like stone, wood, clay, fiber, and food, they were the prosaic materials that could be made luminous, crowned resplendent, and transformed through acts of devotion, skill, and courage.

To be sure, Maya kings used such common understandings as *ahau* to legitimate their particular historical statuses, but these historical "mystifications" are clearly distinguishable from the orthodox beliefs that constrained the possibilities of policy and action. Available evidence from the archaeological record suggests that the institution of *ahau* arose simultaneously throughout the Maya lowland region in the Late Preclassic period as an adaptive response to endemic and pervasive social conditions of de facto elitism and a period of some centuries of early centralization in some regions, such as Peten (Freidel 1986a; Freidel and Schele 1988b; Hansen 1989; Schele 1985). This episode is materially manifested in the regional florescence of central, monumental public architecture (Willey 1977), embodying the principles of power expressed by the kings of such Classic centers as Copan and Palenque. The institution of *ahau* constituted an overall reformulation of Maya culture that rendered elitism natural, rational, and necessary. Because this solution expressed the need felt by Maya society in general for a resolution of the contradiction between an egalitarian ethos and the actuality of hierarchy and inequality, all aspects of the complex religion and cosmology of the Mayas were directly related to the projection of political authority in the institution of *ahau* during the Classic period.

> Centers . . . are essentially concentrated loci of serious acts; they consist in the point or points in a society where its leading ideas come together with its leading institutions to create an arena in which the events that most vitally affect its members' lives take place. It is involvement, even oppositional involvement, with such arenas and with the momentous events that occur in them that confers charisma. It is a sign, not of popular appeal or inventive craziness, but of being near the heart of things (Geertz 1983: 122–23).

An emic interpretation of lowland Maya monumental architecture necessarily leads to the conclusion that these creations combined the sustained labor and skill of constituent populations with the talent and inspiration of the elite to yield viable instruments to amplify and focus the power of rulers. In light of the enormous investment of labor in these objects of power throughout the history and geographic span of the civilization, it is unlikely that their construction was predicated on brute force by the elite. In the investigation of these places we find not merely the grand assertions of kings, but also the remains of their ongoing dialogues with nobility and with the commoner laborers, militia, and taxpayers. The public life of all Mayas, not just the elites, is expressed in these complex communities.

———— *Notes* ————

My notions of Maya ideology are predicated on long-term collaboration with Linda Schele. It is virtually impossible for me to disengage my particular thoughts on the matter from those arising from this collaboration. Although Linda should not be held responsible for the discussions as given, she should be acknowledged for their general thrust.

1. For a clear, engaging, and interesting summary of the major efforts in glyphic decipherment, see Houston (1989).

2. Traditionally spelled *ahau*, *ahaw* is the recommended spelling in the current orthography of Mayan languages (Justeson and Campbell 1984). Although I would like to follow the precepts of my betters in linguistics, *ahaw* simply does not look right to me. Throughout this essay, I have employed the term and discussed the institution as a unified principle of rulership. In fact, the word can

comfortably be glossed as lord, and many nobles besides the king carried it in antiquity.

As observed by Jonathan Haas in discussions during the advanced seminar, the concept of *ahau* itself is subject to ongoing definition among epigraphers and historians of the Classic Maya. The presence of possessive qualifications of the status, *y ahau*, "his *ahau*," in some public texts suggests that a ruler of this status could be subordinate to another. Further, at Bonampak, as noted by Mary Miller (1986: 26–57), the depiction of numerous individuals carrying the *ahau* title in group scenes implies that the status pertains not solely to supreme monarchs, but more generally to the class of people from whom these monarchs may be selected. These complications are particularly evident in texts and scenes dating from the Late Classic period. The Early Classic texts are more firmly focused on *ahau* as king. The qualifier *k'ul* or *ch'ul* is an important one, for it generally pertains to the high king. William Ringle (1988) has discussed the epigraphic argument, and several other scholars, notably David Stuart and John Carlson, also have been working on this term, which generally means holy or divine.

No doubt the institution was dynamic and evolved throughout the history of Maya civilization in ways we can only discern in preliminary fashion (Freidel and Schele 1988b). This essay addresses features of the institution that I regard as central to its original, Late Preclassic period definition, and as relatively stable through its subsequent history. Given the highly volatile nature of our interpretations of Maya civilization as the epigraphic revolution unfolds, any discussion of *ahau* must be regarded as a temporary status report. In the last analysis, the Mayas never did create a separate and unequivocal word for king. This fact may register their ultimate inability to elevate the office conceptually above the nobility, which both required and resented the power of the king.

3. See Cohen (1979) for a succinct summary of the definitional issues surrounding the term *ideology* in anthropology. Shanks and Tilley (1987) mention this issue in passing in their critique of current theory in archaeology. The debate over the intellectual context of archaeology in social theory is interesting, and I have views on the subject in preparation. In terms of priorities, however, that intellectual controversy is less pressing than the need to report the ramifications of breakthroughs in glyphic decipherment and iconographic analysis for Maya field archaeology. My first goal is to bring the ancient Mayas into the arena of comparative, anthropological discussion of social and cultural evolution. I leave it to others, for the moment, to debate the esthetic of my conceptual instruments and exegesis.

4. In his masterwork on shamanism, Eliade (1964) makes it clear, for example, that the *axis mundi* is wherever the shaman manifests it. Ultimately, the vital means of shamanic practice are incorporated into the shaman's person through ecstacy, and all other material means are derivative. We know that Maya

shamans operated in antiquity at the elite level because of their literature and imagery. We know that they have operated at the village level throughout the colonial and national periods. Schele and I (1990) propose that modern Maya village shamanism is the legacy of ancient village shamanism. Given the nature of shamanism viewed cross-culturally, it is much more plausible that the ancient Maya villagers practiced shamanism than the nobility and kings, but presently we can only demonstrate that shamanism occurred among the elite.

5. The subject of shamanism enjoys a rich and extensive literature. I rely here on the definitional discussions of Eliade (1964) but also recommend the fine discussions of Furst (especially 1974).

6. See Schele and Miller 1986, pl. 73, which depicts the Sun God having a vision and embracing the Vision Serpent, a Mayan royal ritual that represents the king communing with the supernatural world. As Linda Schele has pointed out to me, the kings have visions of the supernatural world. Following similar logic, the Sun God is perceived as having visions of the natural world with the same intention of intervention in patterns. Similarly, Schele and Miller 1986, pl. 122, shows the god Chac-Xib-Chac manifesting the World Tree through sacrifice, the world renewal ritual carried out by Maya kings. The natural correlate of this particular event is the rising of Venus, the evening star. Kings, gods, and natural phenomena like stars can be members of the same category of being and can manifest correlative (paradigmatically linked) expressions of the same power dynamics that affect patterns in the natural world.

7. Linda Schele and I have discussed some of the archaeological evidence showing that Late Preclassic definitions of royal practice were shamanic (Freidel and Schele 1988a). Stephen Houston, David Stuart, and Nikolai Grube (personal communications, 1989) have recently identified the ancient Maya glyph for shaman, way, sorcerer, animal protector, spiritual companion (see Houston and Stuart 1989). In specific instances, Maya kings identify themselves with this glyph: for example, King Chan-Bahlum of Palenque. Schele and Freidel (1990) discuss the ritual actions of Classic Maya kings enabling them to pass between this world and the supernatural world.

8. The practice of prophecy through trance communion with the supernatural, clearly shamanic, is well attested and known to archaeologists (Roys 1933). In her seminal work on the dynamics of Maya myth and history, Bricker (1981: 39–40) provides a wonderfully dramatic example of another Maya shamanic practice, the manifestation of the shaman's spiritual alter-ego, his "animal-spirit companion" (uay or way in ancient texts identified by Houston and Stuart [1989] and Nikolai Grube [personal communication, 1989]) during a battle with Spanish forces: "And Captain Tecum, before leaving his town and in front of the chiefs, demonstrated his fortitude and his courage and immediately put on wings with which he flew and his two arms and legs were covered with feathers and he wore a crown. . . . This captain flew like an eagle, he was a great nobleman and a

great sorcerer. . . . And then Captain Tecum flew up, he came like an eagle full of real feathers, which were not artificial; he wore wings which also sprang from his body."

9. J. Eric Thompson's (1966) general point of view; see Schele and Miller (1986) and Houston (1989) for discussions of the history of decipherment of Maya glyphs and speculations about the content of texts.

10. David Stuart is currently crafting a major breakthrough in the economic dimension of Mayan royal rhetoric. Stuart's work on the iconography of "scattering" (Stuart 1984b, 1988) documents a clear connection between the representation of the stuff flowing from the hands of kings in royal ritual and the qualifier *k'ul*, "holy" or "divine," attached to the principal titles of kings. The stuff is certainly the blood of autosacrifice, but it also contains symbols for precious material things—green for greenstone, yellow for precious shell, and mirror elements for iron ores. These exotic commodities appear in the dedicatory offering bowls and plates deposited in buildings. Shell and greenstone were used as currency by the Mayas and other Mesoamericans at the time of the Spanish Conquest (Freidel 1986b). The "scattering" activity may show the king as the source of wealth as well as other forms of power.

11. See Freidel (1986a, 1986b); Freidel and Schele (1988a, 1988b); Schele (1985); and Schele and Miller (1986: chap. 2) for discussions of this framework. Our notion of ancient Maya history is not that it is simply a summary of textual decipherments. Texts and associated art are merely two sources of data, albeit important ones, for the construction of historical interpretations. Other sources include archaeological field data, ecological field data, data from materials analysis, and ethnohistorical and ethnographic data. We have been accused by some colleagues of constructing a monolithic, "fundamentalist" ancient history (Richard R. Wilk, personal communication 1989) that will stifle alternative viewpoints. We could not accomplish this grandiose scheme individually or in cahoots with other Mayanists even if it were desirable which it is not. The very success of the methods of decipherment is measured in the rapid revision of historical interpretations in the wake of new glyphic readings. The synergy with archaeological field data, ecological data, and materials analysis is only just beginning. We conceive of Maya ancient history as the real "middle-range" theory, the bridge between the empirical Maya record and anthropological comparative analysis as attempted by Demarest in this volume (chapter 7).

12. The principal duality is composed of the Ancestral Hero Twins, Hun Ahau (Venus) and Yax Balam (the sun). This duality is mediated by the principle of death sacrifice whereby these archetypical brothers are transformed into parent and child to each other (Freidel 1986a). The transformation, as preserved in the "Quiche Popol Vuh" (Tedlock 1985), is accomplished by magical acts of sacrifice that these boys perform in the court of ballgame sacrifice (Schele and Freidel 1991) in Xibalba, the place of the death lords. They kill each other and bring each other back to life, and in the act of rejuvenation they give birth to each other

as a parent does a child. Sacrifice as a metaphor for the birth of gods is substantiated in the texts of the Classic period (Stuart 1984b). The centrality of the concept of brotherhood to Maya ideology is further expicated by Schele in (1989).

A principal expression of concentric dualism is the relationship between the World Tree and the Trees of the Four Quarters (Roys 1965). The World Tree, a metaphor for the king, is paradigmatically linked with the Vision Serpent, which the king elicits in trances. The Trees of the Quarters are paradigmatically linked to the Celestial Monsters, the arches of heaven: the Pahautuns and Bacabs, the World Bearers. The principal bridging icon is the Double-Headed Serpent Bar, which began in the Preclassic as an architectonic sky frame expressing the homophony between the Mayan words for sky and snake. By the Early Classic period, kings brought the sky frame into the center of their stone stelae, down into their arms where they cradle this conduit of the supernatural.

13. Linda Schele and I have been working on a structural approach to Maya ancient history and archaeology since 1980, independent of the pursuit of a structural archaeology in other domains (see Hodder 1986; Leone 1986). Our intellectual inspiration, for those who are curious, comes from Freidel's exposure to structuralist analysis in the classes of David H. P. Maybury-Lewis and Evon Z. Vogt at Harvard in the late 1960s and early 1970s. It has been empirically shown that Mayan thought is amenable to structural analysis (Vogt 1976); it is a matter of good fortune that they have left a long record that allows structural analysis to yield useful information concerning culture change. As we read more of the British School of symbolic analysis (e.g., Hodder 1986), we are amazed and perplexed by the evident aversion these scholars show to acknowledging and pursuing intellectual anchors in the field of anthropology. From our vantage, the notions of culture and culture change are inextricably anthropological and at the same time central to all discussions of the symbolic.

14. In the Temple of the Cross at Palenque, the glyphic text refers to the object at the center of the main panel, the World Tree, as *wacah chan*, literally "six sky" but also "risen or established sky" (Schele 1987).

15. As of the present, more than forty entries in the Copan Notes series have been written by Linda Schele, David Stuart, and Nikolai Grube and circulated by these scholars among interested professionals.

16. Thus far, no royal residences pertaining to the Copan dynasty have been identified in the settlement zone through epigraphy and iconography. However, Ashmore's (1988) exciting new work in Group 8L-10 through 8L-12 to the north of the acropolis may result in the identification of a royal compound.

7

IDEOLOGY IN ANCIENT MAYA CULTURAL EVOLUTION

THE DYNAMICS OF GALACTIC POLITIES

ARTHUR A. DEMAREST

White (1949:364–65) defines ideology as systems of religion, values, beliefs, or symbols through which human experience finds its interpretation. Here, I would prefer to apply the term more narrowly as it refers to ritual, religion, and explicit cosmology. In most of this chapter, I stress what might be called *religious ideology*, including formal religion as well as the precise guidance of formalized religious institutions or dogmas. In this sense an *ideology* is a set of interrelated ideas that provides the members of a group with a rationale for their existence. A formal *religion* is a particular kind of religious ideology, one based on beliefs in supernatural beings or forces, with a more standardized presentation of these beliefs and, generally, an institutional structure. The political and economic impact of these ideologies is the issue of central concern here, but we should avoid definitions of ideology that are so broad as to be synonymous with political relations, world view, or even "culture." I would prefer to bind my definition more closely to formal, explicit ritual, religion, and cosmology, and only subsequently to examine their broader impact and implications.

The Maya civilization left us with among the richest sets of pre-Columbian evidence on these aspects of culture. Their art, iconography, artifacts, and written texts given detailed views of Maya religion, ritual, and cosmology. Mayanists now have a vast knowledge of Classic Maya world view, myths, and political ideology. It should not, then, be difficult to address the issue of the role of ideology in the history and evolution of the Classic Maya civilization of Central America. Yet, the uneven and incomplete nature of the evidence on Classic Maya economics and subsistence systems makes it difficult to speculate on the relationship between their ideology and their material base. The ongoing revolution in hieroglyphic decipherment and recent discoveries in chronology and subsistence have further complicated the situation by rendering obsolete most of the earlier reconstructions of the nature and dynamics of the Maya state.

It is necessary, then, to begin by assessing the problems of Maya archaeology and the most plausible current interpretations of the Classic Maya state, including its still uncertain functions, its volatile political dynamics, and the apparent sources of power and authority for Maya rulers. In assessing the new evidence on each of these issues, I speculate on the role of ideology and its relationship to other factors in Maya culture history. Finally, I expand earlier discussions (Demarest 1984a, 1986, 1988) of a specific set of analogies drawn from Southeast Asian history that might provide insights into the role of ideology in the evolution and unstable political dynamics of Classic Maya society.

THE PROBLEMATIC MAYA CIVILIZATION: THE ENIGMAS AND MATERIALIST SOLUTIONS

The Maya civilization has always presented a challenge to archaeologists and anthropologists interested in cultural evolution. Unlike the arid river valley systems in which most early states flourished, the Classic Maya civilization flourished in a lowland jungle environment. Moreover, their settlement strategy was dispersed rather than nucleated. Most specific models of cultural evolution have emphasized the role of ecological parameters, such as geographical circumscription, irrigation in arid environments, resource deficiency, and environmental diversity. Yet the Mayas raised their cities and ceremonial centers in seeming contradiction to ecological rationality and achieved their florescence in a dense, subtropical rain forest with generally thin and poor soils, unstable fresh-water supplies, few navigable rivers, and less environmental diversity or environmental circumscription than their highland neighbors.

In light of this ecological situation, it is also interesting that Maya culture was unusually heavily invested in both collective ritual life and individual symbols of ideological power. This investment is manifest in their monuments—ideological statements expressed in millions of tons of stone. Interpreters of ancient Maya culture history have puzzled over a possible relationship between the Maya obsession with ritual and its unusual ecological circumstances as a rain-forest civilization. The easiest solution was simply to dismiss this exasperating tropical civilization by suggesting that the Mayas were a unique culture, that they were a short-lived anomaly, that they never really attained the level of a state, or that Maya states were secondary by-products of more ecologically "normal" highland civilizations (cf. Meggers 1954; Price 1978; Sanders 1962; Sanders and Price 1968; Thompson 1966). These suggestions have never been convincing to most scholars, and archaeologists have continued to puzzle over how and why the Classic Maya sustained elaborate public ritual and architecture in their rain-forest environment.

In the 1960s and 1970s, great strides were made in improving our understanding of lowland Maya ecology, settlement patterns, and written history. Building on these discoveries, some scholars sought to understand Maya civilization by reexamining its ecology and reworking earlier interpretive concepts. Changes in Maya chronology, ecology, and demography seemed to allow for a less paradoxical reconstruction of the early rise of Maya civilization and the managerial functions of the early Maya state. Drawing on this new evidence, the participants in the 1975 School of American Research advanced seminar on Maya origins agreed on a general ecological/demographic model to account for the rise of Maya civilization (e.g., Adams 1977; Ball 1977; Rathje 1977; Sanders 1977; Webster 1977; Willey 1977). This interpretation held that, by the end of the Late Preclassic period, ecological circumstances required a managerial elite and provided them with the means to achieve coercive power. New demographic estimates were believed to show population pressure by Late Preclassic times (Ball 1977). New subsistence evidence seemed to indicate that the Mayas responded to this pressure by intensification of agriculture and the creation of terraces, canals, and raised fields (Adams, Brown, and Culbert 1981; Netting 1977). In turn, these systems would have increased the need for management in their construction and maintenance. Finally, evidence of fortifications implied that in the Late Preclassic period population pressure might have culminated in conflict over resources, creating the need for military leadership (Ball 1977; Webster 1977).

Meanwhile, the ecology and environment of the Maya lowlands was redefined, bringing it into closer alignment with patterns observed for other civilizations. Carneiro (1970) and Webster (1975, 1977) applied a flexible concept of "social circumscription" to redefine the sprawling limestone plain of the Maya lowlands as "socially circumscribed"—

presumably because of the absence of unoccupied zones around it. Sanders (1977) argued that the Maya lowlands could be redefined as "environmentally diverse" since soil qualities, water accessibility, and areas of uplands varied between zones. Rathje (1977) argued that the lack of volcanic stone, salt, and other commodities would further necessitate interregional exchange and symbiosis, creating additional needs for a managerial elite. After these revisions of the evidence, all the factors that had been defined in central Mexico and other world regions as ecological prime movers seemed to apply to the Mayas as well. The Maya lowlanders were believed to have bred themselves into an ecological crisis leading to state formation. By the end of the Preclassic, the responses were agricultural intensification, regional and interregional exchange, and warfare—all responses that helped to generate state leadership.

In the past decade, however, new discoveries have undermined many of these reworkings of the Maya civilization. Recent findings (1) push back the entire chronology for the rise of Maya civilization by four to five centuries, (2) leave the archaeological evidence for warfare several centuries too late for it to be a major factor in the initial rise of Maya states, and (3) generally indicate that settlement patterns suggesting demographic pressure also postdate state formation by at least several centuries (e.g., Andrews V 1981; Andrews V et al. 1984; Demarest 1984a; Freidel 1979; Hansen 1989; Laporte 1986; Matheny 1980; Pendergast 1981; Robertson and Freidel 1986).

In retrospect, it is now clear that we had played some games with terms like "social circumscription," "environmental diversity," and "resource deficiency" in the popular theories of the 1970s. We failed to recognize that these terms are *relative*. Any region can be interpreted as being socially circumscribed or environmentally diverse. Yet, an objective assessment must judge the Maya lowlands as geologically and ecologically *less* diverse and *less* circumscribed than any area of comparable size in Mesoamerica south of the northern Mesa Central of Mexico. Similarly, it is hard to argue for demographic pressure and circumscription before about 100 B.C. Rathje's alleged "resource deficiency" of the Maya lowlands disappears with recent evidence that "needed" goods were available locally (e.g., salt, chert, limestone metates) and long-distance imports were primarily ideological in function (e.g., quetzal feathers, obsidian blades, jade). Thus, problems of both logic and evidence are evident in all of the proposed materialist solutions.

THE INSTABILITY OF MAYA STATES: THE MANY "RISES" AND "FALLS" OF LOWLAND MAYA CIVILIZATION

In the end, efforts to understand Maya ecology and state formation were misled by a flawed chronology. Indeed, current evidence indicates that we may not find a single trajectory and set of causes for the rise of Maya civilization. Instead, we find a complex and heterogeneous civilization, one that may have experienced multiple rises and falls, florescences and declines. The recent research at El Mirador, Cerros, Nohmul, Nakbe, the Mundo Perdido zone of Tikal, and other sites not only provides an earlier general history for the Mayas, it also reveals a multiplicity of contradictory developmental sequences for ancient Maya states (Demarest 1984a; Freidel 1979; Hansen 1989; Laporte 1989; Matheny 1987). Although the rise and decline of El Mirador, Cerros, and Nakbe occurred within the Preclassic period, later and different evolutionary trajectories have been found for other sites.

There is also now evidence for at least three crises between A.D. 0 and 1000: the "decline" at the beginning of the Early Classic, the mid-Classic hiatus, and the southern lowland collapse in the Terminal Classic. Some explanations of these three declines have once again proposed uniform, pan-lowland ecological processes. For example, Dahlin (1983, 1984) has invoked desiccation to explain the Protoclassic or initial Classic collapse of El Mirador, Cerros, and other sites. Sheets (1979, 1983), Sharer (1982), and Dahlin (1979) have suggested that the eruption of the volcano Ilopango in El Salvador was a major factor in the decline of the Late Preclassic centers in the highlands, setting the stage for a Classic period recovery centered on Tikal and the northeastern Peten.

None of these new hypotheses account for the fact that most "declines" of the Maya polities are not chronologically aligned. For example, the Early Classic decline in ceremonial construction activity at El Mirador probably occurs earlier than the parallel declines in Belize. It is also probable that, at least at some lowland sites, the Early Classic population decline has been exaggerated by the persistence of Late Preclassic domestic wares into the Classic period, falsely dating Early Classic houses to the Late Preclassic period (e.g., Hester 1979; Valdez 1987, personal communication 1988; Willey and Mathews 1985). At other centers the Early Classic was a period of great prosperity. For example, Laporte's excavations in the Mundo Perdido zone of Tikal (Laporte 1989; Laporte and Fialko 1985; Laporte and Vega de Zea 1987) exposed a flourishing epicenter with wealth, control over labor, and political development that grew at an accelerated pace right through the Preclassic–Classic interface and into the Early Classic. So, the declines in fortune at some centers, such as El Mirador, were paralleled by florescence elsewhere, as at Tikal. Slightly later Early Classic boom periods were experienced at Altun Ha (Pendergast 1979), Rio Azul (Adams 1986; Adams et al. 1984), and other sites (Mathews 1985).

The so-called sixth-century hiatus has likewise proven to reflect *variability* in the power and construction activity of the major centers rather than a general epoch of decline. Indeed, epigraphic evidence now shows that the sixth- and seventh-century hiatus in northeast Peten was in fact a period of political expansion by centers like Caracol, Belize, and later Dos Pilas, which eclipsed the Tikal regional state (Chase and Chase 1987; Culbert 1988b; Demarest and Houston 1990). The result was a reduction of construction activity by Tikal and its allies. Tikal recovered in the Late Classic, drawing labor and power through its domination of Uaxactun and other sites (Culbert 1988b), but this recovery caused an apparent eighth-century "decline" in construction activity at other sites within Tikal's sphere of influence.

Similar inversely correlated power relations are documented in the hieroglyphic inscriptions, public architecture, and population estimates of other Classic period centers (cf. Willey 1986). Breakthroughs in hieroglyphic decipherments have enabled Mathews and others (e.g., Beetz and Satterthwaite 1981; Culbert 1988b; Houston and Mathews 1985; Mathews 1985, 1988; Mathews and Willey 1990; Riese 1980; Schele and Mathews 1990; Schele and Miller 1986) to plot the boundaries of Maya regional states in the Classic period. These studies have shown that their area was generally small (less than 2000 square kilometers). Stable, large-scale, unified political hierarchies may never have existed in the lowlands (Culbert 1988b; Mathews 1988; cf. Adams 1986; Marcus 1976a), but areas controlled by even small centers could expand or contract by 100 percent in less than a century (Mathews 1988). Some centers, such as Tikal (Culbert 1988b), Caracol (Chase and Chase 1987), and Dos Pilas (Demarest and Houston 1989, 1990; Houston 1987; Houston and Mathews 1985) had episodes of rapid expansion that allowed them to generate large, loose hegemonies.

The picture that emerges from all of the evidence is one of a volatile political dynamic with the fortunes of centers rising and falling throughout the Classic period, and with the networks of subordinate centers correspondingly expanding and contracting. We can presume that their control over labor (voluntary or tributary) for monuments and public architecture varied with these fluctuations, as reflected in episodes of frenzied construction followed by periods of little activity. Similar bursts and declines in construction activity have even been demonstrated in the Preclassic period at Nakbe (Hansen 1989), El Mirador (Demarest 1984a; Matheny 1987), and Cerros (Robertson and Freidel 1986) and in the Classic period at Tikal, Copan, Caracol, and other sites (Ashmore and Sharer 1975; Chase and Chase 1987; Dahlin 1976; Fash 1983). Yet these myriad Maya states were linked together by elite interaction, trade, and ideology into a single, ethnically distinct cultural system—what Freidel, Sabloff, and others have referred to as a "peer-polity" network (Freidel 1986a; Sabloff 1986).

It should be clear from this new historical and archaeological evidence that we can no longer hope to trace a single linear trajectory for lowland Maya civilization. Instead, each regional polity had its own individual developmental history, with large numbers of centers (but not all) aligning only during the ninth-century collapse. In this respect the Maya political landscape resembles that of early competitive states in Mesopotamia and Southeast Asia rather than the more centralized regional polities like Teotihuacan, Tiahuanaco, or Early Dynastic Egypt.

Why is the Maya civilization characterized by heterogeneous and regionalized culture histories? More important, why did they continue to maintain this pattern throughout the Classic period without ever achieving the unification of large regional polities? Local variation in ecology and climate may be a partial explanation, but civilizations that sprawled across far more variable terrains have had much more developmental uniformity and achieved more centralized polities than those characteristic of the Mayas. Any study of Maya history must now address the question of the causes and implications of the political instability as indicated by the archaeological and epigraphic evidence. In turn, the key to understanding the complexity and variability of lowland Maya development may lie in the sources of power in ancient Maya society and the political dynamics that these sources would generate.

SOURCES OF POWER
AND AUTHORITY IN THE CLASSIC MAYA STATES

As in most world regions, discussion of Maya state power has been dominated by functionalist or managerial theories. These theories have designated ecological parameters like arid riverine landscapes (Wittfogel

1955), environmental diversity (Sanders 1968), circumscription (Carneiro 1970), resource deficiency (Rathje 1971), or verticality (Isbell 1978) as responsible for the specific cultural activities (irrigation, markets, territorial warfare, long-distance trade, etc.) that require the development of political leadership for their management or direction. As discussed above, however, because of the new evidence on chronology and environment, the functionalist and environmental theories did not survive the scrutiny of the past decade. Still, we must discover the precise nature of Maya state involvement in local or long-distance exchange, warfare, agriculture, and other activities if we are to understand the unusually volatile dynamics of Maya states. The hard data suggest that Maya rulers were usually most involved in the aspects of each of these activities that relate to ideological authority and political legitimation.

CLASSIC MAYA EXCHANGE SYSTEMS, ELITE INTERACTION, AND IDEOLOGY

Some theories have stressed the role of elite management in Maya exchange systems. Coordination was seen as vital because of ecological pressures for intercenter trade owing to lowland shortages of basic resources (Rathje 1971) or environmental diversity (Sanders 1977)—both of which I criticized above on several grounds (also see Culbert 1977; Dillon 1975; Sharer 1977). From the presently thin evidence on subsistence it would appear that no state-directed complex systems were necessary. The variety of Maya subsistence methods and cultigens (e.g., Hellmuth 1977; Marcus 1982) would have enabled them to balance out any resource deficiencies locally, and each regional Maya polity was probably largely self-sufficient in subsistence goods. Analyses of energetics and transport indicate that throughout Mesoamerica exchange of foodstuffs was limited to the local or intraregional level (e.g., Culbert 1988a; Drennan 1984; Sanders and Santley 1983).

The most recent studies of nonsubsistence exchange systems in the Maya area have also stressed the predominately localized and intraregional nature of Classic Maya economies. Production and exchange of utilitarian objects appear to have been controlled at the level of local communities (Ball and Taschek 1989; Fry 1979; Rands and Bishop 1980; Rice 1987). Long-distance exchange of commodities like obsidian and salt may not have required complex administration (Clark 1986; Drennan 1984; Marcus 1983; Sanders and Webster 1988; Sidrys 1978), but the state was probably involved in trade in exotic goods and high-quality lithics (Belizean chert, obsidian, etc.). Overall, although evidence remains admittedly insufficient, it now appears unlikely that control or management of exchange systems in foodstuffs or utilitarian goods was a principal source of Maya state authority. There is no evidence that these systems were highly evolved or that they were state-controlled.

In contrast, it is clear that rulers and elites were very concerned with exchange of a specific set of nonutilitarian, status-reinforcing goods. Elite trade or gift exchange in status-reinforcing exotic goods was important in *political* interaction. Archaeological research by Ball and Taschek (1989) and compositional studies by Ronald L. Bishop (personal communication, 1988 and 1989) have demonstrated direct elite control of production and exchange of certain fine polychrome ceramic types, eccentric lithics, carved jade, and exotic objects. Other important items of long-distance trade were quetzal feathers, jade, and obsidian. The first two are symbols of rulership, whereas the third had utilitarian uses. However, very fine cherts or highland obsidian obtained by long-distance trade were often used to produce eccentrics for scepters, tools for bloodletting, exotics for tombs and caches, and exquisite spearheads for ritual warfare (e.g., Gibson 1986). Freidel (chapter 6, this volume) and Schele (1984) believe that even simple obsidian blades were often tools for autosacrifice, a hypothesis supported by recent contextual associations with dried blood and bloodletting bowls in temple caches (William L. Fash, personal communication 1986).

Although limited in quantity, these exotic goods were critical in identification of the divine elite class, enhancement of their prestige, and definition of their relations. Sabloff (1986) and Freidel (1986a) have emphasized that these elite exchange networks were critical to peer polity interaction, while limited redistribution of exotics reinforced the loyalty and patronage of nobles and retainers. Thus, the managerial involvement of rulers in trade systems seems to have been focused on items of an *ideological* nature, items that formed a very limited, but politically critical, portion of the lowland economy.

CLASSIC MAYA WARFARE, INTERACTION, AND IDEOLOGY

Warfare was another area in which Maya rulers had a managerial role, yet again the role generally focused on the ideology of political legitimation. Warfare had an early impact on the development of Maya society, probably as a pressure enabling chiefs to extend their power beyond kinship-defined systems (cf. Demarest 1978; Webster 1975). Yet its direct economic impact, positive or negative, appears relatively small when compared to its impact on central Mexico, Peru, or Bolivia (as described by other contributors to this volume). Warfare became less restricted during the last part of the Classic period and in situations of conflict across ethnic boundaries (Cowgill 1979; Demarest 1978; Webster 1975, 1977), but epigraphy and archaeology show that defeat in warfare did *not* usually lead to political domination of the defeated center. For example, it has been demonstrated that Quirigua's famous defeat of Copan (celebrated in many monuments) did not lead to territorial control of Copan by Quirigua or to an economic decline at Copan itself. Indeed, after this defeat, Copan went on to its greatest period of monumental construction. The same occurred after Tikal's defeat in A.D. 678 by Dos Pilas (Demarest and Houston 1990). Tikal's next king, Ruler A, was *not* a vassal of Dos Pilas; rather, he led Tikal into its greatest period of florescence.

Throughout most of the Preclassic and Classic periods, warfare was ritualized and culturally constrained to varying degrees (Demarest 1978, 1984b; Freidel 1986a; Schele 1986). In most cases the spoils of war were probably sacrificial victims, the status reinforcement of the victory itself, access to some captives as slaves, and some amount of tribute (primarily in nonsubsistence exotic goods). As Freidel (1986a) has pointed out, warfare was usually closer in its effects to interdynastic marriage than to territorial absorption; in other words, it was another form of elite interaction, alliance, and information exchange. Moreover, like all of the other forms of elite interaction, Maya warfare was deeply embedded in ritual and religious institutions. Like coronations, period-endings, births, funerals, and other royal events, warfare provided an occasion for the elite visits and elaborate public rituals that helped to hold the Classic Maya world together. Recent syntheses of deciphered Maya texts have detailed the elaborate webs of ritual events and contacts between elites (e.g., Mathews 1988; M. Miller 1986; Schele and Mathews 1990; Schele and Miller 1986).

Still, the economic and political impact of Maya warfare in some cases could be quite significant, especially in the cases of the territorial expansion of conquest states like those of Tikal (e.g., Culbert 1988b), Dos Pilas (Demarest and Houston 1989, 1990), and Caracol (Chase and Chase 1987). Yet even these largest of Maya conquest states controlled extended territories for less than a century before they retracted to "standard" size for Maya polities. In most cases the political or economic gains from warfare came indirectly from ideological effects—the enhancement of the prestige of the victorious ruler and his lineage. For example, the sacrifice of Copan's high king enhanced Quirigua's prestige, legitimated the power of its dynasty, and increased the local power of its rulers over their own populace (Fash 1988; Fash and Stuart 1990; Sharer 1978). The higher status of Quirigua's dynasty was ensured by the public ritual of royal captive sacrifice repeatedly advertised in public monumental sculptures and inscriptions. Thus, the dynasty strengthened its power over the populace and increased its ability to draw on the labor and loyalty of the citizens—an ideological effect that led to very concrete material gains. The same occurred in the case of the defeat of Tikal by Dos Pilas in A.D. 678. Tikal was not dominated, nor did it lapse into deeper decline, but the prestige of Dos Pilas's Ruler 1 was greatly enhanced by the victory, which was celebrated in many stone monuments. The increased prestige helped to launch this young center on its own campaign of expansionism.

INTENSIVE AGRICULTURE AND THE ECONOMIC ROLE OF MAYA LEADERSHIP

The role of the state in constructing or managing agricultural intensification or hydraulics is as yet unclear. In Yucatan, polities may have been involved in the management of fairly substantial agricultural and water-management systems (Harrison and Turner 1978; Matheny 1976; Turner 1974). In the rain forest of the southern lowlands, these managerial activities might have been less crucial. The discovery of raised field and canal systems in some areas led Mayanists to envision intensive agricultural systems across wide stretches of the Peten (Adams 1983; Adams, Brown, and Culbert 1981; Culbert, Magers, and Spencer 1978; Matheny 1976), some of which were identified using SLAR and other satellite and aerial imagery. Some of the SLAR imagery interpretations were questionable, however, and subsequent ground checking has disproven the existence of most proposed systems (e.g., Dahlin, Foss, and Chambers 1980; Dunning and Demarest 1990; Pope and Dahlin 1989). In most areas, soil types and lacustrine hydrology are inappropriate for extensive raised field agriculture (Dunning and Demarest 1990; Pope and Dahlin 1989). These findings cast doubt on theories that raised field agriculture, state-directed or otherwise, was a major subsistence base for the lowlands.

The most recent studies of rain-forest ecosystems view them as incredibly complex and fragile with a wide diversity and dispersal of species. Human systems successfully adapt to rain forests by mimicking this dispersed nature and complexity. Thus, Maya agriculture was probably a complex mix of techniques, each in relatively small units, adapted to the limits and possibilities of specific types of econiches (Dunning and Demarest 1990; Nations and Nigh 1980; Ruthenberg 1981). Again, this finding casts doubt on the need for centralized management—or even its desirability (cf. Flannery 1968a). Certainly, the specific types of agricultural regimes in the lowlands could have been managed by local corporate groups.

Even if large-scale intensive agricultural systems were present in some areas, it does not follow that state control existed. Mayanists sometimes overlook the implications of decades of research in Mesopotamia, which demonstrate that extensive irrigation systems in Ubaid and Early Uruk times were probably locally constructed and managed without major state intervention (Adams 1965, 1966, 1969, 1981; Adams and Nissen 1972). In the southern Maya lowlands the irregular distribution and alternation of swidden plots, raised fields extending outward from uplands, and irregular canal systems can be compared to the Ubaid pattern: growth by accretion of many small, local efforts. An even better example of the disjunction between political power and economic infrastructure can be seen in the rain-forest civilizations of Southeast Asia, the so-called galactic polities or theater states (Bentley 1986; Geertz 1980; Gesick 1983; Tambiah 1976). Some of these states have complex systems of intensive agriculture with an elaborate bureaucracy, yet most analysts agree that the state itself probably had no control over local economic systems (Bentley 1986; Gesick, ed. 1983).

Direct archaeological evidence for state involvement in agricultural management is lacking in the southern lowlands. Hierarchies of administrative centers, unpopulated agrarian landscapes, and highly organized and aligned fields, canals, or raised field systems have not been found. The state-controlled agricultural landscape described by Kolata in the Titicaca basin (chapter 4, this volume) contrasts sharply with the Maya patchwork of garden, slash-and-burn, terrace, and occasionally raised fields. Nor is there evidence or representations of rulers' involvement in agriculture in the extensive, propagandistic Maya monumental art, murals, ceramic art, and artifacts, unlike that found in Egypt, Mesopotamia, and elsewhere. The kinds of metaphorical claims of Maya control over nature described by Freidel (chapter 6, this volume), Freidel and Schele (1988a, 1988b), and Taube (1985) were statements of only a broad spiritual power to invoke prosperity or fecundity. This negative evidence is hardly conclusive, but it does raise doubts about the common assumption of state management based on the mere presence of extensive field or terrace systems in the Maya area.

Thus there is an absence of any clear iconographic, settlement, or administrative evidence for state involvement, and the specific Maya agricultural regimes identified in any one zone were apparently autonomous, diverse, and not extensive. It is probable, then, that the agricultural managerial function was weakly developed in the Maya state. It is rather distressing that after more than a century of archaeological research in the Maya lowlands, we still do not really know the role of the state in Maya agriculture or even the precise nature of the agricultural system itself. Ongoing research is exploring southern lowland agricultural systems on a regional level and looking for evidence of any degree of management or involvement by the elites of regional centers. Given current evidence, however, it seems highly unlikely that control of agricultural systems was a major element of Maya state power.

THE ROLE OF IDEOLOGY IN MAYA POLITIES

One inescapable deduction from the discussion presented above is that both local power and interpolity connections were based heavily on ideological support and sanction: in other words, the role of ritual, religion, public display, and monumental propaganda was central to Classic Maya society. We have seen that this ideological component was critical to elite involvement in both long-distance trade and warfare, and that other economic functions for state leadership may have been poorly developed. Here I would like to stress what should be obvious: religion itself was a principal source, perhaps *the* source, of the power of Maya rulers.

In a recent series of works, Schele, Freidel, Miller, Stuart, and others have detailed the ideology of kingship that held Maya polities together by legitimating the ruler's role, sacralizing the elite class, and specifying rulers' ritual and shamanistic functions (Freidel 1981a, 1986a; Freidel and Schele 1988a, 1988b; Schele 1985; Schele and Freidel 1990; Schele and Miller 1986; Stuart 1984b). As Freidel demonstrates (chapter 6, this volume), the Mayas viewed their leaders as embodiments of the axis of the universe and conduits of communication between the secular and divine worlds. The latter included the world of the Maya earth-sky deities, the world of the revered ancestors, and the world of other divine rulers here on earth. The glyphic and iconographic evidence leaves no doubt that the Mayas themselves considered these roles of *axis mundi,* source of sacred blood, prognosticator, and royal shaman to be the principal functions of the ruler. The bulk of Maya labor was spent in construction of the elaborate stages of their ceremonial centers—plazas, temples, facades, monuments, costumes, exotics, and paraphernalia—all for these ritual events. Warfare and long-distance trade provided, respectively, the captives and goods needed to stage and costume these awe-inspiring displays.

The interaction between elites of different centers reinforced the power drawn from local rituals and religion by sharply defining the class that had access to this power. As Helms has shown (e.g., 1979), the interaction of rulers with their distant peers was similar in its legitimating effect to Maya rulers' claims of contact with the upper worlds of the sky gods or the lower worlds of ancestors and deities. Thus, elite interaction not only defined relations between centers but also enhanced the ruler in his local role as a spiritual leader. We have seen that long-distance trade and warfare were especially concerned with interpolity interaction and elite peer definition.

Other mechanisms of intrapolity interaction reinforced the ties between the major center and its local subordinate centers or rural populations. For example, Vogt (1983, 1985) emphasizes the importance of ritual circuits and movements from center to periphery in ancient and ethnographic Maya culture. The movement of idols from the center to the periphery of sites was critical in all periods as indicated by the ethnohistorical record (Coe 1965; Tozzer 1941) and by the archaeological presence of ceremonial causeways connecting temple complexes within and between sites. On a wider scale, Freidel has stressed the role of religious pilgrimages and periodic markets in Maya settlement patterns (1981b). He points out that these mechanisms enabled the Maya to hold states together against the centrifugal force of the ecologically adaptive rainforest settlement pattern of residential dispersion.

Thus, the ideological role of leaders cannot be dismissed as their own "emic" delusions; they were a very real, direct source of prestige, charisma, and, thus, access to labor and resources. A recent study by Monaghan (1990) of contemporary and ancient Mixtec sacrifice and tribute shows how elites acquired resources through direct payment for religious services. These "gifts" often took the form of status-reinforcing goods that symbolically defined membership in the ruler class. In exchange for privilege and power, elites provided religious services and their role as intermediaries with the spiritual world. Similarly, the impressive public displays carried out on the stage of Maya ceremonial centers were a direct source of support—not merely legitimating, but generating power. The epistemology of many archaeologists in recent years has dictated that ideological factors must be regarded as a reinforcement, legitimation, or simply a "phantasmic representation" of the "real" (generally economic) sources of power. But studies analyzing state power in Southeast Asia and elsewhere have proven that in some states the rituals themselves are a true source of power, and sometimes it is state control of the underlying economic base that is "phantasmic."

SOUTHEAST ASIAN AND MAYA GALACTIC POLITIES: THE DYNAMICS OF IDEOLOGICALLY DEPENDENT STATES

The previous observation leads us inevitably to consider the remarkable similarities between political dynamics in the Maya area and those of Southeast Asia. Striking parallels to lowland Classic Maya states can be found in the historically known polities of Southeast Asia (Coe 1961; Demarest 1984a, 1986, 1988), variously called "galactic polities," *negara, mandala,* or "theater states." I have already reviewed salient characteristics of Maya states, including the competitive dynamics of the peer-polity landscape, the instability of individual polities, and the critical role of rulers in warfare, in trade for prestige goods, and in grand ritual display in the ceremonial centers. All of these features and many more similar traits are found in the polities of Southeast Asia.

GALACTIC POLITIES AND THEATER STATES

To improve our understanding of Maya political dynamics and the role of ideology, particular insights can be gained through application and modification of concepts developed by historians and archaeologists studying Southeast Asian polities (e.g., Bentley 1986; Fritz 1985, 1986; Fritz, Michell, and Rao 1985; Geertz 1980; Gesick, ed. 1983; Higham 1989; Tambiah 1976, 1982, 1984; van Liere 1980). Through comparisons we can benefit from the more complete record of the historical kingdoms of Southeast Asia, a long scholarly tradition of analysis, and the past two decades of debate on the nature and sources of power in these polities. We can also hope that the striking similarities among these rain-forest civilizations might reveal some broader explanatory factors.

All conceptions of the segmentary states of Southeast Asia view them as forming a volatile, competitive, peer-polity landscape (*sensu* Renfrew and Cherry 1986). Like the Classic Maya kingdoms, Southeast Asian polities were highly unstable and had inversely correlated fortunes. Yet, as in the Maya case, these polities shared cultural values and traits that gave the regional civilization an enduring character. Together they formed "a

vast political arena in southeast Asia, made up of a number of principalities, changing boundaries and affiliations and possessing an identity by
virtue of commitment to a religious political ideology, on the one hand,
and of sharing similar economic, demographic, and logistical features, on
the other" (Tambiah 1982:18). As with the Mayas, Southeast Asian civilization endured for millennia, but individual states had complex and
volatile political histories. Each polity consisted of a loose hegemony with
a principal center surrounded by a galaxy of smaller subordinate centers,
which in turn dominated local centers and populations.

The major characteristics of what Tambiah termed the "galactic polities" of Southeast Asia are largely parallel to those of segmentary states
elsewhere, but they are especially similar in structure to the Maya hegemonies described above, particularly in their political dynamics and state
ritual. Tambiah (1976, 1977), Geertz (1980), and Fritz (1986) describe
how the structure of these states and even the physical characteristics of
their centers reflect a cosmological model (*mandala, negara*): an emic vision of the kingdom and the role of the ruler that reinforces both the
ideological functions of the state and its structural instability. The most
salient characteristic of these polities is the great importance of ritual performances in their ceremonial centers and the awe (and authority) that
these displays generated (Geertz 1980; Tambiah 1976, 1977). Other important features include (1) the organization of hegemonies into capital
centers loosely controlling a cluster or galaxy of subordinate centers; (2)
a redundancy of structure and functions between the capital center and
dependencies; (3) an emphasis on control over labor and allegiance rather
than territory; (4) little direct control by the rulers over local economic
infrastructure; (5) an extreme dependency on the personal performance
of the ruler in warfare, marriage alliances, and above all, ritual; and (6)
the tendency of these states to expand and contract in territory, reflecting
the dynamics resulting from all of these features, as dependencies struggle
against authority or shift allegiances or as expanding capitals impose
short-lived attempts at centralization.

Like Maya political structure—and unlike idealized central-place
models—the elements in these Southeast Asian hegemonies were hierarchically organized in power and status but did not represent a strong
hierarchy of functions. According to Tambiah, the major center and its
principal satellites were "a decentralized constellation of units that repli-
cate one another in that they show minimal differentiation of function"
(1976:113) or, as Bentley puts it, "a nested hierarchy of functionally

undifferentiated units" (1986: 292). Because of this redundancy, subordinate centers had less *need* for the affiliation with the capital center than the center had for affiliation with its subordinates, and there was a large potential pool of usurpers for each capital. The rulers of each subordinate center also had their own claims to divine authority, which created circumstances conducive to rebellion by satellites and to competition for those satellites between adjacent major hegemonies. The result was an unstable political landscape that very much resembles the shifting alliances of the Classic Maya world.

The source of power in galactic polities was control over networks of human relationships and labor, rather than physical control of territory. In Southeast Asia this emphasis on labor, rather than land, was related to low population densities and dispersed settlement patterns. As Bentley notes, "the limiting factor on political development throughout the region was not territory but mobilizing sufficient labor to exploit it" (1986: 298; see also Bilgalke 1983; Kirch 1984; Wheatley 1983; Wyatt 1984). "Such labor could be obtained by capturing it or by attracting it" (Bentley 1986: 290). Thus, as with the Mayas, the emphasis is on warfare between elites and on charismatic ritual performance to maintain and expand ideological control of the population. Political allegiance, power, and the degree of centralization of the state were dependent on these networks of personal, political, and religious control that radiated out from the ruler himself through subordinate centers and to their populations. In this sense the *mandala,* like Maya polities, were flexible "center-oriented" networks rather than sharply delineated, "bounded" territories (Tambiah 1977: 74).

Many of these features may relate to the general characteristic discussed earlier: weak involvement of these Southeast Asian states in management, control, or administration of economic infrastructure. "The actual control over men and resources (the political center, so to speak) sat very low in the system" (Geertz 1980: 134). The upper tiers of the political hierarchy extracted labor and support from below, but not efficiently and with little or no administrative control of local units and their agricultural activities. This characterization is remarkable given that these societies were originally considered examples of Wittfogel's coercive "Oriental despotisms." Nonetheless, the past two decades of research in Southeast Asia have produced a consensus on the unusually limited degree of state involvement in intensive agriculture and irrigation: "it appears that in these states both large and small, irrigation control was a localized cooperative affair" (Gesick 1983: 3–4) and "there were no state-owned or state-managed waterworks of any sort" (Geertz 1980: 69). Terrace systems were similarly controlled entirely at the local end (Geertz 1980: 68–86). A few late, unusually large states may have imposed state order on some aspects of agricultural systems, but even this possibility is in doubt. For example, some archaeologists and historians studying the "ultimate" water control system around Angkor Wat have concluded that at this

> locus classicus of "hydraulic despotism," recent archaeological evidence suggests that the foregoing observations are also applicable there, that is, that the irrigation systems of Khmer villages in Angkorian times appear to have been quite separate, localized affairs, unconnected with the spectacular waterworks of the temple complexes, which were designed wholly with ceremonial uses in mind (Gesick 1983: 3–4; cf. van Liere 1980).

As discussed earlier, in the Maya case the data on local economies are too scant to justify a similar conclusion. However, the probable limited economic involvement of the Maya states could help to explain other parallels to the Southeast Asian *mandala*.

THE CENTRAL ROLE OF IDEOLOGY IN ASIAN AND MAYA THEATER STATES

A principal source of a king's power in the Southeast Asian polities was even more directly ideological than that of Maya rulers. His status was most enhanced by (1) the ruler's role in the center's rituals; (2) his supervision of politico-religious rites in subordinate centers; (3) his celebrated periods of study with revered holy men; (4) his acquisition and public worship of heirlooms and renowned idols; and (5) other mechanisms of public ritual and ideological interaction (Geertz 1980; Tambiah 1976, 1977, 1982, 1984; cf. Gesick, ed. 1983). In turn, this increased spiritual status attracted the loyalty of subordinate centers, often manifest in their desire for linkage through political alliance, especially royal marriages. Thus, the expansion of galactic realms was based, above all, on ideological power and prestige generated by these activities and by the ruler's performance in elaborate public ritual. Tambiah notes that the central ruler controls his satellites "not so much by the real exercise of power as by devices and mechanisms of a ritual kind that have performative validity" (1976: 125). Similarly, Geertz's elegant presentation of the rituals of Bali's "theater states" shows how "the state drew its force, which was real enough, from its imaginative energies, its semiotic capacity to make in-equality enchant" (1980: 123).

In fact, the specific, detailed descriptions of Southeast Asian rulers' competitive invocations and manipulations of the spiritual framework of the *mandala* or *negara* are again strikingly similar to the growing body of evidence on the Maya theater states. Descriptions of the Maya cosmogram and its political implications by Freidel and Schele (1988a, 1988b; Schele and Freidel 1990; Schele and Miller 1986; Freidel, chapter 6, this volume) perfectly fit the theater-state model of the "whole polity being held to-gether as an ordered unity by the king's enactment of cosmic rites and his role as the validator of his satellites' credentials" (Tambiah 1976: 123). Even the specific mechanisms used to hold the satellites to the center were similar, including movement of idols, installment rites of local rulers, po-sitions similar to those in cargo hierarchies for local leaders in the kings' courts, and reification of the cosmogram (and its politically legitimating effect) in frequent rites defined by time cycles and involving directional movement and rotation. The historical descriptions (Geertz 1980; Tam-biah 1976, 1982) indicate the importance of the central role of public ritual displays in maintaining the power of kings. Like the Maya *ahau* described by Freidel (chapter 6, this volume), the ruler of a Thai polity was the central axis of state ritual and the personal embodiment of the cosmological principles of the state. The capitals themselves—in both Southeast Asia and the Maya area—incorporate a series of settings for public performances that reenact and reinforce the divine model of the state, structurally replicating the order of the cosmos with the ruler always at its center.

The spectacular and complex nature of the ideological reinforcement (art, ritual, architecture, etc.) involved in maintaining the galactic polities should not seduce archaeologists or historians into misreading them as indicative of great coercive power, centralization, or stability. This heavy investment in ideology was built on little or no control of the economic base and no direct provision of local economic benefits. Because of this ideological dependence, state hegemonies were highly vulnerable to short-term ecological crises, military defeats, interruptions of trade in exotics, or any other factor that might reduce the charisma of the ruler: "behind the doctrines of the exemplary center, of graded spirituality, and of the theater state . . . behind these ritually inflated notions we see the dynamics of poli-ties that were modulated by pulsating alliances, shifting territorial control, and frequent rebellions and succession disputes" (Tambiah 1976:123).

IDEOLOGY AND THE "PULSATIONS" OF CLASSIC PERIOD
SOUTHERN LOWLAND MAYA POLITIES

In Southeast Asia, far-flung polities did sometimes arise that were comparable to the larger Maya hegemonies maintained by Tikal, Caracol, and Dos Pilas for one or two generations. The expansion of these hegemonies occurred when a charismatic leader came to rule a major center and expanded his alliance through warfare, marriages, and ritual display. Also important in episodes of expansionism were exchange and contact with the world beyond Southeast Asia, which were symbolized in exotic goods that reinforced the prestige of the ruler and subordinates by displaying "other worldly" knowledge structurally equivalent to spiritual knowledge (see especially Tambiah 1976, 1984; cf. Helms 1979). Yet, among the Southeast Asian *mandala,* the more widespread hegemonies would usually last at most a few generations, and ultimately, "this process of centralization was abortive" (Tambiah 1976:127). The ideological framework of these theater states held the cultural system together but could not sustain larger, individual states.

The similarities of this system to Maya political dynamics boldly highlight the role of ideology in the Maya world. The Classic southern lowland Maya centers may have had the same redundancy of functions and economic weakness as those in Southeast Asia, along with the corresponding emphasis on ritual, shared cosmology, and elite interaction to hold polities together. In the Maya case these weaknesses also led to the same instability in political control. The rapid but short-lived expansions of the political networks of centers like Tikal, Dos Pilas, and Caracol were also initiated by charismatic leaders who extended their alliances through public performance, marriage alliances, warfare, prestige-reinforcing connections to distant realms, and redistribution to subordinate leaders of exotic symbols of power from those realms.

Specific and now well-documented histories of the expansion and contraction of Maya hegemonies are remarkably parallel to the volatile histories of the segmentary theater states of Southeast Asia. The complex history of the kingdom of Tikal is one example. The impressive religious architecture, sculpture, and ritual settings of the Tikal center in the Middle and Late Classic periods reflect the central ideological component of their expanding hegemony in the fourth and fifth and in the seventh and eighth centuries (Culbert 1988b; Jones 1977, 1990; Laporte 1989; Laporte and Fialko 1985; Mathews 1985, 1988). However, the Tikal hegemony also relied heavily on status reinforcement through contacts with distant capitals like Teotihuacan, redistribution of exotic goods from those regions, and dynastic marriage alliances (Coggins 1975, 1976; Culbert 1988b; Demarest and Foias 1991; Jones 1977; Schele 1986; Schele and Mathews 1990; Taube 1991). Both Early and Late Classic episodes of Tikal's expansion of influence ended with a corresponding contraction of their power and political alliances. Status-shattering defeats reduced both tribute and the ideological pull of that great center (Chase and Chase 1987; Demarest 1990; Houston and Stuart 1990). This contraction is reflected in Tikal's archaeology in dramatic reductions in the monuments and architecture that functioned as the stages of its ritual displays, created and staffed through the state's control of loyal corporate labor.

Another episode of expansion of a galactic polity, that of the eighth-century Dos Pilas hegemony, is currently being documented by archaeology and epigraphy (Demarest 1990; Demarest and Houston 1989, 1990; Houston 1987; Houston and Stuart 1990). Dos Pilas probably relied more heavily than Tikal on warfare and the ideology of militarism. Note, however, that the direction of expansionism (up and down the Pasión River) suggests that control over highland trade routes in exotics was one probable motive for the warfare, again reflecting the demands of elite ideological competition for status-reinforcing goods. The victories of Dos Pilas and subsequent public sacrifice of high-status captives are celebrated in the many stela monuments and hieroglyphic stairways of the Petexbatun and Pasión regions (Houston 1987; Houston and Mathews 1985; Houston and Stuart 1990). Unlike much of the ritualized warfare of the Classic Maya, the wars in the Petexbatun region during the seventh and eighth centuries often resulted in actual conquest and territorial expansion. The ability of the Dos Pilas hegemony to expand, however, may have resulted as much from the success of its propagandistic advertising of the defeat and sacrifice of rivals as from military occupation; the combination of victories, their accompanying rituals, and the monumental propagandaenhanced the prestige of the Dos Pilas rulers and, thus, their ability to contract subordinates through marriage alliances or ritual ties (Demarest 1990:611–612).

In comparisons of the Maya and Southeast Asian political histories, we see remarkable similarity in the specific sets of ideological mechanisms and institutions used to generate, legitimate, and expand royal power. Rituals of temporal cyclicality, center-periphery movements, and rotation of offices and idols were used by both civilizations in their futile attempts to make the center hold. Both civilizations shared an emphasis in art, ritual, and myth on a framing cosmogram, a sacred geography for political action (cf. Tambiah 1976; Freidel and Schele 1988a, 1988b), and both regions have left us a rich corpus of politico-religious art, elaborate rituals, and complex regional histories documenting rulers' charismatic performances or disappointing and brief runs on the stages of these "theater states."

Perhaps, then, the central role of ideology and its particular manifestations in ancient Maya "galactic polities" also can help to explain the contradictory trajectories of Maya regional culture histories—the enigma of the inversely correlated rises and falls of some of the greatest Maya centers. These events need not be seen as idiosyncratic and based on the appearance of "great men" or on imagined ecological crises. Rather, they have a basis in the structural characteristics of the system: the weakness of economic control by centers and the heavy dependence on ideology for state authority. This political framework sets a stage for expansion of spheres of influence through the force of an individual leader's charisma and ability, through propaganda victories in warfare among elites, or through the ideological manipulation of economically trivial foreign contacts. Unfortunately for centers like El Mirador, Cerros, Caracol, Tikal, and Dos Pilas, this political framework was as fragile as it was fluid, resulting in the repeated collapse of the hegemonies it generated.

CONCLUDING SPECULATIONS

I have argued that Maya civilization existed in a state of dynamic instability because of its particular institutional and structural characteristics. In so doing, I seem to contradict ecological and materialist functionalism in positing that a major civilization had states in which economic functions were weak and in which power was heavily based on ideology. The existence of these state-level societies in Southeast Asia, Africa, and the Maya world underscores the problems of the distinction between the *legitimation* of power and the *generation* of power. When embedded in a cultural context with historical inertia, what were identified as the ideological "legitimating" activities of the state may actually be the primary source of power for that state.

Issues of causality must be resolved by demonstrations of chronological priority, but owing to the constant feedback between ideological power and the *reinforcement* of political or economic power, it may not be possible to make chronological and causal distinctions. Still, it is clear that an imposition of a materialist paradigm could *not* explain the inception or the continued existence for thousands of years of either the Southeast Asian kingdoms or southern lowland Maya systems of galactic polities. Only by accepting a major role for ideology as a direct source of power can one understand the institutions of these civilizations, their history, and the elaborate cultural concepts that sustained them.

Despite the apparent disagreement with materialist approaches over the importance of ideology, there is also an implicit admission in this discussion that in long-term cultural evolution, economic and ecologically based power may be more enduring than power based on ideology. The more secure material and coercive bases of power held by states like Teotihuacan or Tiahuanaco may have made them more stable polities. More important, subsequent states built on their economic and cultural institutions, which led to ever more extensive, populous, and energy-intensive political systems. In contrast, the ideologically dependent galactic polities of the Classic Maya lowlands and Southeast Asia seemed doomed to repeat perpetual cycles of internal expansion and decline. In the end, these fragile systems faced overall disintegration, absorption, or externally stimulated transformations to more economically oriented polities. These aspects of the system, especially its dependency on ideology and charismatic leadership, may have resulted in political involution, rather than evolution. Thus, common ground between culture-ecologists and "holists" interested in ideology may be found by focusing on cultural evolution in its longest terms and most grand scale.

8

INCA IMPERIALISM

THE GREAT SIMPLIFICATION AND THE ACCIDENT OF EMPIRE

GEOFFREY W. CONRAD

Students of ancient civilizations, even those who see economic inequality and intrasocietal conflict as the prime movers in social evolution, generally agree that no state has ever endured by force alone. Coercive means of social control have never been sufficient in and of themselves, and any state also has to provide positive motivations for its subjects to participate in its projects—the more enthusiastically, the better (e.g., Godelier 1977, 1978a, 1978b, 1978c; Haas 1982:29; Liverani 1979:297–300; Miller and Tilley 1984:7, 14; Trigger 1985:54). Likewise, even investigators who emphasize intrasocietal conflict agree that one of the primary means of eliciting voluntaristic support is through ideology (e.g., Haas 1982: 174–81; Liverani 1979:297; Miller and Tilley 1984:14).

My goal here is to expand on themes presented in *Religion and Empire* (Conrad and Demarest 1984) by inquiring more deeply into the role of ideology as a motivating force in the growth of the Inca Empire (ca. A.D. 1440–1532). "Ideology" itself is a notoriously elusive concept, subject to multiple definitions (McLellan 1986:1–9). Here I define an ideology as a set of beliefs that provides the members of a group with a rationale for their existence. An ideology tells the members of a group who they are and explains their relations to one another, to people outside the group, to the past and future, to nature, and to the cosmos. These ideas also establish rules for acting properly, given those relationships (Conrad and Demarest 1984:4–5). Depending on perceived circumstances, ideologically proper action may consist of support for or opposition to the status quo.

This definition combines elements of Geertz's (1973:90) definition of religion, followed by Grove and Gillespie (chapter 2, this volume), and Friedrich's (1989:301) view of ideology as "political ideas in action," championed by Kolata (chapter 4, this volume). The definition of ideology advanced here integrates meaning, motivation, and action. If it shades more toward religion than politics, I find that acceptable in the case of the Incas, for whom religious and political thought formed an integrated whole united by belief in a supernatural order (Conrad and Demarest 1984:5).

In brief, I will argue that religious reforms instituted by the founders of the Inca Empire followed one of the classic motivational strategies of propaganda: that of reducing complex, traditional systems of thought to a few simple, powerful ideas. This process, which might be called the "Great Simplification," created a sense of divine mission, enabled Inca leaders to motivate ever-increasing numbers of citizens, and drove a small ethnic polity outward as an irresistible military force. In so doing the Incas were able to achieve material goals and advantages denied to their rivals, which in turn fostered further imperial triumphs.

I will also suggest that this "ideological adaptation" (Demarest and Conrad 1983; Conrad and Demarest 1984:180–83) succeeded far beyond the intent of its instigators. The Inca people were so highly motivated for conquest that they turned their state into a vast empire before their rulers had even defined imperial hegemony as a goal. In other words, the means (religious reforms) overran the original ends to produce an "accident of empire." Although economic motives were unquestionably important in Inca imperialism (Conrad and Demarest 1984:122–24, 173–78), this accidental quality cannot be explained without recognizing the crucial mobilizing power of state religion.

WHY DID INCA MILITARISM SUCCEED?

HISTORICAL BACKGROUND

The Incas were just one of many historically known peoples who emerged in the south-central Andean highlands in the aftermath of the breakdown of Tiwanaku civilization (Kolata, chapter 4, this volume). In the power vacuum produced by this collapse, petty states and chiefdoms fought to establish themselves as the rightful heirs of Tiwanaku and to reap the benefits this dominion would bring.

In part these conflicts stemmed from the environmental diversity of the Andean world, which brought economic advantages to polities able to maintain access to multiple ecological zones (Isbell 1978; Murra 1972).

Political factors were equally important as causes of warfare, however, in that the leaders of local societies had strong vested interests in pursuing militaristic policies. By distributing the spoils of victory to his followers, a successful war leader could build a patronage network to serve as his power base. These political and economic causes worked together to produce a chronic state of petty warfare that lasted from roughly A.D. 1200 to around 1450 (Conrad and Demarest 1984: 94–99, 106–107, 140–44, 178–79).[1]

The Incas rose to imperial power by prevailing in these conflicts, at first locally and eventually across some 4300 kilometers of the Andean world. They began their course of imperialism by emerging victorious from local power struggles after more than two centuries of constant war. To do so, they must have developed an advantage over their neighbors, something that made Inca militarism more successful than that of their competitors. To explain how the Inca Empire arose, then, we need to ask what that decisive advantage might have been.

MILITARY CONSIDERATIONS

In a situation of chronic warfare, a number of factors can confer an advantage on one of the contending groups. The critical difference can be superiority in any of several factors: numbers, supplies and logistics, weapons, tactics, training, discipline, or motivation. Available analyses of Inca militarism (Bram 1941; Murra 1986; Rowe 1946: 274–82) are not as complete as we might wish, and a major new study would be very useful. Nonetheless, the data at hand do offer some basis for assessing the source of the Incas' military prowess.

There is no doubt that in later imperial times the Inca army usually outnumbered its enemies and also had better logistical support, including state storage complexes and llama trains to provision the troops (Bram 1941: 59; Rowe 1946: 274). These advantages were conferred by imperial success: as Rowe (1946: 274) notes, the Incas' military efficiency increased with the expansion of their empire.

It is unlikely, however, that Inca armies enjoyed superior numbers, supplies, or logistics at the beginning of their imperial career. Those advantages seem to have been held by the ethnic polities of the Titicaca basin, most notably the Colla and Lupaqa. These Titicaca basin kingdoms had large populations and highly productive subsistence economies, along with movable food surpluses and vast herds of llamas to carry them

(Murra 1975). The Incas gained control of these riches only *after* their conquest of the northern Titicaca basin (Conrad and Demarest 1984: 94, 106–107, 125, 140–47, 157–63). Thereafter the wealth of the Titicaca basin bankrolled further expansion, but it cannot explain why the Incas originally prevailed in their local power struggles or why they were able to conquer the basin itself.

Likewise, it seems impossible to attribute Inca victories, particularly in the early decades of expansion, to superior weapons, tactics, training, or discipline. Inca armies fought with standard Andean weapons and tactics, and in these matters the Incas and their enemies were evenly matched (Bram 1941: 56–59; Rowe 1946: 274–76). In terms of training, the Inca armies were manned by taxpayers fulfilling one type of labor obligation to the state. At least at first, these draftees served on a rotating basis and received no more military training than the average Andean male. It was not until the empire was already well established that anything remotely approaching professional troops appeared, and even then only in the form of subject ethnic groups whose sole tax obligation was to provide soldiers for the army (Murra 1986: 53–54). Finally, as far as discipline is concerned, Rowe (1946: 278) notes that the battlefield discipline of the Inca armies was so loose that it actually reduced the impact of their numerical superiority.

Numbers, supplies, logistics, weapons, tactics, training, discipline— all seem unable to explain how the Incas first gained a military advantage over their neighbors. We might, therefore, ask whether the decisive factor lay in the realm of motivation.

MOTIVATION AND IMPERIALISM

In his analysis of the Neo-Assyrian Empire, Liverani (1979: 299) argues that "an effective, victorious, enduring imperialism is generally a self-convinced and even fanatical imperialism." Liverani further stresses that material incentives for imperialism always exist but are insufficient in and of themselves. What produces a "self-convinced and even fanatical imperialism" is strong and pervasive ideological motivation (Liverani 1979: 299–302).

I suggest that ideological motivation was, in fact, the key to the Incas' success. What I mean by this claim is that Inca ideology produced a self-conviction that reached the point of fanaticism. This fanaticism gave the Incas the decisive advantage over their neighbors and brought about their initial conquests. In turn, these early victories, particularly the conquest of the northern Titicaca basin, reinforced the ideological motivation with the material advantages that figured so prominently in subsequent campaigns.

IDEOLOGY AND MOTIVATION IN THE INCA STATE

The Inca Empire was born in a moment of crisis, when a hostile group known as the Chankas attacked the Incas and threatened to overwhelm them. At the height of the Chanka crisis, one or more charismatic figures inspired a small group of militant individuals to seize control of the Inca state. Rallying their people behind them, the new Inca leaders repulsed the Chanka invaders, gained a temporary respite, and began to consolidate their power. Among their actions was a series of religious reforms that produced a new central state cult (Conrad and Demarest 1984: 110–12, 144–45).

These religious reforms provided the ideological motivation crucial to Inca imperialism. In the new central cult, the mummies of dead Inca rulers were believed to be the divine sons of the "sun god" Inti, as well as incarnations of Illapa, the thunder or weather "god." These mummies, the embodiment of the gods on earth, were both the visible manifestations of the fertilizing forces of nature (the sun and the weather) and the direct physical links between the Inca people and their pantheon.

Hence these sacred corpses were both economically and ideologically crucial, for they were believed to play central roles in the state's agricultural production and in the Inca cosmos. The Incas' well-being depended on maintaining the prosperity of the royal mummies, and they were treated as if they were still alive. They retained all the property they ever owned, while the living emperor was forced to conquer new territories in order to ensure his own eternal support (Conrad and Demarest 1984: 112–21, 145–47).

This revamped state religion necessitated imperial expansion in ideological terms. Proper treatment of the royal mummies *in perpetuity*, which was required for the Incas' very existence, was made dependent on Inca victories. The state cult also rewarded ferocious warriors with earthly advancement and places of honor in the afterlife. In so doing, Inca state religion integrated economic, social, political, and ideological factors into a unified cult of imperial expansion. The net result was to instill the Inca people with a sense of divine mission that propelled them to their initial conquests (Conrad and Demarest 1984: 121–25, 147, 180–83).

Following the lead of Cowgill (1975a), Demarest and I have emphasized the need to examine this ideological motivation on the level of individuals and social subgroups, not just society as a whole. Seen from this perspective, it becomes apparent that in the initial decades of imperial growth Inca leaders succeeded in motivating ever-increasing numbers of people, beginning with small nuclear groups and eventually reaching entire societies. The reforms instituted by the new regime came to drive all ethnically Inca citizens both as individuals and as members of various social subgroups. Families, larger kin units, ruling elites, lesser administrators, priests, rural farmers—all were impelled by the central state cult. To some extent the motivating effect even spread to citizens from subject ethnic groups, who contributed their labor to their conquerors' fields, public works, and armies—in part because of the threat of coercive force, but also in part because of ideologically induced consent (Conrad and Demarest 1984: 123–24, 147, 173–78; Godelier 1978c: 13).

PROPAGANDA, IDEOLOGY, AND MYTH

What gave the Inca religious reforms sufficient power to activate citizens to serve the political and economic ends of the state? To help answer this question, we might look for parallels. Today the use of ideology for political motivation falls under the heading of "propaganda," one of the most pervasive features of the modern world. Propaganda sustains all contemporary social orders (Doob 1935: 85; Ellul 1965: 32), but probably its most dramatic contribution has been the fomenting of the great totalitarian revolutions that have done so much to shape the twentieth century (Ellul 1965: 288).

Scholars who have considered this question have recognized that propaganda was also a pervasive feature of early civilizations (Jowett and O'Donnell 1986: 38–39; Lasswell, Lerner, and Speier 1979). Specific cases that have been examined include Sumer, Akkad, Assyria, and Babylonia (Finkelstein 1979), Vedic India (Sharma 1979), imperial China (Wright 1979), and the Mexica Aztec (Conrad and Demarest 1984: 33–44, 76–77; Townsend 1979). Particularly relevant is Liverani's (1979) analysis of propaganda in the Neo-Assyrian Empire, which foreshadows some of the arguments raised here, including the notion of the Great Simplification. Accordingly, I believe the study of ancient and modern propaganda can offer valuable insights into the active role of religious beliefs in the Inca state.

Propaganda is information disseminated to serve a cause. Specific definitions vary (e.g., Doob 1935: 71–90; Ellul 1965: 61–87; Jowett and O'Donnell 1986: 16), but all authorities agree that propaganda is fundamentally an attempt to mobilize individuals by influencing their attitudes (Doob 1935: 3–4, 31, 89; Ellul 1965: 30–31, 61; Jowett and O'Donnell 1986: 15–16). In this context an "attitude" refers to an individual's state of mind in regard to some particular matter—that is, to a cluster of thoughts that predisposes the individual to act in a certain way toward that matter. Most attitudes are formed on the basis of stereotypes, which may be defined as pictures individuals construct about the world, or knowledge people imagine they possess (Doob 1935: 29–36).

Effective propaganda must be based on ideologies and myths that already exist and are widely shared within a society (Ellul 1965: 32, 38–39; Jowett and O'Donnell 1986: 116, 163). If propaganda is to succeed in appealing to enough people to achieve its ends, it cannot run counter to a society's collective beliefs. Instead, it must manipulate established beliefs to create new myths and stereotypes that are prior justifications for whatever goals the propagandist will eventually seek to instill in his audience. In so doing, propaganda "furnishes him [the individual] with a complete system for explaining the world, and provides immediate incentives to action" (Ellul 1965: 11).

THE GREAT SIMPLIFICATION

SIMPLIFICATION IN MODERN PROPAGANDA

The "Great Simplification" is my name for an essential technique by which ideology is transformed into propaganda: the reduction of a traditional system of thought to a few simple ideas. The importance of the Great Simplification as a motivational tool has been explicitly formulated as a guiding principle by all of the foremost modern practitioners of propaganda. For example, *Mein Kampf* stresses this point repeatedly. The chapter on war propaganda (Hitler 1939: 227–42) is full of exhortations to simplify the message.

A belief in the efficacy of the Great Simplification is not confined to demagogues and street agitators. All leading scholars of propaganda have stressed the fact that reducing ideologies to a few basic concepts makes them more forceful motivators (e.g., Doob 1935: 96–98; Ellul 1965: 38, 200; Jowett and O'Donnell 1986: 46). Complicated ideas will be obscure or inaccessible to many people and are therefore ineffective. In contrast, a message that has been simplified to the point where it can be repeated over and over in sloganlike fashion has a much greater chance of being heard and heeded.

THE ROLE OF THE CORE GROUP

A key feature of the Great Simplification is that it begins with a core group. The core group is a small nucleus of people endowed with great strength of conviction who take upon themselves the task of spreading the new doctrine through whatever propagandistic means lie at their disposal. They use the Great Simplification to make the masses become their adherents. In this way the core group builds an organization with itself at the head (Ellul 1965: 12, 204, 288; Hitler 1939: 846–67).

THE GREAT SIMPLIFICATION IN THE ANCIENT WORLD

To date, most studies of propaganda in ancient civilizations have been descriptive and have not spoken to the questions at issue here. In one case, however, an interpretive study suggests that a Great Simplification may have taken place. In his analysis of Neo-Assyrian imperial ideology as propaganda, Liverani (1979: 299–302) repeatedly emphasizes that the propagandistic message was effective only because it was able to reach all social levels and groups. The message achieved this global pervasion because it was simplified as it moved outward from the Assyrian ruling class.

Liverani (1979: 297–99) also stresses the need for the core group, in this case the Assyrian ruling class, to believe its own message—that is, to be itself ideologically motivated. To Liverani, the Assyrian ruling class had strong political and economic motives for imperialism, but those concerns alone were not sufficient to rouse anyone to action. It was ideological motivation that gave the members of the Assyrian ruling class their credibility, both to themselves and to others, and thus their effectiveness. The result was, in Liverani's (1979: 299) phrase, "a self-convinced and even fanatical imperialism."

THE GREAT SIMPLIFICATION IN INCA RELIGION

My contention is that the royal mummy cult of the Incas exhibited the characteristics of a Great Simplification. First, like all effective propaganda, it was grounded in already existing ideologies. Second, it simplified those existing ideologies, which were highly complicated, and distilled from them a few central ideas that served as powerful motivating forces in the Inca expansion. Finally, we can trace the spread of the cult outward from a small core group to the rest of society via propagandistic means.

GROUNDING IN EXISTING IDEOLOGIES

There is no doubt that the reformed state cult was deeply rooted in traditional beliefs and practices. In fact, the reforms were acceptable and effective precisely *because* they represented logical reworkings of established religious concepts (cf. Adams 1979:59). The beliefs and practices underlying the imperial cult were already present in pre-imperial Inca society, which in and of itself is enough to make them traditional in the eyes of ethnically Inca citizens at the time of the transformation. In fact, though, the basic concepts were considerably more ancient and widespread (Conrad and Demarest 1984:99–105, 116–18, 140, 146).

The creation of the royal mummy cult involved the crystallization of a solar patron deity, Inti, out of a multifaceted sky god complex. It also represented a manipulation of ancestor worship and, even more fundamentally, cults of the dead. These underlying phenomena—manifold sky gods, ancestor worship, and more general cults of the dead—were traditional elements in the ideologies of south-central Andean peoples.

The "sun god" Inti, the divine ancestor of the ruling dynasty, was actually one facet of an overarching divine complex composed of countless individual aspects. Demarest (1981) has shown that manifold "high gods" of this nature were found throughout the south-central Andean highlands at the time the Inca state emerged. The original form of the divine complex was a generalized creator/sky/weather deity that could be unfolded into different subcomplexes, or clusters of aspects, in different rituals. This basic form dates back *at least* to Tiwanaku times and may be considerably older (Demarest 1981).

Cults of the dead have considerable antiquity in the Andean world. In fact, they appear to be the basic form of Andean religion. The archaeological data on the earliest manifestations of Andean religions are still spotty. Nonetheless, the elaborately prepared Chinchorro mummies of northern Chile (Allison et al. 1984) suggest that cults of the dead centered around the actual possession of mummies developed in some areas as early as 6000 B.C., roughly 7500 years before the rise of the Inca Empire.

These cults eventually became manifest in a tradition of formalized ancestor worship that "formed the core of Peruvian religion" (Zuidema 1973:16). Throughout the Andean world in late prehistoric times the local kin group's ancestors were venerated as its protectors, and their bodies were treated as sacred objects. Typical expressions of these beliefs included sacrifices to the dead and the periodic repetition or recelebration of funeral rites, with renewals of grave offerings (Anonymous 1919; Arriaga 1968; Avila 1966:156–57; Bandelier 1904; Cieza de León 1959: 311–13; Conrad and Demarest 1984:101–105, 142–43; Hernández Príncipe 1923; Polo de Ondegardo 1916:116–19; Zuidema 1973, 1983, 1985, etc.).

Ancestor worship and cults of the dead were by no means uniquely ethnically Inca or upper-class phenomena. Inca ideology was imposed on conquered peoples less than a century before the Spanish Conquest and was never fully integrated with local religions. In provincial areas, uniquely Inca beliefs were easily eliminated by Spanish campaigns against idolatry, but ancient and widespread concepts proved to be far more durable (Kubler 1946:396–97). Native rituals of ancestor worship, including the veneration of mummies, were still being practiced throughout the central Andes in the mid-1600s, more than a century after the Spanish Conquest (Bandelier 1904). In fact, veneration of ancestors has persisted among Andean Indians into modern times (Mishkin 1946:465; Valcárcel 1946:474). In view of this enduring strength, the fundamental and pervasive importance of cults of the dead in Andean religion cannot be overstated.

SIMPLIFICATION OF EXISTING IDEOLOGIES

Pease (1973), Duviols (1967, 1976, 1979), and above all Zuidema (1964, 1973, 1977a, 1977b, 1982, 1983, 1985) have helped to elucidate aspects of traditional Andean ideologies. Highland Andean civilizations developed extremely complicated systems of belief encompassing calendrics, astronomical movements and alignments, the geography of the Andean world, and social divisions, any of which could be symbolically transformed into the others. Within this general system of thought lay an upper pantheon composed of the multifaceted divine complex discussed above (Demarest 1981).

The Incas simplified these belief systems by stressing the solar associations of the ancient divine complex. They eventually isolated one solar aspect, Inti, as a national symbol and dynastic ancestor. Note that this simplification consisted of giving the overarching divine complex a clearly defined primary emphasis. The other aspects did not disappear, but they did tend to fade into the background and to become increasingly esoteric details of state religion—knowledge primarily of concern to specialists. The aspect most forcefully promulgated to the public was the newly defined central focus, the cult of the national patron.

Similar simplifications took place with regard to the ancient institutions of ancestor worship and cults of the dead. Zuidema (e.g., 1973, 1983, 1985) has shown that ancestor cults and mummy worship were thoroughly integrated with a virtually incomprehensibly complicated body of ideas about the order of the cosmos, the segmentation of time, the division of geographical space, and social organization. Again, the Inca religious reforms simplified these ancient, more diffuse beliefs and practices by giving them a sharply defined focus. Ancestor worship was directly linked to the central solar aspect of the pantheon. The Incas were to provide eternal support for the mummies that embodied the sun in the world of humans. This starkly simple idea formed the militant core of state religion.

MOTIVATIONAL IDEAS

Through the Great Simplification of their religion, the Incas succeeded in doing what none of their competitors had been able to do—integrate economic, social, political, and religious factors into a unified cult of warfare and conquest. This new cult made militaristic expansion an ideological necessity. The royal mummies—supernatural beings on whom society's welfare, and in fact the Incas' very existence, depended—had to be supported in proper fashion. The Incas' living dead demanded perpetual income, and continual warfare and conquest would guarantee these paramount necessities for each ruler in his turn (Conrad and Demarest 1984:116–21, 146–47, 181–83).

In other words, the Incas developed a stereotype of themselves as a chosen people; in league with their pantheon through their ancestors' divine corpses, they acted to ensure the preservation of their world. Conquest was not merely their right, but their sacred duty. This sense of divine mission generated an intense devotion to the state and its causes, institutionalized drives for conquest, and transformed Inca society into a ferocious war machine. The Inca Empire's initial victories were brought about by the virtually fanatical motivation of its armies.

PROPAGATION BY A CORE GROUP

Of the individuals who rose to power through the Chanka crisis, Inca oral tradition emphasized one figure—Pachakuti, who became the first emperor. In fact, official state histories credit the invention of the Incas' royal ancestor cult to Pachakuti. Although these accounts probably slight the contributions of other members of the new regime, it does seem certain that the Great Simplification of Inca religion was the work of the militant faction that took control of the Inca state during the Chanka crisis (Conrad and Demarest 1984: 110–21, 144–47).

This core group used every means at its disposal to disseminate the new cults. Inca state ritual took on overt tones of propaganda. Certain state ceremonies were accompanied by processions of dead rulers, in which their descendants sang of their heroic exploits (some of which must have been highly exaggerated, if not completely fabricated). The new regime was quick to take over whatever formal means of education existed in order to spread the message to the youth (Conrad and Demarest 1984: 124–25, 147).[2] In these ways the core group rapidly instilled the new cult throughout Inca society and thereby activated the war machine that carried it to imperial power.

Ultimately the Inca ruling class assumed the primary responsibility for promulgating the royal mummy cult. As Liverani (1979: 297–99) argues in his analysis of the Neo-Assyrian Empire, it is important to understand that the Inca ruling class believed its own ideological propaganda and was motivated by it. Events of the early Spanish colonial era reveal the awesome motivational power of the central state cult. Members of the Inca nobility surrendered their wealth and endured excruciating tortures—including being burned alive—to protect the royal mummies from the Spaniards who sought to destroy them (Conrad and Demarest 1984: 115–16, 145–46, 186). People who will impoverish themselves and die hideous deaths to hide a sacred corpse have surely succumbed to what propaganda strives to provide: "an organized myth that tries to take hold of the entire person" (Ellul 1965: 11).

THE PROBLEM OF INTENTIONALITY

Because they were grounded in traditional but simplified versions of ideology and included the creation of powerfully motivating ideas that were disseminated by a core group, the Inca religious reforms display all the characteristics of a Great Simplification. One question remains: was it consciously intended? Did members of the original core group reason that traditional ideology had become too complicated and confusing to inspire anyone, and that a simplified version would be a much more effective motivator? Or did the militant faction inadvertently stumble upon one of the major principles of political propaganda?[3]

The question of intentionality is extremely difficult for archaeologists. Although we can learn the results of people's decisions in the past, it requires a leap of faith to say—on the basis of archaeological data alone—that these consequences were the desired ones. Even the documentary sources available to ethnohistorians are of dubious help. In the standard chronicles the actions of Pachakuti's core group are described as parts of a conscious, comprehensive plan (Conrad and Demarest 1984: 110–21). The chronicles are at least in part politically motivated rewritings of history, however, and I take it as an axiom of politics that if something works, somebody is going to stand up and say it was planned that way.

These cautions notwithstanding, there is reason to believe that the Great Simplification of Inca religion was indeed intentional—provided we are careful to distinguish between short- and long-term consequences. Occurring not only in a time of chronic warfare, but at a moment when the Chanka onslaught threatened the very existence of the Inca state, the rise of Pachakuti's core group and the reworking of Inca religion had all the hallmarks of a "revitalization movement" (Wallace 1956) or a "crisis cult" (Jones and Kautz 1981: 23–33; LaBarre 1971). In conditions of crisis, when it is widely perceived that traditional beliefs and practices can no longer cope with overwhelming problems, "a new religious movement is very likely to develop . . . aimed at the dual goal of providing new and more effective rituals of salvation and of creating a new and more satisfying culture" (Wallace 1966: 157–58).

In this sense, the short-term consequences of the Incas' Great Simplification do seem intentional. In a time of crisis, Pachakuti and his core group saw that Inca religion had become too complicated; it had lost hold of or failed to identify what they perceived as its central truths. If those central truths could be defined or reestablished, and then reinforced, the Inca people would have "new and more effective rituals of salvation and . . . a new and more satisfying culture" (Wallace 1966: 158). Their ideological motivation would be reinvigorated, they would have a decisive advantage over their neighbors, they would survive the immediate crisis, and they would prevail in local power struggles. These goals were consciously desired, and the Great Simplification of Inca religion was meant to achieve them.

Long-term consequences must be treated separately, however. The available evidence suggests strongly that they were *not* intentional; the Great Simplification surpassed its original ends and transformed the Inca state far beyond the intent of Pachakuti's core group. The Incas broke out of the confines of local power struggles without ever intending to do so. Their fanatically motivated armies won victories on an imperial scale before their leaders even realized they could be imperial powers and resolved to act accordingly. It is this process—the means superseding original ends and creating new ones—that leads me to speak of the "accident of empire."

THE ACCIDENT OF EMPIRE

Some evidence for this accidental creation of empire can be found in accounts of specific military campaigns—most notably the Incas' defeat of their strongest opponent, the kingdom of Chimor. As described by the chronicler Cabello Valboa (1951:312–20, 332) and analyzed by Rowe (1948:42–45), the conquest of Chimor began when Pachakuti sent out a raiding and exploring expedition under the command of one of his half-brothers. The expedition had strict orders not to proceed beyond a specific point. A contingent of non-Inca troops deserted, however, and an overzealous pursuit by the rest of the army led to a victory over the kingdom of Cajamarca, well beyond the prescribed stopping point and hundreds of miles from the nearest Inca-controlled territory. Although the eventual result was the destruction of the Incas' most powerful rival, the accidental victory at Cajamarca "committed the Inca state to a lightning expansion for which Pachacuti was probably not ready and a war with Chimor which he had hoped to postpone" (Rowe 1948:43).

Even more significant, perhaps, is the fact that Inca official state histories assigned the role of great lawgiver and consolidator to the second emperor, not the original head of the core group. Late in life, Pachakuti appointed his son Topa Inca as coregent and head of the army. When Topa Inca took the throne, the Inca state seems to have been an empire without a vision of itself as such, and without the institutions to sustain itself. Topa Inca is treated as the first Inca ruler to realize that imperial hegemony was feasible ambition and to define it as a conscious goal.

In traditional oral histories Topa Inca is described as the first Inca ruler to envision himself as master of the entire civilized world: he vowed not to stop his conquests until he reached the "uttermost sea" (Cieza de León 1959:243; Cobo 1979:144; Rowe 1946:208). Topa Inca is also depicted as the great lawgiver of the Inca Empire: he is credited with the creation of the institutional framework that held the conquered lands together (Brundage 1963:222; Cabello Valboa 1951:346–47, 352–54; Cobo 1979:142; Sarmiento de Gamboa 1942:132).

I do not know which of these accounts reflect real historical events and which are allegorical. Nonetheless, it does seem significant that they are all attributed to the *second* ruler of the Inca Empire. I suggest that they reflect overly rapid expansion during the first decades of imperial rule as the powerfully motivating central cult drove state growth far beyond the original, much more limited ambitions of the new regime. The political and economic goals of Pachakuti's core group called for slower and more locally contained growth, but the ideological reforms increased the pace and scale of state expansion far beyond anyone's intent.

Traditional dynastic histories acknowledge this accident of empire by attributing the creation of consciously imperial policies and institutions to Topa Inca rather than Pachakuti. In fact, Tom Zuidema (personal communication, 1985) suggests that Topa Inca may actually be a composite figure. If so, it seems even more likely that the Inca state became a de facto empire first and that only afterwards did its rulers slowly recognize and respond to the reality of their situation.

CONCLUSION

In view of the foregoing discussions, it seems to me that assessing the causal roles of ideology and economics in Inca imperialism as an "either/or" proposition is not very useful. Ideology and economics were both indispensable parts of the chain of causality. Clearly, the Inca expansion had economic causes, goals, and consequences. However, a propagandistic state religion also played a highly active role in motivating state expansion and driving it far beyond its original goals. If this ideological element is discounted, it seems impossible to explain why the Incas gained the initial advantage over their competitors or why their empire grew as swiftly as it did. What shaped Inca history was the mutual causal interdependence of material and ideological factors.

——— *Notes* ———

1. In general, I have foregone extended discussions and citations of the ethnohistorical sources when I am recapitulating arguments presented in *Religion and Empire*. To save space, I have simply referred the reader to the relevant pages of Conrad and Demarest (1984), where the sources are cited and analyzed. In

the case of arguments not developed in *Religion and Empire*, the ethnohistorical sources are cited more fully.

2. Margaret Mead (1979: 28–29) has noted how quickly new customs can be made to seem traditional to young people in societies where the control of information is in very few hands. In later imperial times, education in the Inca capital of Cuzco was mandatory for young men from native provincial aristocracies who were being groomed for important administrative positions. Those youths were indoctrinated with the Incas' propagandistic ideology and charged with spreading the message to their own peoples (Conrad and Demarest 1984: 124, 147).

3. In fact, as Doob (1935: 76–80, 89) argues, it is a mistake to think that all propaganda must be intentional. Even in the modern world, much propaganda is unintentional.

9

POINT COUNTERPOINT

ECOLOGY AND IDEOLOGY IN THE DEVELOPMENT OF NEW WORLD CIVILIZATIONS

ROBERT L. CARNEIRO

From the inception of their discipline, archaeologists have always had a materialist bent. Dedicated as they are to the recovery of material objects from the ground, it is understandable that they should focus their attention on palpable, tangible things. This underlying tendency was further strengthened in the 1960s when the New Archaeology introduced a theoretical outlook that regarded ecological forces and processes as of primary importance in explaining the dynamics of culture.

During the past decade, however, the pendulum has begun to swing the other way. We now find archaeologists turning increasingly to speculations about the ideas that lay behind the materials of prehistory. Some are even beginning to reverse the arrow of cultural causation and are looking more and more to ideology as providing the principal impetus to cultural change.[1]

The contributors to this book are, if not confirmed idealists, at least receptive to the notion that ideology may have played a key role in molding the societies whose remains they excavate. It is my assigned task to examine the views they have put forward and to assess how successfully they have argued them.

In doing so, I do not claim to be a completely impartial observer. My role in the advanced seminar out of which these papers grew was to serve as a counterpoise to the ideological views presented in it. Thus my aim here is to find whatever flaws there may be in the arguments of my colleagues. At the same time, I will be ready to recognize the validity of any of their assertions that strike me as true. Indeed, toward the end of the paper, I will offer a few examples of how ideology has played a positive role in the development of culture.

IDEOLOGY: ITS PROPONENTS AND ADVERSARIES

Most of the contributors to this volume take pains to spell out just what they mean by ideology. Demarest (chapter 7) tells us that "ideology refers to ritual, religion, and explicit cosmology." Conrad (chapter 8) defines ideology as "a set of beliefs that provides members of a group with a rationale for their existence." And Freidel (chapter 6) thinks of ideology as "the interconnected, fundamental ideas held by the elite and common-ers alike about the order of the cosmos and everything it contains."

But ideology is more than just ideas held in the mind. It has a social function. As Kolata says, quoting Friedrich (1989:301), ideology is "a system . . . of ideas, strategies, tactics, and practical symbols for promot-ing, perpetuating, or changing a social and cultural order; in brief, it is political ideas in action."

All well and good. Everyone seems agreed on what ideology *is* and what it *does*. But differences of opinion arise when we try to ascertain the role of ideology in effecting change. On this issue, theoretical positions are arrayed over much of the intellectual spectrum. At one extreme we have the philosophy of pure idealism, which in its classical Platonic form holds that "ideas come first; they are the real things; they endure for-ever; material objects and sensory experiences are merely imperfect and ephemeral manifestations of the Ideas . . . [which] are the original seeds, the prime movers" (White 1949:46–47, 233).

At the other end of the spectrum we have the materialist view, first fully enunciated by Karl Marx. According to this perspective, societies are divisible into an infrastructure and a superstructure. The infrastructure consists of environmental, technological, ecological, and economic fac-tors, along with, if we follow Marx, the "relations of production." It is here that the forces of change originate and the basic dynamic process begins. The superstructure of a society consists of ideas, beliefs, values, attitudes, philosophies, and related social forms that stand upon the infra-structure and are determined by it. Between these two polar views exists a wide range of intermediate positions.

Within anthropology, the cultural materialist position was first ex-pressed by Leslie White and is today most vigorously championed by Marvin Harris. The idealist end of the spectrum, which has been gaining adherents in recent years, is, surprisingly enough, espoused (among oth-ers) by scholars who label themselves Marxists. We see this, for example, in the structural Marxism of Maurice Godelier who, Kolata observes, "collapses . . . superstructural elements, such as kinship and politico-religious ideology, downward into the infrastructure by recharacterizing these key elements as relations of production" (chapter 4, this volume). Among non-Marxist archaeologists, Ian Hodder may be counted among the leaders of the idealist movement. Quoting Hodder's concept of the idealist position, Grove and Gillespie (chapter 2, this volume) maintain that "causes will not have social effects 'except via human perception and evaluation of them' (Hodder 1986:13)."

The authors represented in this volume are of course not all cut from the same theoretical cloth. Some are more ideological than others. But by and large, they appear to be more open-minded than doctrinaire. Conrad, for example, concludes that "What shaped Inca history was the mutual causal interdependence of material and ideological factors" (chapter 8, this volume). Wilson also takes pains to be even-handed and notes that "however complex the relationship between ideology and other societal variables, there is clearly a mutually causative chain of relationships among all systemic variables, including ideology." Thus, according to Wilson, "it seems better to fall back on the democratic assertion that causation is equally top-down and bottom-up" (chapter 3, this volume).

Wilson's democratic leanings, though, seem to be misplaced. Just because the relationships between two variables are *reciprocal* does not mean they are *equal*. Indeed, in his own reconstruction of the prehistory of the Santa Valley, Wilson shows clearly that ideology generally reflected ecological conditions rather than originated spontaneously and independently of them.

THE ARGUMENT PRESENTED

Let us take a closer look at the ideologist's argument and the materialist's rejoinder. In presenting their case, ideologists will say, "Look, wherever you encounter a new form of behavior, you will find that it was immediately preceded by an idea. To be sure, ideas do not arise out of nothing. They come from somewhere. But in explaining cultural change we prefer to begin with ideas and dwell on how they came to modify behavior." To this, the cultural materialists reply: "We prefer to take a different view and to regard ideas as dependent rather than independent variables, as something requiring explanation rather than as the prime instigators of change."

Cultural materialists readily admit that ideas are always present and active, that they form a necessary link in the causal chain leading to overt behavior. But they do not *start* with ideas, nor do they accept ideas as *given*. They insist on trying to account for ideas, and they feel that the most promising way to account for them is to turn to ecological factors.

In his discussion of causation, Kolata remarks that in the cultural materialist's attempt to explain behavior, "belief systems, ideas, values, and cognitive categories rank rather near the bottom in the hierarchy of causal agents" (chapter 4, this volume). But this is not quite the way to put it. It is not that materialists put ideology "near the bottom" of the causal sequence. It is that they make ideology only the *proximate* cause, the immediate term in the series of events leading to overt behavior. Although ideas must be in people's heads for them to act, antecedent conditions, usually of a material nature, precede these ideas, giving them form and substance and injecting them into the minds of individuals. *That* is what produces behavior.

I would also take issue with Kolata when he speaks of the cultural materialist's "embedded notions of an a priori hierarchy of causative agents." There is nothing a priori in the materialists' turning to ecological and technological conditions for the causes of things. They do so not by fiat but because they have found *empirically*, through repeated trial and error, that this approach offers the best avenue for understanding the process underlying cultural change.

To be sure, no cultural materialist maintains that ideology counts for naught. The question is, just exactly what role does it play? Demarest (chapter 7, this volume) clearly sees that the fundamental issue regarding ideology, the battleground on which idealists and materialists contend in their attempts to account for the rise of the state, is "the distinction between the *legitimation* of power and the *generation* of power." He says, very properly, that for any particular case, this issue "must be resolved by demonstrations of chronological priority."

Unfortunately, it is not always that easy. Owing to the restricted and selective nature of the archaeological record, it may be impossible to make this determination to everyone's satisfaction. In the absence of consensus, researchers generally fall back on their theoretical preferences to search for an answer. And for Demarest, "Only by accepting a major role for ideology as a direct source of power can one understand the institutions of these civilizations [those of the Mayas] . . . and the elaborate cultural concepts that sustained them" (chapter 7, this volume).

IDEOLOGY AND THE RISE OF THE STATE

No one denies that ideology, skillfully applied, may help to gain acceptance—indeed, even enthusiastic support—for a political regime. But what role did ideology play in giving rise to this regime in the first place? This issue is an important one in many of these papers. My own view is that the initial changes that take place in a society are most often prompted by altered conditions of existence. At some point, if it is not to perish, the society must *adapt* to these changes, both structurally and ideologically. As structural changes take place, an ideology arises aimed at gaining acceptance for these changes and thus providing order and stability to the society undergoing them.[2] As this ideology is internalized by individuals, it provides the motives that impel them to do whatever is appropriate and adaptive under the circumstances.

Grove and Gillespie tell us that ideology is "a symbolic system that acts to establish powerful, pervasive motivations in people" (chapter 2, this volume). True enough. But although this proposition is true, its converse is not. What motivates people to act in new and different ways need not be symbolic. It can simply be a direct perception of reality or necessity, unrefracted through the lens of symbolism. Ideology may thus not be essential for a significant new adaptation to arise. For example, ideology was not necessary for the invention of agriculture; the only requirement was a practical knowledge that game was becoming scarce and that certain seed plants, carefully tended, yielded more than when harvested wild. Nor was another great technological achievement—the Industrial Revolution—inspired by any elaborate ideology. The immediate practical need to develop machinery that could pump water out of flooded coal mines was the initial stimulus that led, step by step, to the invention of the steam engine, the Industrial Revolution's great prime mover.

All the papers in this volume (except for chapter 2) deal with ideology as it was manifested by societies already at the level of the state. But ideology occurs at lower levels as well. There is ideology in a simple Neolithic village. It is an ideology of autonomy, equality, generosity, cooperation, and comradery—an ideology appropriate to the type of society it serves. But this type of ideology can be an impediment to the development of new forms of society. Thus Neolithic ideology must be swept away and replaced by a very different one once simple agricultural villages lose their autonomy and become part of a chiefdom or state. This new and more appropriate ideology must be ready to countenance, indeed promote, such things as inequality, subordination, obedience, obligation, duty, and even reverence.

It is on the ideology that develops concurrently with the growth of chiefdoms and states that the papers in this volume focus. Accordingly, let us look at the rise of Mesoamerican and Andean states as discussed by the authors of this book and see how their individual views on ideology emerge from these discussions.

None of these authors subscribe to any recognized unitary theory of the origin of the state. In fact, they are generally critical of these theories. Demarest, for instance, says that "materialistic solutions" fail to explain the origin of Maya states, and that "functionalist and environmental theories" that attempted to do so "did not survive the scrutiny of the past decade" (chapter 7, this volume). Cowgill asserts (with justification, I think) that Wittfogel's hydraulic hypothesis is not supported by the evidence from the Valley of Mexico (chapter 5, this volume). It is fair to say that the authors of these chapters lean more toward a "mosaic" theory in which a number of factors are seen at work, producing an intricate pattern of causation, with no one factor playing a preponderant role.

Demarest states that "we may not find a single trajectory and set of causes for the rise of Maya civilization," adding that "we find a more complex and heterogeneous civilization, one that may have experienced multiple rises and falls, florescences and declines." But two separate issues are involved here. Civilizations produced by a single set of causes may nevertheless rise, fall, and rise again, in undulating fashion. *Unilinearity* of origin does not imply *rectilinearity* of trajectory. Moreover, development and decline are not mirror images. *Variable* causes of decline are not incompatible with a *unitary* process of development. Demarest may be able to show that each Maya state had a different reason for declining, but he has not proved thereby that they all arose by dissimilar means.

THE CHIEFDOM AND ITS CAUSES

State formation results from the continued development of chiefdoms, but of the various cultures discussed in this book, only one—the Olmec—was (apparently) at the chiefdom level.[3] The picture presented by Grove and Gillespie (chapter 2, this volume) of how Olmec chiefdoms arose and what held them together avoids materialist explanations and leans heavily on ideological, voluntaristic ones. Grove and Gillespie adopt Service's view of the chiefdom as emerging peacefully, and of paramount chiefs acquiring and maintaining their position through redistribution (Service

1975). They also follow him in believing that the authority of the paramount chief rested on his powers as a shaman rather than his success as a military leader.

But Service's portrait of the chiefdom as a peaceful theocracy with the chief as a redistributor has come under increasing attack (Carneiro 1981:61–63; Peebles and Kus 1977; Rountree 1989:14–15, 144–45). More and more evidence is accumulating to show that the chiefdom arose, not through peaceful acquiescence, but through military imposition. And "redistribution," once considered the open sesame to chiefdom formation, is now seen in a very different light. Only when it stopped being a voluntary contribution and became an exacted tribute did it constitute an avenue to chiefly power.

Grove and Gillespie also say of the Olmec that "the chief was elevated above society by his sacred quality" (chapter 2). But how do they know? Their statement is little more than a surmise. Even if the archaeological evidence should show that the Olmec were a well-established chiefdom whose leader was imbued with religious authority, that still would not tell us how he had originally obtained his power.

IDEOLOGY AND ICONOGRAPHY

A society's iconography certainly bears some relation to its ideology. But how close is this relationship? And how easily can it be interpreted in the absence of direct observation of a society or of extensive written records of that society? Wilson is, I think, on solid ground when he argues that the parietal art covering the walls of one Moche structure "depicting military iconography . . . was aimed at serving the ideology of the Moche state: namely, to ensure that potential recalcitrants at the local level were constantly aware of the dangers of rising up in rebellion against it" (chapter 3, this volume). Oftentimes, though, iconography is less clear-cut. In these cases, interpretations tend to reflect one's theoretical predilections.

As an example, the iconography of the site of Chavin de Huantar is usually taken to represent a religious cult that spread peacefully through much of the Andes. To me, however, this interpretation seems wide of the mark. If the Chavin cult was so pacific, why should its dominant symbols have been jaguars and eagles instead of, say, butterflies and guinea pigs?

Wishing to portray Olmec chiefs in a rather benevolent light, Grove and Gillespie say of the famous Olmec heads, now thought to be representations of paramount chiefs, that "motivations other than utilitarian need or the threat of physical force could have accounted for public participation in the erection . . . of the monuments" (chapter 2, this volume). Maybe so. Perhaps by the time the heads began to be carved, the Olmec chiefdom was already so firmly entrenched and so wrapped in the aura of religion that faith alone could move, if not mountains, at least monuments. But that still leaves at issue how this religious power originated. A chiefdom that, through time, has evolved into a peaceful theocracy may still have had strong military roots (Carneiro 1990: 208– 10).

Moreover, if Olmec heads were indeed portraits of actual chiefs rather than representations of gods, this finding in itself points to the strong political power they were able to wield. After all, it was *they*, and not the gods, who were being portrayed.

Iconography not only reflected ideology, Grove and Gillespie tell us, it also imparted it. Indeed, they go so far as to claim that widespread ceramic motifs served to convey the notion of order to societies that were "searching for order at a time of social disorder" (chapter 2, this volume). But is this not asking a bit too much of pottery designs?

At best, iconography is an uncertain key to ideology. It is often very sparse, as in the Santa Valley of Peru (Wilson, chapter 3, this volume), but even where it abounds, as in the Maya lowlands, it must be treated with restraint. In interpreting Maya polities, for example, we are at the mercy of what is carved on the stelae.

Maya stelae do tell us a lot, but they don't tell us everything. And they tell us only what Maya rulers chose to make public. They do not tell us, for instance, about the everyday rules of conduct and the secular means of enforcing them (Demarest, chapter 7, this volume). Conceivably, every transgression in Maya society was thought to bring down the wrath of the gods on the miscreant. But does any Mayanist really believe that these threats were sufficient to keep an entire populace in line? Must there not have been purely secular means for dealing with wrongdoers? On this score the glyphs are, apparently, silent.

European history amply attests to the fact that art and iconography do not necessarily tell us all we want to know about the kinds and frequencies of actual behavior. Christian iconography during the Middle Ages provides much evidence of the glory of God but precious little about the military relations between feudal principalities. If churches and Bibles alone had survived from that period, what a skewed picture we would have of medieval life. Even a full recovery of the paintings of the age would not redress the balance. For every battle scene there would be, no doubt, twenty Adorations of the Virgin!

What I have said about iconography in particular applies (if not as strictly) to archaeology in general. As Grove and Gillespie admit in their discussion of temples and public buildings, "the material and ideological motivations stimulating those labor efforts cannot easily be extracted from the archaeological record" (chapter 2, this volume). The evidence of archaeology, then, is generally too tenuous, uncertain, and ambiguous to allow us to say just what role ideology played in the rise of chiefdoms and states. Thus, it seems unlikely that archaeology alone is in a position to refute the notion that material determinants played a leading role in this process.

WARFARE AND THE ARCHAEOLOGICAL RECORD

Archaeology is very often able to reveal the previous existence of a trait; it is seldom able to demonstrate its absence. This may well have been the case with warfare, an element which, I believe, played a key role in the rise of chiefdoms and states. Once it is highly developed, warfare can, of course, leave unmistakable traces of its presence. A string of fortresses, for example, allows for very little doubt that warfare was once common and important. Iconography can also demonstrate the presence of war. The bound prisoners depicted in the Bonampak murals do this, as do the figures of captives and war victims carved on the outer walls of the main temple at Cerro Sechin. Even a single Moche pot, as Wilson (fig. 3.13) shows, can tell us a good deal about the treatment of war prisoners in that culture.

Warfare can be present, however, and still leave little or no evidence of itself, especially when it is fought among small, autonomous villages. What evidence will a future archaeologist find, for example, of Yanomamö warfare? Thus, when Demarest (chapter 7, this volume) tells us that "the archaeological evidence for warfare [among the Mayas] is several centuries too late for it to be a major factor in the initial rise of Maya states," I question how strongly he can make this assertion. Let us recall that until the discovery of the Bonampak murals, the Mayas were generally regarded as a peace-loving people (Carneiro 1970: 734, 738n.).

The role warfare may have played in creating chiefdoms and states in Central and South America is, nevertheless, a critical issue. It is discussed in most of the chapters, especially those dealing with the Mayas, Teotihuacan, Tiwanaku, and the Incas. These chapters clearly show us ideology at work in the service of militant, expansionist states. They show ideology giving warfare a greater goal, helping to mobilize men to fight, and reconciling defeated populations to the yoke of conquest. But was an explicit ideology required for a society to have taken the first steps in state formation? Could this ideology have engendered a state without the instrument of war?

Demarest, as we have seen, believes war appeared too late among the Mayas to have been a significant factor in their rise. Perhaps he is not entirely convinced, however, because he goes on to say that "warfare had an early impact on the development of Maya society, probably as a pressure enabling chiefs to extend their power beyond kinship-defined systems" (chapter 7, this volume). He appears, then, to recognize that coercion was necessary to surmount the autonomous village level that once characterized the Mayas. At least he suggests no other mechanism for the creation of chiefdoms and states from autonomous villages.

Demarest is correct when he observes that Maya civilization arose in an area considered inauspicious for the development of high culture by most theories of state formation. Its lack of aridity made it an unlikely place by the standards of the hydraulic hypothesis, and the absence of sharp geographic boundaries made it unpromising for strict formulations of the circumscription theory. But states did arise in the Maya lowlands, and something had to account for it. In his chapter on the Mayas, Freidel says that "kingship is the key to the main span of Maya civilization from the first century B.C. through the ninth century A.D." (chapter 6, this volume). If this statement is true, it seems appropriate to try to unearth the roots of Maya kingship.

MAYA "PEER POLITIES" AND THEIR SIGNIFICANCE

Of the earliest stage of Maya political development, when for the first time villages were being aggregated into chiefdoms, there is little archaeological evidence. For the period by which the Mayas had developed a number of small states, however, archaeology is much more revealing.

Demarest characterizes these petty Maya kingdoms as "peer polities" and talks about a "peer-polity landscape" and a "peer-polity network" (chapter 7, this volume). "The picture that emerges from all of the evidence," he says, "is one of a volatile political dynamic [of competing kingdoms] with the fortunes of [individual] centers rising and falling throughout the Classic period." This decline in the fortunes of particular polities led many Mayanists to believe in a general decline of Maya culture in the sixth century A.D. But Demarest contends that "The so-called sixth-century hiatus has proven to reflect *variability* in the power . . . of the [individual] major [Maya] centers rather than a general epoch of decline."

Reflecting the views of some Mayanists, Demarest refers to the recurring ups and downs of Maya states as unusual and puzzling. Thus he speaks of "the enigma of the inversely correlated rises and falls of some of the greatest Maya centers" and points to the "remarkable similarities" between these ups and downs and those reported for various petty states of Southeast Asia (Demarest, chapter 7, this volume).

But is this change of fortune of individual Maya states really puzzling? I think not. Rather than enigmatic and unusual, these inverse correlations strike me as commonplace and expectable. Parallels to it are to be found, not just in the "galactic polities" of Southeast Asia, but in many other areas of the world as well. For example, among the Heptarchy, the seven small states into which Anglo-Saxon England was long divided, we find now Northumbria, now Mercia, and now Wessex gaining ascendancy. And among the *taifas*, the petty kingdoms into which Moorish Spain broke up during the eleventh and twelfth centuries, first one *taifa* and then another became dominant.

The rise and fall, expansion and decline of individual states is, in fact, a regular process in "peer-polity interaction" everywhere. Thus, the picture of Maya polities Demarest paints shows them to be much less unique than once supposed, and more and more in line with the development of early states in general.

Even if (as I believe) war played a vital role in Maya history, it was not a single-minded and unending struggle for territory. "Throughout most of the Preclassic and Classic periods," Demarest tells us, "warfare was ritualized and culturally constrained" (chapter 7, this volume). I have no doubt that this statement is true; however, there is such a thing as placing war too firmly in a ritual context. And this seems to be what Demarest is doing when he turns the execution of the king of Copan by the victorious Quirigua—a violent physical act—to the service of ideology. The same may be true when he quotes Freidel (1986a) to the effect that Maya warfare "was usually closer in its effects to interdynastic marriage than to territorial absorption," thus making it "another form of elite interaction, alliance, and information exchange" (Demarest, chapter 7, this volume). A bold attempt, this, to co-opt the harsh domain of war for the benign kingdom of ideology!

Even where Maya warfare was admittedly serious business, as in the region of Dos Pilas, where Demarest's own work shows an expansionist militaristic state in operation, he tries to hammer the sword of war into the plowshare of ideology. Thus he writes that "the ability of the Dos Pilas hegemony to expand . . . may have resulted as much from the success of its propagandistic advertising of the defeat and sacrifice of rivals as from military occupation" (chapter 7, this volume). To use a humble analogy, this seems to me like saying that a pitcher might give Babe Ruth an intentional base on balls because he had *heard* that Ruth was a great slugger rather than because he *was*.

TEOTIHUACAN AND
THE MAYAS, A STUDY IN CONTRAST

Referring to the ups and downs of Maya states, Demarest says, "In this respect the Maya political landscape resembles that of early competitive states in Mesopotamia and Southeast Asia rather than the more centralized regional polities like Teotihuacan, Tiahuanaco, or Early Dynastic Egypt" (chapter 7, this volume). Although he points out this difference, he fails to use all the material factors he might have to account for it. Let me therefore venture to do so, harking back to the circumscription theory, which early in his chapter Demarest dismisses, perhaps too readily, as inapplicable here.

In discussing why the "galactic polities" of the Classic Maya lowlands "seemed doomed to repeat perpetual cycles of internal expansion and decline," while Teotihuacan and Tiahuanaco were not, Demarest points to "the more secure material and coercive bases of power held by [these] states" that "may have made them more stable polities" (chapter 7, this volume). Let us see just what Teotihuacan's "more secure material and coercive bases of power" might have been.

Teotihuacan was, unquestionably, the greatest aboriginal urban center ever to arise in the New World. Not only was it large and imposing, it was also enduring. Cowgill alludes to "the seven centuries of Teotihuacan's dominance in central Mexico" and talks of the "explosive growth" of the city as early as the Patlachique phase, 150–1 B.C., a period that saw "a spectacular increase in population" (chapter 5, this volume).

Cowgill offers no clear-cut, unitary explanation for this remarkable growth. Population pressure has never appealed to him as a determinant of cultural development, and he remains cool to the idea, saying that even while tens of thousands of persons were coming together in the city of Teotihuacan, there was still enough land in nearby areas of the Valley of Mexico to feed them all. To the extent that he tries to explain Teotihuacan's striking cultural florescence at all, Cowgill says that it was "due to some combination of commercial success, military prowess, strong leadership, a good location, luck, and some special religious appeal" (chapter 5, this volume).

Let me attempt to do what Cowgill has refrained from doing: namely, to account for the early rise and rapid growth of Teotihuacan in specific and concrete ways. In doing so I propose to use two of the factors Cowgill himself alludes to—"military prowess" and "a good location"—and one factor he specifically rejects—population pressure.

The Valley of Mexico offers a prime example of an environmentally circumscribed area. The arable land within it is sharply bounded by a ring of mountains. Even before the introduction of agriculture, the basin contained bountiful sources of wild food in the form of fish, reptiles, amphibians, and aquatic birds, all of which served to attract people to it in substantial numbers (Carneiro 1987:254). Once agriculture was introduced, a further impetus was given to population growth. The build-up in human numbers in the Valley of Mexico would thus have started well before the founding of Teotihuacan.

It is hard for me to imagine that, with population growing rapidly, the arable land freely available to each autonomous village within the valley would not soon have been curtailed. This shortage of land would sooner or later have led to fighting. This warfare, as I have argued elsewhere (Carneiro 1970, 1981:63–65), would eventually have caused the transcending of village autonomy and the establishment of chiefdoms. Nor would fighting have ceased once chiefdoms emerged. The scale of warfare would simply have increased. Now it was chiefdom against chiefdom as the existing polities continued to struggle for arable land.

Competition over land in the Valley of Mexico may have accounted for much of the warfare Cowgill notes when he speaks of "the evidence, now very clear and abundant, for the importance of military elements in the society" (chapter 5, this volume). This warfare, he believes, may have occurred at least as early as the Patlachique phase, 150–1 B.C. Thus, in addition to the religious and commercial factors that he entertains as playing a role in Teotihuacan's development, Cowgill says that "a plausible speculation is that Patlachique growth was based on . . . military effectiveness. . . ." This militarism continued; during the subsequent Tzacualli phase (A.D. 1–150), although religion may have loomed larger than before, "it is highly unlikely that military effectiveness would have become unimportant" (Cowgill, chapter 5, this volume).

By the Tzacualli phase, the Teotihuacan state was near its apogee and controlled not only the Valley of Mexico but also a number of outlying areas. By now, Cowgill tells us, "the rulers at Teotihuacan had extraordinary power to affect people's behavior in much of the basin, presumably by means of some combination of coercion, ideological appeal, and economic inducements" (chapter 5, this volume).

The fact that Teotihuacan was located in an environmentally circumscribed area was, I maintain, a major factor in its initial rise out of a cluster of autonomous villages. Its location also helped it to develop, in relatively short order, into a single, large, and powerful state. The "peer polity" type of organization described by Demarest for the Mayas, though it may once have existed in the Valley of Mexico, would have been only fleeting. Ecological conditions militated against the continued existence of a number of small, coequal states, struggling to maintain their position ·in an unstable equilibrium. Instead, the circumscribed nature of the Valley of Mexico, because it impeded the retreat of defeated groups, favored rapid unification.

Once Teotihuacan's military hegemony was established, it seems to have been complete and long lasting. If its rulers "were able to suppress the development of foreign rivals for many centuries without costly struggles," writes Cowgill, "this situation would go far to explain the long duration of Teotihuacan's dominance in central Mexico" (chapter 5, this volume).

Teotihuacan's undisputed suzerainty had some interesting consequences. Despite Cowgill's careful efforts not to slight religion and ideology in his attempt to account for the rise of Teotihuacan, he notes that a powerful secular state might have been able to dispense with much of its supernatural trappings after having gained complete control. Once "free of any need to be deeply concerned with any human rivals," Cowgill suggests, the lords of Teotihuacan no longer felt that "a divine pedigree" was important "to legitimize high office" (chapter 5, this volume).

The lack of an exterior military threat seems also to have been reflected in Teotihuacan ritual and art. Cowgill remarks that "The absence of victory celebrations may be because Teotihuacan had long since won all the important wars in the core area that it controlled." The fact that militarism itself was likewise not represented in Teotihuacan art could be similarly explained (Cowgill, chapter 5, this volume).

With these developments in a circumscribed region like the Valley of Mexico as a background, let us see if we can account for the different course that political evolution took among the Mayas.

A SUGGESTED EVOLUTION FOR THE MAYAS

Unlike the Valley of Mexico, the Maya lowlands were relatively unbounded, and they were not endowed with as wide a variety of wild food
resources. Consequently the area would not as readily have attracted
people to it in the first place and thus would not have begun to fill up as
early. Even when population began to grow following the adoption of
agriculture, population pressure, building up slowly here and there,
would have been relieved by the still-existing possibility of moving one's
village and settling elsewhere. Because of this absence of severe restrictions on outward migration, it would have taken longer for the pressure
of human numbers on the land to develop. Thus warfare over land, with
the resulting consequences of conquest and amalgamation of villages,
which eventually led to state formation, would have been delayed.

I have already noted that Demarest questions the idea that population
pressure was a cause of Maya state formation since, he says, "settlement
patterns suggesting demographic pressure . . . postdate state formation by
at least several centuries" (chapter 7, this volume). However, I think archaeologists often seriously underestimate the point at which population
pressure can be said to begin. Indeed, it may start even when the type of
agriculture being practiced is still only slash-and-burn.

Consider the following circumstance. If a village that normally fallows
its abandoned garden plots for twenty years is impinged upon by its
proliferating neighbors so the accustomed twenty-year fallow must be reduced to, say, fifteen years, this circumstance already constitutes population pressure. Of course, the pressure may not be apparent to someone
casually walking through the area and noting only that most of the land is
still under forest. How, then, can an archaeologist, excavating the same
area centuries later, be able to tell? The fact remains, though, that a farmer
who can no longer allow his abandoned garden plot to recover its full
fertility before having to recultivate it is already feeling the pinch of diminishing land resources and may be ready to take drastic measures to
relieve the situation.

These drastic measures include fighting for land. Yet, very little evidence of this warfare might be found on the ground, since the weapons
of war would very likely be the same as those of the chase, and fortifications may not yet be used, as is often the case in Amazonia today. Then
too, whatever evidence of warfare existed might also be missed, especial-
lyby archaeologists whose attentions were focused on what was happening in ceremonial and urban centers dating to a later period. Thus, I am

convinced it is a mistake to discount population pressure and war as active elements in the rise of Maya states. The evidence for it might not yet be there, but conclusive evidence against it can hardly be said to exist.

The slower pace of state formation characterizing the Maya lowlands as opposed to the Valley of Mexico is precisely what we would expect on theoretical grounds. When only social rather than environmental circumscription is at work to keep growing populations from dispersing, polities fragment more readily, and political evolution proceeds more slowly. And, as among the Mayas, political unification of the entire region may never be achieved.[4]

The continued existence of many states, cheek by jowl, jostling each other, warring at times, growing and declining by turns in some sort of cyclical pattern, all of which characterized the Mayas, is just what the circumscription theory would lead us to expect in an unbounded area. Thus the similarity Demarest finds between the Mayas and the states of Southeast Asia, which also developed in an uncircumscribed rain-forest environment, is simply a case of like conditions producing like effects.

IDEOLOGY AND THE INCAS

We have gotten away from ideology. Now it is time to return to it. Let us do so by taking up Conrad's explanation of the growth of the Inca Empire, which he attributes in large measure to the conscious devising of an ideology of conquest.

That a great empire should have arisen in the Andes was not unexpectable. After all, it had happened at least twice before. But which of the hundreds of competing petty states that dotted the Andean landscape around A.D. 1400 was to achieve it? What particular set of circumstances would determine that the Incas, and not some other group, would successively defeat and engulf their enemies? Conrad sets the stage:

> The Incas rose to imperial power by prevailing in these conflicts, at first locally and eventually across some 4300 kilometers of the Andean world. They began their course of imperialism by emerging victorious from local power struggles after more than two centuries of constant war. To do so, they must have developed an advantage over their neighbors, something that made Inca militarism more successful than that of their competitors. To explain how the Inca Empire arose, then, we need to ask what that decisive advantage might have been (chapter 8, this volume).

Conrad begins by dismissing a number of factors to which the Incas' military success might have been assigned. "It seems impossible," he says "to attribute Inca victories, particularly in the early days of expansion, to superior weapons, tactics, training, or discipline." The answer, he thinks, lies in a new militaristic cult based on the requirements of the royal mummies. The "Incas' living dead," he writes, "demanded perpetual income, and continual warfare and conquest would guarantee these paramount necessities for each ruler in his turn." This new cult thus "made militaristic expansion an ideological necessity." By its prescriptions, the deceased Incas "retained all the property they ever owned, while the living emperor was forced to conquer new territories in order to ensure his own [as well as the mummies'] eternal support" (Conrad, chapter 8, this volume).

The cult of the dead Incas seems to have been rather complicated at first. Accordingly, those in power decided that to mobilize the masses into an effective fighting force, the ideology would have to be simplified. The sophisticated Mayas might be able to get along with ideologies consisting of "dualities mediated by triadic principles," as Freidel (chapter 6, this volume) suggests, but Andean peasants evidently needed something less subtle. Thus came to pass what Conrad calls the Great Simplification. The "few simple, powerful ideas" to which the new Inca ideology was then reduced "created a sense of divine mission," which "drove a small ethnic polity outward as an irresistible military force" (Conrad, chapter 8, this volume). The "ferocious war machine" thus created, propelled by a religious fanaticism, carried the Incas from a petty polity around Cuzco to the largest aboriginal empire ever seen in the New World.

If the Inca Empire represented a triumph of ideology, however, it was not a simple and unalloyed triumph. Warfare was, after all, the means by which the Incas defeated and subjugated their enemies. Although warfare may have its ideological components, it is basically as ecological as one can get. The outcome of war often makes the difference between survival and extinction, expansion and contraction—between wealth and glory on the one hand and impoverishment and ignominy on the other. Whatever the ideological motivations behind Inca aggrandizement, the instrument of its execution was warfare.

Remember too that warfare existed among the Incas before the new ideology. Indeed, it had already led to the rise of a small Inca state. It had been the means by which earlier Inca rulers had attained their power and gained the awe that made them exalted in life and venerated in death. And it was their revered mummies, the desiccated corpses of previous successful war leaders, who now called for further wars—unrelenting wars that would continue to bring them in death the fruits they had enjoyed in life. So, if ideology is to be credited with giving the critical impetus to the formation of the Inca Empire, it seems to me that warfare must share equal billing.

To further emphasize the importance of war in Inca political development, consider that the Great Simplification was made, not in peacetime, but "in a time of chronic warfare" (Conrad, chapter 8, this volume). Note also that the royal mummies were not the only ones who had an important stake in successful military campaigns. "The state cult also rewarded ferocious warriors with earthly advancements and places of honor in the afterlife."

Finally, even if "the Inca empire's initial victories were brought about by the virtually fanatical motivation of its armies," as Conrad holds, would all the religious fervor in the world have triumphed without adequate numbers, good generalship, effective discipline, the skilled use of weapons, and other military attributes? What Inca ideology did, then, was to take a phenomenon already present and active in Inca culture—warfare—and imbue it with a higher purpose and a stronger will.

Let us turn away from warfare to Inca ideology itself. How sure can we be that the ideology that the Incas claimed had inspired the conquests of their predecessors was actually as they portrayed it? Even assuming that it was, did it really play the role it was said to? Over the ensuing years had there not, perhaps, been a Great Simplification of the Great Simplification? Could Inca history have been distorted to give a purpose and a motive to early Inca conquests beyond what they actually had? In sum, may not what survived of Inca origins be *ideology* rather than history?

It may not be out of place here to quote the words of a professional historian:

> Most historians preside over the construction of the collective memory. And they are not architects whose patrons have given them a free hand. They are under pressure to design an impressive, even a glorious facade that may bear only a tangential resemblance to the structure of events concealed behind it. . . . It has all too often been the historian's assignment to assist his culture in remembering events that did not happen, and in forgetting events that did. The culture wants a past it can use (Gay 1988:206).

IDEOLOGY REAPPRAISED

All that I have said up to now is not meant to deny that ideology may indeed help significantly in marshaling human efforts toward great and dangerous enterprises, such as conquest warfare. Inherent in all war is the possibility of death, and who is willing to risk his life unless coerced by overriding force or driven by very stirring motives? A belief in the righteousness of one's cause is tremendously effective in mobilizing men to fight and to fight well. Of two warring groups otherwise evenly matched, victory is likely to go to the side more highly inspired by powerful ideals.

Some of the most notable military expansions in history were propelled by religious ideology. The breakout of Muslims from the Arabian peninsula and their rapid spread across North Africa and into Spain cannot easily be explained without recourse to the concept of *jihad*, or holy war, derived from the teachings of Mohammed. When the vigor of the first wave of Arabs who conquered Spain had been spent and the Umayyad dynasty had eroded and collapsed, it was the Almoravids, imbued with the fighting zeal of a newly preached version of Islam, who triumphed over a fragmented Muslim Spain, reunited it, and pushed back the Christian kingdoms. Then, when the Almoravids themselves declined and again allowed the breakdown of Moorish Spain into the tiny *taifa* states, once more it was a new fundamentalist Islamic sect, the Almohads, who, energized by a fresh set of tenets, invaded Spain, reunited its disparate Muslim elements, and again rolled back the kingdoms of León, Castile, and Aragón.

Still, it must be emphasized that it was not ideology, pure and simple, that triumphed. It was ideology as applied through the point of a lance and the edge of a sword. Thus, one should never lose sight of the fact that only as implemented through material means can ideology conquer lands and subjugate people.

THE INTEGRATIVE FUNCTION OF IDEOLOGY

Ideology is, of course, most dramatic when it leads men to score great victories and found huge empires, but its role does not end there. Indeed, its most enduring contribution is in the less obvious way in which it helps to run a society once it is established. Ideology serves to impart order, stability, and coherence to a society. This function is especially important when a society consists of disparate, even antagonistic elements, recently brought together. As Kolata remarks, although states may be created by raw power, "coercive mechanisms, when applied indiscriminately, inevitably generate instability and hostility in subject populations" (chapter 4, this volume). Thus, a wise ruler of a conquered people dons a velvet glove over his iron fist.

How does ideology work? In fact, it has a double edge. It is persuasive and it is coercive. Durkheim (1964: 2) was right when he said that rules of conduct "are not only external to the individual but . . . endowed with coercive power, by virtue of which they impose themselves upon him." Thus, impressing itself on a person, ideology may force him to act, no less than the point of a sword.

Yet culture operates most effectively the less coercive it appears. People follow rules more willingly the more these rules seem, not mandates from above, but impulses from within. One complies most readily when spoken to by that wee small voice of conscience, often unaware that, as Shakespeare shrewdly noted, "Policy sits above conscience" (*Timon of Athens*, act 3, scene 2).

Erich Fromm put the matter very neatly when he said that a society works best when people *want* to do what they *have* to do. Rulers see to it, therefore, that ideas of duty, obedience, and fealty are thoroughly instilled in their subjects. In this way, onerous and even odious tasks, like obeying restrictive laws, paying taxes, and risking life and limb in time of war, are made bearable. Indeed, if sufficiently imbued with societal goals, subjects come to feel that fulfilling these demands is their patriotic duty. And when devotion to duty is conspicuously rewarded with honor, glory, wealth, and rank, compliance with the desires and interests of the ruler becomes even more assured.

Let me present just one example of the cultural softening, even sweetening, of an obligation. Ordinarily, paying taxes is regarded as a cheerless burden by any population, but chiefs on the island of Fiji had found a way to make it a pleasant occasion. According to the missionary Thomas Williams (1870: 31–32),

> Tax-paying in Fiji, unlike that in Britain, is associated with all that the people love. The time of its taking place is a high day; a day for the best attire, the pleasantest looks, and the kindest words; a day for display: whales' teeth and cowrie necklaces, . . . the newest style of neck-band. . . . The Fijian carries his tribute with every demonstration of joyful excitement, of which all the tribe concerned fully partake. Crowds of spectators are assembled, and the king and his suite are there to receive the impost,

which is paid in with a song and a dance, and received with smiles and applause. From this scene the tax-payers retire to partake of a feast provided by their king.

To which Williams adds, "Surely the policy that can thus make the paying of taxes 'a thing of joy,' is not contemptible" (Williams 1870: 32).

When political obligations, lightened in this way, are in addition infused with religious meanings and sanctions, the silken cord of ideological coercion is drawn still tighter. When the desire of the chief also becomes the will of the gods, and compliance with it is rewarded with promises of a glorious hereafter or other supernatural recompense, who would willingly demur? And to stiffen the spine of those who might, there is often added the threat of swift and terrible reprisals by the gods should they fail to do so.

Grove and Gillespie appear firmly opposed to this view of the workings of ideology, however, and in arguing their case they raise the following objection: "The assumption that ideology merely legitimates the status quo, and that it 'dupes' the masses into accepting the dominance of their masters, treats humans as automatons bereft of creativity and incapable of independent thought" (chapter 2, this volume).

To this I reply, "yes and no." Ideology is important precisely because human beings are *not* automatons. They are not mere neuro-sensory-muscular organisms, acting solely by reflex and tropism. They need ideas to inspire and direct them, to give their actions meaning and purpose. Still, that does not mean they are not, in a very real sense, "duped." As I stated above, one function of ideology is to make the members of a society feel that the ideas they are quietly absorbing from around them, which lead them to act for the good of the state—often to their own detriment—are *their* ideas, springing from their own inner being and, ultimately, whatever travails they may occasion at the moment, leading to a just and proper outcome.

THE LIMITS OF IDEOLOGY

Again let me return to my dissenting role. No ideology is all-powerful. Never does it exert such complete control over a people that secular sanctions are entirely superfluous. Moreover, to be effective, an ideology must flow in the same general direction as the current of the culture. An ideology grossly at variance with prevailing conditions and attitudes is destined to fail. Thus, an ideology of peace when war is pervasive has little chance of succeeding. Consider the following example:

Confucius had wandered from one state to another in a vain
attempt to persuade the rulers of his time to forsake the struggle
for power and return to the enlightened path of the Sage kings.
But most men of this later age [the Warring States period,
453–221 B.C.] realized that peregrinations devoted to the promotion of pacific and ethical objectives were a waste of time.
The most pressing problems were those of practical statecraft;
of internal administration and foreign policy. The crucial aspects
of the latter were . . . to preserve and enrich the state and enhance its power and influence at the expense of enemies either
actual or potential (Griffith 1963: 28–29).

Not only may ideology fail to achieve any positive result, it may actually produce a negative one. The Spanish Inquisition offers a prime example. In the name of upholding Christian doctrine, the Inquisition put
to death many of the leading thinkers of Spain and intimidated those it
didn't kill. Thus it succeeded in stifling innovative thought and blocking
advances in science, technology, and commerce, ultimately causing Spain
to fall from being the leading nation in Europe to a third-rate power.

RETURNING TO THE ANDES

Having left the Andes to examine other topics and areas, let us return to
it and consider another Andean empire, Tiwanaku. The rise of Tiwanaku,
says Kolata, preceded the Incas by more than a thousand years. Its most
striking archaeological feature is an elaborate system of raised fields around
the southern margins of Lake Titicaca. This system was so extensive and
so efficient that it provided ample food for a large and growing population.
    Unlike his predecessor, David Browman, who states that Tiwanaku
arose by essentially peaceful means, Kolata depicts the Tiwanaku state as
an aggressive, expansionist polity that eventually extended its domains
from an original nucleus along the shores of Titicaca to areas far beyond
it. The appearance of this empire was relatively early. By the Tiwanaku III
phase, beginning around A.D. 200, the raised field system was in place
and a large centralized polity had emerged. No oral histories survive to
afford concrete details of how Tiwanaku arose, but Kolata sees this expansion, like that of the Incas, as having been carried out by military means.
Unable to spell out a specific ideology for Tiwanaku conquests, as Conrad
did for the Inca, Kolata says merely that "the Tiwanaku state imposed
a regional political unification of the Titicaca basin with an eye to-

ward expanding its agricultural production and thereby its fundamental sources of wealth, economic vitality, and political power" (chapter 4, this volume).

Although he sees coercion as the genesis of the Tiwanaku state, Kolata does not think coercion alone was sufficient to maintain it. Ideology played a prominent role as well. A subject population's acquiescence, he argues, is essential if a state is to survive and endure. And he offers "the nearly 1000-year reign of the lords of Tiwanaku" as proof that they possessed an ideology that kept the large and varied population of the empire more or less contented over the course of centuries.

By the period beginning around A.D. 400 (which was some 200 years *after* the Tiwanaku state had emerged), "one element of Tiwanaku imperial policy was the forced imposition of a state cult" (Kolata, chapter 4, this volume). Although he cannot enumerate the details of this ideology, Kolata is willing to speculate about it: ". . . I would further hypothesize that the ancient and probably pan-Andean divisions of labor . . . between pastoralists and agriculturalists were formalized by the Tiwanaku state into a unified ideological system that emphasized and commemorated in monumental public display the necessary, complementary interaction between these two great touchstones of the high plateau economy" (chapter 4, this volume).

The message conveyed by this cult, Kolata thinks, was that "the kings of Tiwanaku nourish and sustain the common people. Through direct intercession and identity with the divine forces of nature, they will guarantee the agricultural and reproductive success of the nation" (chapter 4, this volume).

When the Tiwanaku state went to war, so did its religious ideology. Perhaps the gods of one side did not actually engage in celestial combat with the gods of the other, but at any rate, when Tiwanaku won, its gods did too, and their rival deities were taken captive. Thus, when Tiwanaku defeated the enemy state of Pukara, they appropriated the emblems of the latter's deities and, in effect, held them hostage.

WAS IDEOLOGY PRESENT AT THE BIRTH?

Kolata has argued plausibly for the need Tiwanaku's rulers felt to develop and implant a coherent ideology in the minds of its citizens. But he has not shown what role, if any, ideology played in giving rise to the Tiwanaku state in the first place. So we are back to the familiar dilemma we have faced so many times before—whether ideology can be said to have played a major role in the *origin* of chiefdoms and states. Everyone agrees that an established state develops an ideology calculated to command the allegiance and promote the acquiescence of its citizens. But what role did ideology play in the very inception of the state? To this question, the data we have for Tiwanaku afford no conclusive answer.

Indeed, every polity described in this volume (except the Olmec) was already a state at the period they are first presented to us. Each had had centuries during which their foundations were being laid and their ideologies formulated, modified, and crystallized. How can anyone tell, then, what these ideologies were like when wars first brought chiefdoms and states into being or, indeed, if they played a major role in these early conquests and amalgamations?

THE IDEOLOGICAL CONCOMITANTS OF CHIEFDOMS

Of course, when the earliest chiefdoms were emerging, people's heads were not empty. They contained ideas, and these ideas reflected the prevailing conditions. Just what ideas had been generated in people's minds to provide a link between ecological conditions and political consequences?

As I have discussed elsewhere (Carneiro 1970, 1981), several factors led Neolithic villages to transcend local autonomy and create the multivillage polities we call chiefdoms. These conditions were, essentially, the presence of agriculture, the existence of environmental or social circumscription, population pressure, and warfare. Together, these factors formed the necessary and sufficient conditions for triggering the process. Once they were present, they led, almost irresistibly, to the rise of chiefdoms.

Now, given the presence of these conditions, into what concrete ideas would they have been translated as chiefdoms began to be formed? It seems to me that the ideas involved would have been few in number and could have occurred to any ordinary mind. Certainly they would have come easily to a would-be paramount chief. They amounted to little more than this:

1. Defeat neighboring villages by force of arms.
2. Incorporate them and their territory into your political unit.
3. Take prisoners of war and make them work for you as slaves.
4. Use your close supporters to administer conquered territory if local leaders prove rebellious.
5. Require your subjects to pay tribute to you periodically.

6. Require them also to provide fighting men in time of war.

These scant half-dozen ideas were quite enough to provide the intellectual armamentarium involved in creating a chiefdom. Could any half-dozen ideas be simpler? Could they not have occurred to anyone? Could they fail to occur to a village chief faced with the problem of insufficient land and covetous and troublesome neighbors?

That these ideas were indeed simple and did occur to many a chief is amply demonstrated by the facts. Look around the world during late Neolithic and early Bronze Age times and you see *hundreds* of chiefdoms emerging. In terms of their basic structure, these chiefdoms all looked pretty much alike. In fact, the more we learn about chiefdoms, the more we are struck by the similarities they possess. And multiple recurrences of the same phenomenon argue against the necessity for any elaborate and difficult set of ideas to bring it about. Quite the contrary. Rather than subtle, abstruse, and profound, the ideas that underlay the chiefdom were easy and obvious. In fact, chiefdoms were the predictable outcome of a specifiable set of circumstances. Whenever these conditions were present, chiefdoms arose. It was that simple.

WHAT ROLE DID RELIGION PLAY?

This straightforward, materialistic view of the matter is not generally shared by my colleagues in this volume. Thus, when the archaeological evidence for the causes of chiefdom or state formation in their areas is scant—as it usually is—their tendency is to flesh out the bones of their reconstructions with an assortment of ideologies.

One of the major elements of almost any ideological superstructure is religion, and Freidel finds in it the initial causes of Maya political development. Since even at the height of Maya rule the basis of the king's power, Freidel thinks, was essentially shamanic, he projects this source of authority deep into the Maya past. "Shamanism," he asserts, "was and remains the foundation of Maya ideology" (Freidel, chapter 6, this volume).

A shamanic basis for chiefly power appeals to Grove and Gillespie as well, who, as we have seen, employ this model to account for Olmec chiefdoms. "On the Gulf coast," they tell us, "chieftainship seems to have emerged from an earlier shamanic role as mediator with underworld forces" (chapter 2, this volume). However, they neglect to suggest how, if shamanic power lay at the root of chiefly power, some ancient Olmec shaman was able to evolve into a powerful chief when shamans the world over have generally persisted in remaining shamans.

In addition to seeing them as political leaders, Grove and Gillespie regard Olmec chiefs as intercessors between the populace and the supernatural. That may have been, but it is still only speculation, and arguing for this notion is a step toward embracing a more unlikely possibility. Grove and Gillespie tell us that Olmec heads were mutilated before they were buried. The simplest and most obvious interpretation of this fact, it seems to me, is that this defacing was done by a victorious chief intent on humiliating and diminishing the leader of a defeated enemy. But Grove and Gillespie propose a different explanation. They believe the mutilation of Olmec heads was done at the chief's death by his own subjects "to neutralize any remnant supernatural power they may have contained" (chapter 2, this volume). This explanation, it seems to me, flies in the face of probability.

SHALL THE TWAIN EVER MEET?

In the preceding pages I have taken issue with my colleagues in this volume when I felt their ideological interpretations to be unwarranted or overdrawn. I must concede, though, that in much of what they say I have found these authors neither dogmatic nor doctrinaire. Indeed, scattered throughout their chapters are statements that are at least compatible with, if not actual expressions of, cultural materialism. In this concluding section I would like to assemble examples of what I consider sound and solid interpretations on their part.

In the chapters by Cowgill, Kolata, and Wilson one can hardly find an ideological leaning. I have already noted Cowgill's even-handedness in parceling out degrees of influence to various classes of determinants. Thus, he is not about to seize on religion as the key to explaining other features of Teotihuacan society. He does not, for example, see temples as the nucleus around which the early city of Teotihuacan crystalized. Indeed, he suggests that these temples were "more a consequence than a cause of the growth of the city" (Cowgill, chapter 5, this volume).

Kolata is also even-handed in his interpretation of the rise of Tiwanaku. Rather than coming down on the side of ideology, he offers "a trial synthesis . . . of the articulation between economic and ideological behavior" (chapter 4, this volume). And he is quick to dismiss any "idealist" interpretation of Tiwanaku he considers unsound, such as the notion that Tiwanaku arose as "a pilgrimage center of great prestige that became the nexus of multiple, far-flung caravan routes" (Kolata, chapter 4, this volume).

Wilson likewise makes clear his disinclination to cast his lot with either theoretical extreme: "we must be ecological anthropologists/archaeologists, not cultural materialists (bottom-uppers) or symbol-oriented ideologists (top-downers)" (chapter 3, this volume). Yet much of his paper shows environmental and material forces doing the lion's share of the work in molding cultural development in the Santa Valley. He finds evidence of warfare in the valley as early as 1000 B.C. and considers it to indicate that enemies from valleys to the south, running out of arable land themselves, tried to take possession of the fertile fields along the Santa.

Unlike most Peruvian coastal rivers, he tells us, the Santa drains an entire mountain valley before breaking through the Andes and making its way to the Pacific. Because of the great amounts of water it carried, the Santa provided its coastal valley with a more assured harvest than did other coastal rivers, including those immediately to the south. Thus, once population pressure in these adjacent southern valleys had increased to a critical point, their inhabitants sought, by military means, to take over at least parts of the Santa Valley.[5]

Wilson's interpretation of Santa Valley warfare shows the reasonableness—indeed, the persuasiveness—of ecological explanations. If he is unwilling to label this interpretation as "cultural materialist," I regard this unwillingness to be more a disagreement of words than of substance.

Leaving Peru and returning to Mesoamerica, I previously expressed misgivings about Grove and Gillespie's readiness to invoke a highly ideological interpretation of the Olmec and their stone heads. I should point out, however, that they also make statements like the following: "ideological systems are not . . . static. . . . They are constantly redefined and transformed by the dialectical processes involved in fitting the constructed order of existence to actual historical events" (chapter 2, this volume). As a statement of cause-and-effect relationships in the culture process, this could hardly be improved on. And in another instance they refuse to succumb to a facile ideological interpretation. Some archaeologists, Grove and Gillespie tell us, try to explain the occurrence of chiefdoms over much of Preclassic Mesoamerica as a result of the diffusion of "the *idea* of the chiefdom" from the precocious Olmec. Very sensibly, though, Grove and Gillespie argue that there is no need to derive Mesoamerican chiefdoms from an Olmec archetype. Chiefdoms, they maintain, may well have arisen independently in various parts of Mesoamerica out of purely local circumstances.

Here and there, Freidel also gives a balanced appraisal of the interplay of forces determining the development of the Mayas. Asserting that ideology is not static, he speaks of "the 'reinvention' of Maya ideology to cope with pervasive and debilitating social crises" (Freidel, chapter 6, this volume). At a certain point, he says, the Mayas felt a need to resolve "the contradiction between an egalitarian ethos and the actuality of hierarchy and inequality. . . ." This need led to "the projection of political authority" through "all aspects of the complex religion and cosmology of the Mayas," which in turn produced "an overall reformulation of Maya culture that rendered elitism natural, rational, and necessary" (Freidel, chapter 6, this volume).

Elsewhere in his paper Freidel again argues in a similar vein. He tells us, for example, that "Maya public buildings were the declared and commissioned work of kings and lesser rulers of the hereditary elite designed to express the power of their governments and the relationships within and between realms" (chapter 6, this volume). If this is ideology, it is ideology trumpeting hard, secular political reality.

So, then, where do we stand? Certainly, the ideological component of a chiefdom or state is one of its significant features. And it is to the role played by ideology in creating and maintaining such polities that the contributors to this volume have largely addressed themselves. Yet, as the passages just quoted show, the material conditions of existence are so basic to the origin, growth and florescence of any polity that they obtrude into the formulations of even the staunchest ideologist.

──────── *Notes* ────────

1. A couple of readers of this chapter have felt that at times I have set up an ideological straw man, an adversary with little more strength and stature than a caricature. I would ask these critics to consider the following pronouncement by William H. Durham (1990:188): "Swayed by the arguments of recent culture theorists [and he cites Clifford Geertz and Roger Keesing] I specifically limit the meaning of 'culture' to ideational phenomena . . . and thus include the values, ideas, and beliefs that guide human behavior, *but not the behavior itself*" (emphasis added). When felling a tree with a stone axe is no longer a part of culture, we have let ideology run rampant.

2. Of course, ideology can be directed toward fomenting revolution as well as upholding the established order. Since this volume is devoted almost entirely to ideology that was meant to advance and enhance established order rather than destroy it, however, we can dismiss revolutionary ideology from further consideration here.

3. It is instructive to note that two of the leading students of the Olmec,

Michael Coe and Richard Diehl, who in fact have co-authored a major monograph on them, nevertheless disagree on whether the Olmec were a chiefdom or a state (Diehl 1989:29)! This disagreement points to the great gulf that often exists between archaeological *fact* and its *interpretation*.

4. No doubt the existence of dense tropical rain forest as the natural vegetation of the Maya lowlands presented an impediment to conquest, just as it did, more than a thousand years later, to U.S. armed forces in Vietnam. This impediment may have afforded another reason for the long survival of peer polities among the Mayas.

5. I continue to differ with Wilson on the question of whether chiefdoms in the Santa Valley arose peacefully and voluntarily, as he thinks, or through warfare, as I think. To me, the many early citadels he found in the valley indicate *intra*valley warfare, leading to chiefdom formation, whereas to him they suggest defense against attack from adjacent valleys. I have stated some of my views on this issue in Carneiro 1988:508–509.

10

IDEOLOGIES

UNITY AND DIVERSITY

ROBERT McC. ADAMS

At least until quite recently, ideology would have been thought of as lying along—if not beyond—the outermost margins of fields of inquiry to which archaeologists might usefully turn their attention. It required a leap of faith, unguided by any existing body of theory, to get from mute artifacts, evidence of subsistence systems, or any conceivable contextual or associational data elicited by archaeological or related means to the realm of directive ideas. We now know that much can be done with imaginative use of ethnohistorical sources. Also immensely widening our horizons are giant strides in the understanding of contemporary written records, like those fundamental to the accounts given here for the ancient Mayas. But each of these developments is still a fluid mix of promise and performance. Remaining to be fully disentangled from many fascinating but less than conclusive leads and surmises is a solid core of replicable analysis that is demonstrably applicable to the subject at hand.

So perhaps two questions should be asked directly at the outset: To what extent is the whole line of inquiry taken in this volume the product of the belated discovery by archaeologists that other, "ancillary" fields of investigation can powerfully supplement—or replace—their own when it comes to dealing no longer only with the routines of daily life but with the rationales as well as structural principles of hierarchical organization? Second, is it possible to address the subject of ideology in nonliterate cultures by archaeological means alone? If answers to these questions were negative or discouraging, the auspices of this volume probably were inappropriate. Fortunately, however, the essential principles of a positive response recently have been boldly sketched and brilliantly illustrated by David Keightley (1987) with reference to early China:

I believe that material culture expresses and also influences, often in complicated, idealized, and by no means exact ways, social activity and ways of thinking, and that the goal of archaeology must be *comprendre* as well as *connaître*. . . .

The essence of my argument is twofold. First, I assume that the way people act influences the way people think and that habits of thought manifested in one area of life encourage similar mental processes in others. I assume in particular that there is a relationship between the technology of a culture and its conception of the world and of man himself, that 'artefacts are products of human categorization processes,' and that style and social process are linked. It is this assumed linkage that encourages me to think in terms of mentality, whose manifestations may be seen in various kinds of systematic activity. . . .

Second, I assume that one of the essential features that distinguished Bronze Age from Neolithic mentality, in China as elsewhere, was the ability to differentiate customs that had hitherto been relatively undifferentiated, to articulate distinct values and institutional arrangements, to consciously manipulate both artifacts and human beings. This is not to claim that prehistoric man did not make distinctions or that he was not conscious of what he was doing. The difference is one of degree. In the prehistoric evidence, accordingly, I shall be looking for signs of enhanced differentiation, for signs of increasing order in both the material and mental realms, for signs of what Marcel Mauss called the 'domination of the conscious over emotion and unconsciousness' (Keightley 1987:93–94).

Here, then, is both a method and a strategic approach suitable for our field of inquiry. When we also take into account the growing, potentially crucial streams of epigraphic and ethnohistorical evidence that can contribute to it, this effort is as timely as it is important.

POLITICO-RELIGIOUS CONTINUUM

I do not mean to imply that consensus or closure is at hand on the concept of ideology itself. One understanding of it, borrowed by Kolata (chapter 4, this volume) from the works of Paul Friedrich, speaks fairly narrowly of "political ideas in action" and focuses on "the attempts of elite interest groups to carve out and promote their domination over economically valuable resources, principally labor and territory." The choice of wording, it will be noted, brings us to if not beyond Keightley's threshold of domination of the conscious over the unconscious, and it approaches Marx's classic distinction between a class of itself and a class for itself. This extension of the concept of ideology is also apparent in Kolata's suggestion that "the intended meaning of the metaphoric association between the images of agropastoral productivity and the representation of royal office . . . could not be more clear: the kings of Tiwanaku nourish and sustain the common people. Through direct intercession and identity with the divine forces of nature, they will guarantee the agricultural and reproductive success of the nation" (chapter 4, this volume).

I think this statement may overcompress or oversimplify a wide range of politico-religious motivations and processes. It attributes intentionality not merely to an individual's personal rationalizations for action but to those developed and propagated by a coherent, self-conscious elite. Were the elites already identifying and pursuing their own interests in this way by the time of the Tiwanaku state? Ethnohistoric sources can provide little direct assistance in answering this question, since this period was still many centuries before the Conquest.

Closer to my own understanding is another formulation that contextualizes ideology more explicitly and diffuses (without denying) the element of intentionality within it:

> Ideology, far from being an independent factor, is deeply affected by the social, economic, even technological and ecological realities. In a sense, it is their justification, it is the way a reality of unequal socio-economic relations is made acceptable to people. Therefore ideology should be studied against its social, economic, even technological background . . . as being determined by socio-economic reality, and as overturning it (Liverani 1990: 294).

Conrad may share my concern to broaden the range of early ideology, since his discussion "shades more toward religion than politics" (chapter 8, this volume), at least in the case of the Incas. A further step in the same direction is taken by Monaghan (1990), with his still more sweeping suggestion that ideology is "a definition of the social order." Monaghan then considerably qualifies it, however, and focuses on the allocation of power and asymmetries in personal obligations and the distribution of resources. That focus seems entirely acceptable (to me at least) insofar as sacrificial cults in late pre-Conquest Mesoamerica are his principal point of departure

But did a concept like "power" have the same meaning and behavioral substance eight or nine centuries earlier? And how much before that? A recent study of the Roman imperial cult by S. R. F. Price (1984) reinforces the doubt implicit in my questions:

> The notion of power as a possession of political leaders is . . . highly questionable. There are objections at two different levels. Firstly, it is surely wrong, as is usually done in historical studies, to treat power in realist terms as a simple datum. . . . As Foucault argues, "clearly it is necessary to be a nominalist: power is not an institution, a structure, or a certain force with which certain people are endowed; it is the name given to a complex strategic situation in a given society." . . . The second-level objection to the conventional view of power is that it does not necessarily reside primarily in politics, or the "efficient" aspects of the state. If power is taken as an analytical term, . . . there are manifold relations of power which pervade and constitute society. Religion just as much as politics is concerned with power. . . . (Price 1984:241–42).
>
> A Christianizing theory of religion which assumes that religion is essentially designed to provide guidance through the personal crises of life and to grant salvation into life everlasting imposes . . . a distinction between religion and politics. But a broader perspective suggests that religion need not provide answers to these particular questions, and the imposition of the conventional distinction between religion and politics obscures the basic similarity between politics and religion: both are ways of systematically constructing power (Price 1984:247).

Or, at least, of rationalizing its implementation and seeking to make it more palatable!

> Ideology, presupposing as it does contradiction, potential conflict, or periodic violence in society, is part of a set of assumptions that may be strongly at odds with the finished products of functionalism, systems theory, and much of ecological theory. The concern is not smooth functioning per se but how conflicts or contradictions are masked or neutralized (Leone, Potter, and Shockel 1987:284).

But should we go as far as Grove and Gillespie (chapter 2, this volume), who explicitly extend Geertz's definition of religion fully to embrace ideology as well? Or, *a fortiori*, as far as Freidel, who sees ancient Maya ideology as "the interconnected, fundamental ideas held by elite and commoner alike about the order of the cosmos and everything it contains" (chapter 6, this volume)? With this extension the word becomes indistinguishable from holistic world view. I think ideology is analytically useless if it is applied this broadly, and it has the further weakness that the totality of its reconstruction and application—to the entirety of the Maya populace and to the entirety of its thought—will remain forever speculative.

SOCIAL AND INDIVIDUAL CHOICE

A further set of problems emerges from the conflicts and collisions of interest assumed even in this definition. How far are we justified in assuming that the whole of a given society can be identified with a dominant, corresponding ideology? How far are ideologies autonomously generated, as opposed to being functionally integrated with, and expressive of, underlying "adaptive" requirements? Ideally, written sources following the advent of "history" might provide unambiguous answers to these questions. In practice, however, until relatively modern times both the subject matter and the audience for virtually all categories of textual materials were elites—whose identity of views with their presumed followers is precisely what is problematical. When we turn to purely prehistoric, preliterate contexts, it is of course obvious that even for elites, the reconstruction of their ideologies is extremely difficult and doubtful at best.

Given the reach of imagination (some will still say, suspension of disbelief) required, it is gratifying to find that the concern of this volume's authors with such refractory problems of ancient ideologies as these does lead to a little light at the end of the tunnel. Specifically, it brings us into congruence with a significant shift of emphasis within the larger domain of the social sciences. Among many indications of this trend are altered meanings for the concept of culture itself:

> While it was once seen as a map *of* behavior it is now increasingly seen as a map *for* behavior. In this view, people use culture the way scientists use paradigms—to organize and normalize their activity. Like scientific paradigms, elements of culture are used, modified, or discarded depending on their usefulness in organizing reality. In a sense the term *culture* is now used as nearly equivalent to the term *ideology*, but without the latter's pejorative connotations. Sociologists now recognize that people

continuously choose among a wide range of definitions of situations or fabricate new ones to fit their needs (Peterson 1979: 159–60, emphasis added).

As this quotation suggests, choice and intentionality are among the key signposts pointing toward a new orientation. The doctrine of methodological individualism invokes a parallel stress: "[A]ll social phenomena—their structure and their change—are in principle explicable in ways that only involve individuals—their properties, their goals, their beliefs and their actions" (Elster 1985: 5). Granted that this form of reductionism may not always be timely and can never be absolute (e.g., individuals often have relational properties), "to go from social institutions and aggregate patterns of behaviour to individuals is the same kind of operation as going from cells to molecules" (Elster 1985: 5; cf. Levine, Sober, and Wright 1987).

The prescription I detect, and share, is that efforts to provide causal explanation are incomplete if they fail to probe deeply for variability within and among what are interpretively reconstructed as templates of cognition and behavior, or if they are content to accept those templates as givens—anonymous, unproblematic outcomes of collective, unconscious processes. Cultural patterns and social institutions obviously do persist and undergo change, dominating our view of not only the contemporary but the archaeological landscape. But they do so as a consequence of the combined action of individuals who do not constitute—have never constituted—an undifferentiated mass. What we see instead are interactive products of continuous, semiautonomous exercises of variable, highly imperfect knowledge and rationality by individuals (Boudon 1982: 9).

An argument for the greater prominence of intentionality and choice is necessarily premised on the existence of wide creative capabilities for rationalizing social change or continuity that reside with individuals rather than social aggregates. This premise is at the opposite epistemological pole from Carneiro's mechanistic interpretation of the human brain as a "neurological mixmaster," capable of nothing more than endless recombinations of external inputs. The enabling microprocesses are probably as follows:

> We pose a problem by giving the state description of the solution. The task is to discover a sequence of processes that will produce the goal state from an initial state. Translation from the process description to the state description enables us to recognize when we have succeeded. The solution is genuinely new to us. . . .

The correlation between state description and process description is basic to the functioning of any adaptive organism, to its capacity for acting purposefully upon its environment (Simon 1981: 223, 229).

To be sure, psychological mechanisms may seem somewhat far afield from the principal concerns of this volume. Its concern is overwhelmingly at the societal rather than individual level, focused on the complex interpersonal and intergroup processes by which institutions or movements both shape and are shaped by the ideologies that rationalize and energize them. Yet as exemplified by Kolata (chapter 4, this volume), the other authors tend to reject Carneiro's sweeping behaviorism. Seemingly a "mainstream" position for the group was Kolata's acknowledgement that "mental schemata and the material conditions of life are mutually interpenetrating, mutually implicatory elements of any explanatory framework." Although Wilson's repeated references to "cultural adaptive systems" may suggest some convergence with Carneiro's evolutionary approach, he too joins in stressing the existence of "an important mutual causal relationship between ideology and other societal and environmental variables in cultural adaptive systems" (chapter 3, this volume).

Whatever their other connotations, ideologies are expressions of the more or less bounded rationalism with which people move beyond their primordial groupings to form other, more-or-less durable associations for selected, common ends. Systematized goals and similar assessments of life chances are symbolic constructs that act as the cement holding these associations together. If we were, by contrast, to approach ideologies on the basis of rigorously materialist premises, as Carneiro advocates and is at least right in recognizing, they virtually disappear as significant social forces or issues.

CONSTRUCTIONS OF CAUSALITY

Archaeology, the primary means of apprehending most early civilizations, is driven in the direction of a fundamentally materialist outlook by the nature of its data and methods. Yet it is only fair to characterize the view of a substantial majority of the authors of this volume (and coincidentally my own) as multidimensional and antideterministic. They (we) see the emergence of civilization as an uneven and regionally variable process resulting from shifting complexes of forces, rather than as a smooth and unilinear progression governed in the last analysis by a limited set of prime movers. Hence an underlying tension exists between, on the one hand, this volume's subject matter of ideology and, on the other, the greater part of the infrastructure of method, theory, and data on which it must draw. Not surprisingly, the tension remains near the surface, emerges at odd moments, and is not resolved.

Pejorative connotations of the term *ideology*, already alluded to, are a further source of tension. "The most elusive concept in the whole of social science," it is typically applied to "someone *else*'s thought, seldom our own" (McLellan 1986: 1):

> The familiar parodic declension suggests the problem: "I have considered views of social reality, you have political opinions, he has an ideology." The Archimedean point from which one examines this topic or any social science question is thus brought into question, and the struggle for objectivity as regards it is the greater (Culture and Ideology Working Group 1990:480).

An additional difficulty with the term goes to the heart of the process by which people, having framed options or made choices within some personally constituted sphere of autonomy, attempt to identify common goals or programs of action. Available ideologies, in any historical setting, do not offer a smooth continuum of possibilities from which to choose. Elster (1983:110), drawing on a general theory of choice propounded by Veyne (1976:706), succinctly but convincingly suggests "(*i*) that options come in bundles that cannot be disassembled and reassembled at will, (*ii*) that people tend to go to extremes and (*iii*) that the choices, once made, retroactively influence the preferences." In short, the discontinuous classes of ideologies can never be fully reconciled with a given materialist base. In addition, we must ask whether the direction of the causal arrow runs predominantly from a presumed materialist base to the associated ideological superstructure, or the other way around.

> Although it is plausible that interests inform our opinions, subtly predisposing us to believe those things that it benefits us to believe, it is equally obvious that interests do not have the field of belief to themselves. Where new ideas must make way in the face of entrenched belief, their reception depends in part upon their attraction for others besides those who benefit directly. Certainly, to attract support, ideas must be capable of serving more interests than their authors'; which is another way of saying that the ideas must facilitate the attainment of widely shared

goals. Equally troublesome from a theoretical point of view is Marx's insistence that people holding similar ideas must have formed alliances prior to the acceptance of the ideas rather than subsequently. Marx's explanation for the formation of classes and ideology is grounded on his contention that group loyalties grow out of economic relations, that people joined by a common interest in a system of production adopt similar beliefs, which further cements solidarity. Such a developmental sequence rests on Marx's belief that it is in and through action that thought arises. However, since ideas are more often selected than created, it could well be that men coalesce into a new ruling class in recognition of commonly held opinions. In this case, the origins of the agents of historical change would be less important than the shared attitude to material changes from people of differing backgrounds (Appleby 1978: 11).

Little in this volume suggests that the authors are any more ready than most of our colleagues to approach this question of the dominant direction of causality as an open, empirically determined one. Most of us long ago paid our dues and made our choice on this matter, and the tortuous processes by which those initial choices may be later shifted or qualified seldom have much to do with lessons ineluctably following from any given body of data.

The same applies to a related basis of theoretical divergence, that of distinguishing historical from evolutionary approaches. The evolutionary avenue is associated with trying to identify a relatively strong, simple signal emitted by determinate sequences of transformation from the irregular noise of random, short-term events. Consistent with other aspects of their stance already mentioned, most authors in this volume hold a less unilinear view of causality. Although differing in many other respects, they would argue that new configurations emerge continuously and not wholly predictably, as in a rotating kaleidoscope, and are the product of heterogeneous prior conditions and ongoing forces.

Often associated with the evolutionary standpoint is a tendency to take for granted a real and important distinction between long-term processes of change that are grounded in materialist infrastructures and the short-term ebb and flow of "mere" events. On the historical side, which finds greater favor here, the distinction between signal and noise, as well as other distinctions between long-term and short-term and between infrastructure and superstructure, are viewed with greater skepticism.

Truthfulness is sought in details rather than macrostructures—in a progressively fuller and more precise specification of the uncertainties as well as the intricacies of causality.

Still another unbalanced division among the contributors concerns the relative openness of cultural systems. As articulated in some of these papers and elsewhere, the materialist position is that environmental, subsistence, and technological factors are essentially external and thus can act unilaterally. The opposing view is less unitary, but it involves substantial doubt as to the independence and externality of these (or any) putative prime movers. Population pressure, for example, may exist not only as a result of a supposedly inevitable, Malthusian excess of births over deaths within a naturally circumscribed area, but also because of culturally generated attitudes toward family size and security, inheritance patterns, and boundary-maintaining mechanisms. Institutional patterns, cultural (-ideological) preferences, and hierarchies of values interact continuously.

EVOLUTIONARY INFRASTRUCTURE
AND POLITICAL SUPERSTRUCTURES

Even though ecologically based, gradualist, evolutionist, and materialist positions in fully articulated form are in short supply in this volume, their appearance in more mixed modes of analysis is fairly frequent. How hierarchically rigid and authoritarian, for example, was Maya society? Given the supposed simplicity, individualism, and dispersion of swidden agriculture in the Peten rain forests, materialists for a long time tended to deprecate the strength and permanence of its politico-religious superstructures. Then for a period, as Demarest (chapter 7, this volume) recounts, the evidence seemed to point toward greater subsistence complexity and population density. Now, he argues, it is tending to undermine that apparent drift—at least for what now appears to be Maya civilization's gestational period. He, at least, is keenly aware that arguments for the solidity, complexity, and continuity of Maya states tend to wax and wane in direct proportion to the plausibility of the case for a relatively stronger or weaker subsistence base. The question of how secure Maya state power could have been if it were not associated with a managerial requirement remains, for him, both salient and troubling.

Regrettably, as yet no clear answers are available regarding how tenuous Maya rulership really was. Demarest stresses the existence of "a volatile political dynamic," with centers and their dependencies tracing different trajectories at one another's expense. Freidel, choosing to ignore infrastructural issues and apparently relying on the lengthy sequences of royal succession and the immense efforts that must have been involved in monument construction, takes a more integrative, positive view (chapter 6, this volume). What can be deduced from scale and monumentality is indeed an arresting question that fully deserves a closer, more detailed scrutiny than it has heretofore received. Although the royal lineages testify to considerable formal continuity, however, they tell us little about the powers rulers actually exercised or about the prevailing pattern of their interrelationships.

Freidel may be correct in his characterizations of Maya elites as "especially parasitic and ultimately dysfunctional" and their activity as "somehow epiphenomenal to the adaptive forces operating through the common folk." These opposing characterizations are surely extreme positions, however, and their polarity does little to clarify what is ultimately a matter of degree. In Mesopotamia, I might note, only the masses of economic and administrative texts, for which there is no Maya counterpart, permit us to establish the nature and importance of the administrative functions of early Mesopotamian religious and political leaders.

A great deal of ancient Near Eastern evidence may have a bearing on Maya peer-polity interactions. A pathbreaking, primarily documentary study of the Late Bronze Age has recently assembled unparalleled documentation of the (cultural-) ideological patterning reflected in the correspondence between ruling families:

> If we must summarize it in two words, we should probably speak about refined ceremoniality—or perhaps better suspicious formalism. There are rules for everything: how to address each other and how to send greetings, how to make war and how to make peace, how to give and how to bargain, how to get a wife or ask for a physician. Inside a compact culture there are always such rules (their sum being in fact the culture itself); but here we are at the intersection of different cultural traditions, in search for an adjustment (Liverani 1990: 286).

Freidel (chapter 6, this volume) briefly suggests a relationship between the popular effort involved in producing great monuments and the degree to which Maya lords and commoners may have been bound together by a common ideology of rulership. He readily concedes that Maya social segmentation was not all sweetness and otherworldly light. In principle, moreover, one must greet with heavy skepticism the notion that those on the beneficiary end of an exploitative relationship can provide credible testimony of the views about that relationship held by majority from whom we hear nothing directly. But there is some potential leverage here on the nature and role of early ideologies that deserves our attention.

Characteristic of the initial stages of state formation in most if not all parts of the world has been a striking quality of labor-intensiveness that seems almost certain to have a common ideological basis. It is well represented by the immense efforts required to obtain the large stones employed in the Olmec monuments, with which Grove and Gillespie deal, and by the colossal Teotihuacan pyramids to which Cowgill draws attention. Similar phenomena can be cited elsewhere: the lack of later parallels for Old Kingdom Egyptian pyramids; the lengthy (although not permanent) decline in the size of Mesopotamian ziggurats or temple platforms after the initial period of urban growth; the similar absence of later equivalents of Middle period temple platforms in Peru; the lack of concern for any invisible, internal finishing in the ceremonial constructions of Postclassic Mayapan. In general, then, early monumental architecture is not only often more massive than later examples but also more painstakingly executed in ways that may suggest a qualitatively different degree of commitment and intensity affecting the work force as well as the ruling elite.

I do not have a convincing explanation for this phenomenon. It may be related to what has sometimes been called a trend toward secularization, and thus to the stadial sequences moving (with variable terminology) from "theocracies" to more "militaristic" polities that were at one time commonly proposed for the prehispanic civilizations of the New World. But secularization is too sweeping a description. Its original employment was dependent on simplistic form-function identifications (e.g., "temples" and "palaces") that Freidel rightly observes are no longer admissible.

Nonetheless, a strong case remains for the emergence of politico-military hierarchies that gradually came to be seen more as expressions of the will of human elites and less as those of otherworldly forces or deities for whom human attendants were mere mouthpieces. If that is indeed a general trend, it certainly must be assumed to have had powerful ideological ramifications that deserve further consideration. Intuitively, the emphasis given to individual representation in portraiture, possibly together with the substitution of military for ceremonial accoutrements, would appear to be a fruitful avenue for the investigation of this trend. The differences between Teotihuacan and the Maya region in these respects, to which Cowgill makes reference (in chapter 5, this volume), are especially noteworthy. They should play a considerable part in attempts to reconstruct and compare the respective ideological systems on the basis of their iconographic differences.

As the above discussion makes clear, it is still highly uncertain at what point, and accompanied by what series of qualitative as well as quantitative changes, coercive political elites made their appearance in any New World developmental sequence. The authors collectively fail to put forward even speculative suggestions on what is surely a central issue within this volume's range of concerns. This absence of attention to a fundamental turning point in incremental processes of scalar expansion and structural elaboration is somewhat embarrassing, at least if the somewhat iconic reference to "evolution" in some chapters really has any significance.

THE CASE OF ASANTE

Particularly when we must operate with archaeological evidence alone, it is important to recognize the danger of assuming a one-to-one correspondence of a society with its ideology. The historically well-documented West African kingdom of Asante provides a good illustration of this danger and is especially valuable in that its status as an expansionistic state, or even nation-state, is quite unambiguous. Eighteenth-century European travelers, "who were not liberal in their use of that term for Africa" (Wilks 1989), characterize it repeatedly as a state. These accounts provide us with rewarding insights into ongoing processes of change, and into both the chronology and the substance of the pattern of imperial expansion and corresponding modes of governance. A well-documented and comprehensive study carefully documents the dynamics of change in Asante's political economy (Wilks 1989), but the following brief summary is primarily drawn from a succinct and penetrating analysis that is more relevant to the subject at hand (Chazan 1988).

Pre-state Asante myths all associate its beginnings with the clearance of forests and the introduction of agriculture. This massive, labor-intensive effort relied heavily on the procurement of slaves. The slave trade, an element in the very early development of long-distance trade, was also linked to the development of indigenous craft technologies, including implements for forest clearing, articles of brass, ornamental pottery, sophisticated weaving for export purposes, and gold.

The first rulers apparently were military elites at the head of dominant groups of kinsmen, who were primarily engaged in agricultural production. These military formations, which at first were primarily concerned with the maintenance of trade routes, subsequently developed a more achievement-oriented orientation than the ascriptive groups from which they were drawn. Through time, the inherent tension between these co-existing kin and functional elite groups led to a "gradual separation of the political culture from the broader cultural context in which it was nurtured" (Chazan 1988: 76).

With the vast expansion of the empire, these tensions were greatly exacerbated. On the one hand, "the kinship principle did not contain answers to questions of political communication, resource extraction, resource aggregation, and legitimation. In these circumstances, some deviation from ascriptive norms had to take place, if only to tackle the minimal details of governing." On the other hand, successful military expansion also "altered the Asante attitude toward commerce. While wars were conducted initially as a means of preventive action or to enlarge the agricultural work force, in time they took on an economic momentum of their own. The steep cost involved in going to war could be defrayed neither by the war tax nor by distribution of booty after the successful completion of a military engagement. Gradually trade for trade's sake, as a means of enhancing profits and obtaining goods, became an object in its own right" (Chazan 1988: 89–90).

What is important for present purposes is that through this process of separation, "two distinct types of state came into being in precolonial Asante. The first was concerned with the strengthening of the cohesion of society through symbolically ratified consensus, while the second imposed a system of domination of a functionally defined ruling group whose existence was facilitated by secularization. An incipient, mediatory state in a socially stratified context was beginning to emerge when Asante succumbed to external pressures" (Chazan 1988: 97).

Introduction of the Asante case raises several pertinent questions: What can be said about the importance of *differentiated* elites in the New World civilizations we are primarily considering? To the extent that they were present, are we able to identify the ideologies separately associated with some or all of them? Since different elites presumably arose in response to different developmental processes—for example, peer-polity interactions vs. monocentric states—how were the dynamics of their synergisms and rivalries reflected in the modification or fusion of their respective ideologies?

An ancient Egyptian version of these differences in standpoint, which admittedly reflects stylized viewpoints rather than accurately recorded statements, opposes the positions of officials and their pharaoh as follows:

We are at ease holding our part of Egypt. Elephantine is strong, and the midland is with us as far as Cusae. Men till for us the finest of their land; our cattle are in the papyrus marshes. Spelt is trodden out for our swine. Our cattle are not taken away. . .

To what end am I cognizant of it, this power of mine, when a chieftain is in Avaris, and another in Kush, and I sit in league with an Amu and a Negro, every man holding his slice of this Egypt? (Liverani 1990: 67).

The answers to questions concerning these issues of differentiation will rarely be easy, and when we are dependent on archaeology alone they may completely evade us. Myths, legends, or other recorded political and religious traditions greatly improve our chances. But even when we discern what may be direct allusions to differing elite orientations, as in the complex Quetzalcoatl-Texcatlipoca succession in central Mexico, our interpretations are likely to remain speculative unless they can be painstakingly confirmed with independently converging lines of evidence.

Were documentation available, we would like to be able to follow in detail the emergence of stratified societies as this process impacted, and in turn was impacted by, ideologies. Presumably the significant axes of change involved the mobilization of labor for elite-supporting as well as less ambiguously public ends, and the establishment of inequalities in access to productive resources (e.g., land, traded materials, craft-produced products). These phenomena may not be appropriate research topics for societies at an early or even incipient stage in the stratification process, however, since few of them become visible until a fairly late stage in a society's development. It may be more productive to focus attention instead on the extent to which an ancestor cult, for example, or an expansionist ideology was genuinely communicated to and shared by the ordinary population and thus was a significant force in the motivation of the population for arduous military service at increasing distances from their home districts.

Conrad (chapter 8, this volume) insists that motivation of an elite was not enough. Because warfare involves risk of death or injury, Inca expansion additionally required enhanced motivation of the common soldier. Awards to the rank and file in the Inca army were in some cases material, although in others they merely conveyed prestige and access to Inca ethnic accoutrements. The real question is the process—possibly lengthy and subject to reversals—by which warfare was transformed from a small-scale affair involving elites in hand-to-hand engagements in pursuit of prisoners, as in the Maya Classic, into a late Postclassic activity involving mobilized masses of ordinary people. Nor should we assume that elites were ever fully successful in establishing, maintaining, or monopolizing consensus through any of the measures they took.

CONCLUSION

The burden of most of the foregoing comments is that oversimplification of ideologies and their modes of attachment to other cultural phenomena may well be the distortion that most seriously threatens to undermine studies of ideologies in early states and civilizations. This oversimplification may involve, for example, assumptions of congruence of material expressions and conceptual content; invention of "efficient" motives, explanations, and systemic properties; identification of surviving expressions with the original totality; as well as overemphasis on coherence and standardization and consequent neglect of subtle and indirect clues to internal social tensions or contradictions.

It may be useful, in conclusion, to view this question of oversimplification through another set of disciplinary lenses. A recent exchange between a social historian and a political sociologist, although immediately concerned with the French Revolution, introduces somewhat opposed positions that will be familiar to those who have examined the studies in this volume. William Sewell, the historian, argues for the "autonomous power of ideology in the revolutionary process," viewing it as "anonymous, collective, and as constitutive of social order" (1985:58, 61). Theda Skocpol, by contrast, finds this position "unrealistically totalistic and synchronous":

> Dangerous pitfalls lurk when students of complex, changing, highly stratified sociopolitical orders rely upon anthropological ideas about cultural systems. It is all too easy to suppose the existence of integrated patterns of shared meanings, total pictures of how society does and should work. Given the impossibility of face-to-face fieldwork contact with diverse societal groups acting and arguing in real time, there is an inevitable temptation to read entire systems of meaning into particular documents. . . . Most risky of all, one is tempted to treat fundamental cultural and ideological change as the synchronous and complete replacement of one society-wide cultural system by another. . . .

Historians, sociologists, and political scientists are not well served by supposing that sets of ideas—whether intellectual productions or cultural frameworks of a more informally reasoned sort—are "constitutive of social order." Rather, multiple cultural idioms exist, and they arise, decline, and intermingle in tempos that need to be explored by intellectual and sociocultural historians (Skocpol 1985:89–91).

What is argued here is a case for more appropriate recognition of the scale and complexity of the phenomena with which we deal when our attention turns to states, civilizations, and empires. The cultural holism of the traditional anthropological view no longer provides an effective analytical framework (if indeed it ever did) and should itself be recognized as a form of ideological expression.

We encounter instead a pluralistic, strife-ridden, only loosely bounded world of contending individuals and groups who share some elements of a world view but diverge or even clash in others. Rare hinges of change or historical conjunctures may exist at which forces in disparate institutions or areas of activity converge to create the sense of a broadly synchronous transformation reaching into many realms of individual and collective behavior. But we must expect to find that changes are more commonly uncoordinated or dialectically counterposed, and that continuity of goals often is only a remote observer's teleological construct. Ideologies play an important part in this mix and are fully worth the painstaking, often frustrated effort to elicit vestiges of them from the highly refractory record. We are bound to be disappointed, however, if we turn away from the full range of other physical as well as mental constructs of early civilizations to seek in them a unifying, explanatory vision.

REFERENCES

Adams, Richard E. W.
  1983 Ancient land use and culture history in the Pasión River region. *In* Prehistoric settlement patterns: essays in honor of Gordon R. Willey. Evon Z. Vogt and Richard M. Leventhal, eds. Albuquerque: University of New Mexico Press.
  1986 Rio Azul. National Geographic 169:420–51.
Adams, Richard E. W., ed.
  1977 The origins of Maya civilization. Albuquerque: University of New Mexico Press, School of American Research Advanced Seminar Series.
Adams, Richard E. W., W. E. Brown, Jr., and T. Patrick Culbert
  1981 Radar mapping, archaeology, and ancient Maya land use. Science 213:1457–63.
Adams, Richard E. W., G. D. Hall, I. Graham, F. Valdez, S. L. Black, D. Potter, D. J. Connell, and B. Connell
  1984 Rio Azul Project report 1: final 1983 report. San Antonio: Center for Archaeological Research, University of Texas.
Adams, Robert McC.
  1965 Land behind Baghdad: a history of settlement on the Diyala Plains. Chicago: University of Chicago Press.
  1966 The evolution of urban society: early Mesopotamia and prehistoric Mexico. Chicago: Aldine.
  1969 The study of ancient Mesopotamian settlement patterns and the problem of urban origins. Sumer 25:111–24.
  1972 Patterns of urbanization in early southern Mesopotamia. *In* Man, settlement and urbanism. Peter J. Ucko, Ruth Tringham, and G. W. Dimbleby, eds. London: Duckworth.
  1979 Late prehispanic empires of the New World. *In* Power and propaganda: a symposium on ancient empires. Mogens Trolle Larsen, ed. Mesopotamia: Copenhagen Studies in Assyriology 7. Copenhagen: Akademisk Forlag.
  1981 The heartland of cities: surveys of ancient settlement and land use on the central floodplain of the Euphrates. Chicago: University of Chicago Press.
Adams, Robert McC., and Hans J. Nissen
  1972 The Uruk countryside: the natural setting of urban societies. Chicago: University of Chicago Press.
Allison, Marvin J., Guillermo Foccaci, Bernardo Arriaza, Vivien Standen, Mario Rivera, and Jerold M. Lowenstein
  1984 Chinchorro, momias de preparación complicada: métodos de momificación. Chungará 13:155–73. Arica, Chile.
Andrews, E. Wyllys, V
  1981 Dzibilchaltun. *In* Supplement to the handbook of Middle American Indians, vol. 1: archaeology. Jeremy A. Sabloff, ed. Austin: University of Texas Press.
  1987 Spoons and knuckle-dusters in Formative Mesoamerica. Paper presented at the symposium "Olmec, Izapa, and the development of Maya civilization," University of Texas, Austin.
Andrews, E. Wyllys, V, William M. Ringle, Philip J. Barnes, Alfredo Barrera R., and Tomás Gallareta N.
  1984 Komchen: an early Maya community in northwest Yucatan. Proceedings of the XVII mesa redonda de la Sociedad Mexicana de Antropología. San Cristóbal, Chiapas, Mexico.
Anonymous
  1919 Idolatrías de los indios huachos y yauyos [1613]. Revista Histórica 6:180–97. Lima.

Appleby, Joyce Oldham
1978 Economic thought and ideology in seventeenth-century England. Princeton: Princeton University Press.

Ardener, Edwin
1971 The new anthropology and its critics. Man, n.s. 6:449–67.

Armillas, Pedro
1964 Northern Mesoamerica. In Prehistoric man in the New World. Jesse D. Jennings and Edward Norbeck, eds. Chicago: University of Chicago Press.

Arriaga, Pablo Joseph de
1968 The extirpation of idolatry in Peru [1621]. L. Clark Keating, trans. and ed. Lexington: University of Kentucky Press.

Ashmore, Wendy A.
1986 Peten cosmology in the Maya southeast: an analysis of architecture and settlement patterns at Classic Quirigua. In The southeast Maya periphery. Patricia A. Urban and Edward M. Schortman, eds. Austin: University of Texas Press.
1988 Proyecto Arqueológico Copan de Cosmología/Copan North Group Project: June–July 1988. Report submitted to the Instituto Hondureño de Antropología e Historia and the National Geographic Society.

Ashmore, Wendy A., and Robert J. Sharer
1975 A revitalization movement at Late Classic Tikal. Paper presented at the Area Seminar in Ongoing Research, West Chester State College, New York.

Avila, Francisco de
1966 Dioses y hombres de Huarochirí [ca. 1598]. Fuentes e Investigaciones para la Historia del Perú, Textos Críticos 1. Lima: Instituto de Estudios Peruanos.

Ball, Joseph W.
1977 The archaeological ceramics of Becan, Campeche, Mexico. Middle American Research Institute Publication 43. New Orleans: Tulane University.

Ball, Joseph W., and Jennifer T. Taschek
1989 Small center archaeology and Classic Maya political organization: the Mopan-Macal Triangle Project. Paper presented at the Society for American Archaeology Annual Meetings.

Bandelier, Adolph F.
1904 On the relative antiquity of ancient Peruvian burials. Bulletin of the American Museum of Natural History 20:217–26.

Barbour, Warren
1975 The figurines and figurine chronology of ancient Teotihuacan, Mexico. Ph.D. dissertation, Department of Anthropology, University of Rochester.

Becker, Marshall J.
1975–76 Moieties in ancient Mesoamerica: inferences on Teotihuacan social structure. American Indian Quarterly 2:217–36, 315–30.
1983 Kings and classicism: political change in the Maya lowlands during the Classic period. In Highland-lowland interaction in Mesoamerica: interdisciplinary approaches. Arthur G. Miller, ed. Washington, DC: Dumbarton Oaks.

Beetz, Carl, and Lincoln Satterthwaite
1981 The monuments and inscriptions of Caracol, Belize. Monographs of the University Museum 45. Philadelphia: University of Pennsylvania.

Bender, Barbara
1978 Gatherer-hunter to farmer: a social perspective. World Archaeology 10:204–22.

Bentley, G. Carter
1986 Indigenous states of southeast Asia. Annual Review of Anthropology 15:275–305.

Bernal, Ignacio
1969   The Olmec world. Berkeley: University of California Press.
Berrin, Kathleen, ed.
1988   Feathered serpents and flowering trees: reconstructing the murals of Teotihuacan. San Francisco: The Fine Arts Museums of San Francisco. Seattle: University
of Washington Press.
Beyer, Hermann
1979   Estudio interpretativo de algunas grandes esculturas [1922]. *In* La población del
valle de Teotihuacán, vol. 1. Manuel Gamio, ed. Mexico, DF: Instituto Nacional
Indigenista.
Bigalke, T.
1983   Dynamics of the Torajan slave trade in south Sulawesi. *In* Slavery, bondage, and
dependency in southeast Asia. A. Reid, ed. New York: St. Martin's Press.
Blanton, Richard E.
1976a   Anthropological studies of cities. Annual Review of Anthropology 5:249–64.
1976b   Comment on Sanders, Parsons, and Logan. *In* The Valley of Mexico: studies in
pre-hispanic ecology and society. Eric Wolf, ed. Albuquerque: University of
New Mexico Press, School of American Research Advanced Seminar Series.
1976c   The role of symbiosis in adaptation and sociocultural change in the Valley of
Mexico. *In* The Valley of Mexico: studies in pre-hispanic ecology and society.
Eric Wolf, ed. Albuquerque: University of New Mexico Press, School of American Research Advanced Seminar Series.
1978   Monte Alban: settlement patterns at the ancient Zapotec capital. New York: Academic Press.
1980   Cultural ecology reconsidered. American Antiquity 45:145–51.
Blanton, Richard E., Stephen A. Kowaleski, Gary Feinman, and Jill Appel
1981   Ancient Mesoamerica. Cambridge: Cambridge University Press.
Blucher, Darlena K.
1971   Late Preclassic cultures in the Valley of Mexico: pre-urban Teotihuacan. Ph.D.
dissertation, Department of Anthropology, Brandeis University.
Boggs, Stanley
1950   "Olmec" pictographs in the Las Victorias Group, Chalchuapa Archaeological
Zone. Notes on Middle American Archaeology and Ethnology, no. 99. Washington, DC: Carnegie Institution.
Boksenbaum, Martin William, Paul Tolstoy, Garman Harbottle, Jerome Kimberlin, and
Mary Neivens
1987   Obsidian industries and cultural evolution in the Basin of Mexico before
500 B.C. Journal of Field Archaeology 14:65–75.
Bottomore, T. B.
1956   Marx's social theory. London: Watts.
Boudon, Raymond
1982   The unintended consequences of social action. New York: St. Martin's Press.
Bove, Frederick
1978   Laguna de los Cerros, an Olmec central place. Journal of New World Archaeology 2(3):1–56.
Braithwaite, M.
1982   Decoration as ritual symbol: a theoretical proposal and an ethnographic study
in southern Sudan. *In* Symbolic and structural archaeology. Ian Hodder, ed.
Cambridge: Cambridge University Press.
1984   Ritual and prestige in the prehistory of Wessex c. 2200–1400 B.C.: a new dimension to the archaeological evidence. *In* Ideology, power and prehistory.

Daniel Miller and Christopher Tilley, eds. Cambridge: Cambridge University Press.

Bram, Joseph
1941   An analysis of Inca militarism. American Ethnological Society Monograph 4.

Bray, Warwick
1978   Civilising the Aztecs. *In* The evolution of social systems. Jonathan Friedman and M. J. Rowlands, eds. London: Duckworth.

Bricker, Victoria R.
1981   The Indian Christ, the Indian king: the historical substrate of Maya myth and ritual. Austin: University of Texas Press.

Browman, David L.
1978   Toward the development of the Tiwanaku (Tiahuanaco) state. *In* Advances in Andean archaeology. David L. Browman, ed. The Hague: Mouton.
1981   New light on Andean Tiwanaku. American Scientist 69:408–19.

Brumfiel, Elizabeth
1976   Regional growth in the eastern Valley of Mexico: a test of the "population pressure" hypothesis. *In* The early Mesoamerican village. Kent V. Flannery, ed. New York: Academic Press.

Brundage, Burr C.
1963   Empire of the Inca. Norman: University of Oklahoma Press.

Burger, Richard L.
1988   Unity and heterogeneity within the Chavin horizon. *In* Peruvian prehistory. Richard W. Keatinge, ed. Cambridge: Cambridge University Press.

Cabello Valboa, Miguel
1951   Miscelánea antártica [1586]. Lima: Instituto de Etnología, Universidad Nacional Mayor de San Marcos.

Cabrera C., Rubén, and Saburo Sugiyama K.
1982   La reexploración y restauración del Templo Viejo de Quetzalcoatl. *In* Memoria del proyecto Teotihuacan 80–82. Rubén Cabrera C., Ignacio Rodríguez G., and Noel Morelos G., eds. Mexico, DF: Instituto Nacional de Antropología e Historia.

Cabrera C., Rubén, Ignacio Rodríguez G., and Noel Morelos G., eds.
1982a Memoria del proyecto arqueológico Teotihuacan 80–82. Mexico, DF: Instituto Nacional de Antropología e Historia.
1982b Teotihuacan 80–82: primeros resultados. Mexico, DF: Instituto Nacional de Antropología e Historia.

Cabrera C., Rubén, Saburo Sugiyama, and George L. Cowgill
1991   The Temple of Quetzalcoatl Project at Teotihuacan: a preliminary report. Ancient Mesoamerica 2:77–92.

Cabrera C., Rubén, George Cowgill, Saburo Sugiyama, and Carlos Serrano
1989   El proyecto Templo de Quetzalcoatl. Arqueología 5:51–79. Mexico, DF.

Carlson, John B.
1981   Olmec concave iron-ore mirrors: the aesthetics of a lithic technology and the Lord of the Mirror. *In* The Olmec and their neighbors. Elizabeth P. Benson, ed. Washington, DC: Dumbarton Oaks.

Carneiro, Robert L.
1970   A theory of the origin of the state. Science 169:733–38.
1981   The chiefdom: precursor of the state. *In* The transition to statehood in the New World. Grant D. Jones and Robert R. Kautz, eds. Cambridge: Cambridge University Press.
1987   Further reflections on resource concentration and its role in the rise of the state. *In* Studies in the Neolithic and urban revolutions: the V. Gordon Childe Collo-

quium, Mexico, 1986. Linda Manzanilla, ed. British Archaeological Reports, International Series 349. Oxford.

1988   The circumscription theory: challenge and response. American Behavioral Scientist 31:497–511.

1990   Chiefdom-level warfare as exemplified in Fiji and the Cauca Valley. *In* The anthropology of war. Jonathan Haas, ed. Cambridge: Cambridge University Press, School of American Research Advanced Seminar Series.

Carrasco, Pedro, and Johanna Broda, eds.

1978   Economía, política, e ideología en el Mexico prehispánico. Mexico, DF: Instituto Nacional de Antropología e Historia.

Caso, Alfonso

1937   ¿Tenian los teotihuacanos conocimiento de tonalpohualli? El Mexico Antiguo 4:131.

1967   Dioses y signos teotihuacanos. Teotihuacan: onceava mesa redonda 1:249–75. Mexico, DF: Sociedad Mexicana de Antropología.

Ceja Tenorio, Jorge Fausto

1985   Paso de Amada, an Early Preclassic site in the Soconusco, Chiapas, Mexico. Papers of the New World Archaeological Foundation, no. 49. Provo, UT: Brigham Young University.

Chagnon, Napoleon

1973   Studying the Yanomamö. New York: Holt, Rinehart and Winston.

1977   Yanomamö: the fierce people. 2nd. ed. New York: Holt, Rinehart and Winston.

1979   Mate competition, favoring close kin, and village fissioning among the Yanomamö Indians. *In* Evolutionary biology and human social behavior: an anthropological perspective. Napoleon A. Chagnon and William Irons, eds. North Scituate, MA: Duxbury Press.

Chase, Arlen, and Diane Chase

1987   Investigations at the Classic Maya city of Caracol, Belize: 1985–1987. Pre-Columbian Art Research Institute Monograph 3. San Francisco.

Chávez, Sergio J.

1975   The Arapa and Thunderbolt stelae: a case of stylistic identity with implications for Pucara influences in the area of Tiahuanaco. Nawpa Pacha 13:3–26.

Chazan, Naomi

1988   The early state in Africa: the Asante case. *In* The early state in African perspective: culture, power, and division of labor. S. N. Eisenstadt, Michael Abitbol, and Naomi Chazan, eds. Studies in Human Society 3. Leiden: E. J. Brill.

Childe, V. Gordon

1954   Prehistory. *In* The European inheritance. E. Barker, G. Clark, and P. Vaucher, eds. Oxford: Oxford University Press.

Cieza de León, Pedro de

1959   The Incas of Pedro de Cieza de León [1553]. Harriet de Onis, trans., and Victor W. von Hagen, ed. Norman: University of Oklahoma Press.

Claessen, Henri, and Peter Skalnik, eds.

1978   The early state. The Hague: Mouton.

Clark, John E.

1986   From mountains to molehills: a critical review of Teotihuacan's obsidian industry. Research in Economic Anthropology, supplement 2:23–74.

1987a   The formation of ranked societies in Chiapas, Mexico. Paper presented at the American Anthropological Association Annual Meetings.

1987b   Politics, prismatic blades, and Mesoamerican civilization. *In* The organization of core technology. J. K. Johnson and C. A. Morrow, eds. Boulder: Westview Press.

Clark, John E., and Thomas E. Lee, Jr.
  1984   Formative obsidian exchange and the emergence of public economies in Chiapas, Mexico. *In* Trade and exchange in early Mesoamerica. Kenneth G. Hirth, ed. Albuquerque: University of New Mexico Press.

Clark, John E., and Tamara Salcedo Romero
  1989   Ocos obsidian distribution in Chiapas, Mexico. *In* New frontiers in the archaeology of the Pacific coast of southern Mesoamerica. Frederick Bove and Lynette Heller, eds. Anthropological Research Papers, no. 39. Tempe: Arizona State University.

Clark, John E., Michael Blake, Pedro Guzzy, Marta Cuevas, and Tamara Salcedo
  1987   Final report to the Instituto Nacional de Antropología e Historia of the Early Preclassic Pacific Coastal Project. Provo, UT, and San Cristóbal de las Casas, Chiapas, Mexico: New World Archaeological Foundation.

Cobean, Robert M., Michael D. Coe, Edward A. Perry, Jr., Karl T. Turekian, and Dinkar P. Kharkar
  1971   Obsidian trade and San Lorenzo Tenochtitlan. Science 174:666–71.

Cobo, Bernabé
  1979   History of the Inca empire: an account of the Indians' customs and their origin together with a treatise on Inca legends, history, and social institutions [1653]. Roland Hamilton, trans. and ed. Austin: University of Texas Press.

Coe, Michael D.
  1961   La Victoria: an early site on the Pacific coast of Guatemala. Papers of the Peabody Museum of American Archaeology and Ethnology, vol. 53. Cambridge, MA: Harvard University.
  1965   A model of ancient community structure in the Maya lowlands. Southwestern Journal of Anthropology 21:97–114.
  1968   San Lorenzo and the Olmec civilization. *In* Dumbarton Oaks conference on the Olmec. Elizabeth P. Benson, ed. Washington, DC: Dumbarton Oaks.
  1970   The archaeological sequence at San Lorenzo Tenochtitlan, Veracruz, Mexico. Contributions of the University of California Archaeological Research Facility, no. 8:21–34. Berkeley.
  1974   Photogrammetry and the ecology of Olmec civilization. *In* Aerial photography in anthropological field research. Evon Z. Vogt, ed. Cambridge, MA: Harvard University Press.
  1977   Olmec and Maya: a study in relationships. *In* The origins of Maya civilization. Richard E. W. Adams, ed. Albuquerque: University of New Mexico Press, School of American Research Advanced Seminar Series.
  1981a Religion and the rise of Mesoamerican states. *In* The transition to statehood in the New World. Grant D. Jones and Robert R. Kautz, eds. Cambridge: Cambridge University Press.
  1981b San Lorenzo Tenochtitlan. *In* Supplement to the handbook of Middle American Indians, vol. 1: archaeology. Jeremy A. Sabloff, ed. Austin: University of Texas Press.

Coe, Michael D., and Richard A. Diehl
  1980   In the land of the Olmec, vol. 1: the archaeology of San Lorenzo Tenochtitlan. Austin: University of Texas Press.

Coggins, Clemency C.
  1975   Painting and drawing styles at Tikal: an historical and iconographic reconstruction. Ph.D. dissertation, Department of Anthropology, Harvard University.
  1976   Teotihuacan at Tikal in the Early Classic Period. Acts of the 42nd International Congress of Americanists 8:251–69.

1983a An instrument of expansion: Monte Alban, Teotihuacan, and Tikal. *In* Highland-lowland interaction in Mesoamerica: interdisciplinary approaches. Arthur G. Miller, ed. Washington, DC: Dumbarton Oaks.

1983b The stucco decoration and architectural assemblage of Structure 1-sub, Dzibil-chaltun, Yucatan, Mexico. Middle American Research Institute Publication 49. New Orleans: Tulane University.

Cohen, Abner
1979 Political symbolism. Annual Review of Anthropology 8:87–113.

Cohen, Ronald, and Judith D. Toland, eds.
1988 State formation and political legitimacy. Political anthropology, vol. 6. New Brunswick, NJ: Transaction Books.

Conkey, Margaret W., and Janet D. Spector
1984 Archaeology and the study of gender. *In* Advances in archaeological method and theory, vol. 7. Michael B. Schiffer, ed. New York: Academic Press.

Conrad, Geoffrey W.
1981 Cultural materialism, split inheritance, and the expansion of ancient Peruvian empires. American Antiquity 46:3–26.

Conrad, Geoffrey W., and Arthur A. Demarest
1984 Religion and empire: the dynamics of Aztec and Inca expansionism. Cambridge: Cambridge University Press.

Cook, Sherburne F.
1946 Human sacrifice and warfare as factors in the demography of precolonial Mexico. Human Biology 18:81–102.

Cowgill, George L.
1974 Quantitative studies of urbanization at Teotihuacan. *In* Mesoamerican archaeology: new approaches. Norman Hammond, ed. London: Duckworth.

1975a On causes and consequences of ancient and modern population changes. American Anthropologist 77:505–25.

1975b Population pressure as a non-explanation. *In* Population studies in archaeology and biological anthropology: a symposium. Alan C. Swedlund, ed. Society for American Archaeology Memoir 30.

1979 Teotihuacan, internal militaristic competition, and the fall of the Classic Maya. *In* Maya archaeology and ethnohistory. Norman Hammond and Gordon R. Willey, eds. Austin: University of Texas Press.

1983 Rulership and the Ciudadela: political inferences from Teotihuacan architecture. *In* Civilization in the ancient Americas: essays in honor of Gordon R. Willey. Richard M. Leventhal and Alan L. Kolata, eds. Albuquerque: University of New Mexico Press.

Cowgill, George L., Rubén Cabrera C., Saburo Sugiyama, and Carlos Serrano
1991 Discoveries in 1988–89 at the Feathered Serpent Pyramid, Teotihuacan. Ancient Mesoamerica. In press.

Culbert, T. Patrick
1977 Maya development and collapse: an economic perspective. *In* Social process in Maya prehistory: essays in honour of Sir J. Eric S. Thompson. Norman Hammond, ed. New York: Academic Press.

1988a The collapse of Classic Maya civilization. *In* The collapse of ancient states and civilizations. Norman Yoffee and George L. Cowgill, eds. Tucson: University of Arizona Press.

1988b Political history and the decipherment of Maya glyphs. Antiquity 62:135–52.

Culbert, T. Patrick, P. Magers, and M. Spencer
1978 Regional variability in Maya lowland agriculture. *In* Prehispanic Maya agricul-

ture. Peter D. Harrison and B. L. Turner II, eds. Albuquerque: University of New Mexico Press.

Culture and Ideology Working Group
1990   Culture and ideology. *In* Leading edges in social and behavioral science. R. Duncan Luce, Neil J. Smelser, and Dean R. Gerstein, eds. New York: Russell Sage Foundation.

Dahlin, Bruce H.
1976   An anthropologist looks at the pyramids: a Late Classic revitalization movement at Tikal, Guatemala. Ph.D. dissertation, Department of Anthropology, Temple University.
1979   Cropping cash in the Protoclassic: a cultural impact statement. *In* Maya archaeology and ethnohistory. Norman Hammond and Gordon R. Willey, eds. Austin: University of Texas Press.
1983   Climate and prehistory on the Yucatan Peninsula. Climatic Change 5:245–63.
1984   A colossus in Guatemala: the Preclassic city of El Mirador. Archaeology 37(3): 18–25.

Dahlin, Bruce H., John E. Foss, and Mary Elizabeth Chambers
1980   Project Acalches. *In* El Mirador, Peten, Guatemala: an interim report. Ray T. Matheny, ed. Papers of the New World Archaeological Foundation, no. 45. Provo, UT: Brigham Young University.

Deevey, E. S., Don S. Rice, Prudence M. Rice, H. H. Vaughan, Mark Brenner, and M. S. Flannery
1979   Mayan urbanism: impact on a tropical karst environment. Science 206:298–306.

Demarest, Arthur A.
1976   The ideological adaptation of the Mexica Aztec. Manuscript in the possession of the author. Department of Anthropology, Vanderbilt University.
1978   Interregional conflict and "situational ethics" in Classic Maya warfare. *In* Codex Wauchope: festschrift in honor of Robert Wauchope. M. Giardino, M. Edmonson, and W. Creamer, eds. New Orleans: Tulane University.
1981   Viracocha, the nature and antiquity of the Andean high god. Monographs of the Peabody Museum 6. Cambridge, MA: Peabody Museum Press.
1984a Conclusiones y especulaciones. *In* Proyecto El Mirador. Arthur A. Demarest, ed. Mesoamerica 7. South Woodstock, VT: Centro de Investigaciones Regionales de Mesoamerica.
1984b Overview: Mesoamerican human sacrifice in evolutionary perspective. *In* Ritual human sacrifice in Mesoamerica. Elizabeth H. Boone, ed. Washington, DC: Dumbarton Oaks.
1986   The archaeology of Santa Leticia and the rise of Maya civilization. Middle American Research Institute Publication 52. New Orleans: Tulane University.
1987   The archaeology of religion. *In* The encyclopedia of religion. Mircea Eliade, ed. New York: Macmillan.
1988   Political evolution in the Maya borderlands: the Salvadoran frontier. *In* The southeast Classic Maya zone. Elizabeth H. Boone and Gordon R. Willey, eds. Washington, DC: Dumbarton Oaks.
1989   The Olmec and the rise of civilization in eastern Mesoamerica. *In* Regional perspectives on the Olmec. Robert J. Sharer and David C. Grove, eds. Cambridge: Cambridge University Press, School of American Research Advanced Seminar Series.
1990   Resumen de los resultados de la segunda temporada. *In* Informe preliminar #2: segunda temporada (1990) del Proyecto Arqueológico Regional Petexbatun. Arthur Demarest and Stephen Houston, eds. Report submitted to the Instituto de Antropología e Historia de Guatemala.

Demarest, Arthur A., ed.
  1984   Proyecto El Mirador. Mesoamerica 7. South Woodstock, VT: Centro de Investi-
          gaciones Regionales de Mesoamerica.
Demarest, Arthur A., and Geoffrey W. Conrad
  1983   Ideological adaptation and the rise of the Aztec and Inca empires. *In* Civilization
          in the ancient Americas: essays in honor of Gordon R. Willey. Richard M. Lev-
          enthal and Alan L. Kolata, eds. Albuquerque: University of New Mexico Press.
Demarest, Arthur A., and Antonia Foias
  1991   Mesoamerican horizons and the cultural transformations of Maya civilization.
          In Latin American horizons. Don S. Rice, ed. Washington, DC: Dumbar-
          ton Oaks.
Demarest, Arthur A., and Stephen D. Houston, eds.
  1989   Informe preliminar de la primera temporada (1989) del Proyecto Arqueológico
          Regional Petexbatun. Report submitted to the Instituto de Antropología e His-
          toria de Guatemala.
  1990   Informe preliminar #2: segunda temporada (1990) del Proyecto Arqueológico
          Regional Petexbatun. Report submitted to the Instituto de Antropología e His-
          toria de Guatemala.
Diehl, Richard A.
  1981   Olmec architecture: a comparison of San Lorenzo and La Venta. *In* The Ol-
          mec and their neighbors. Elizabeth P. Benson, ed. Washington, DC: Dumbar-
          ton Oaks.
  1989   Olmec archaeology: what we know and what we wish we knew. *In* Regional
          perspectives on the Olmec. Robert J. Sharer and David C. Grove, eds. Cam-
          bridge: Cambridge University Press, School of American Research Advanced
          Seminar Series.
Diener, Paul, Donald Nonini, and Eugene Robkin
  1978   The dialectics of the sacred cow: ecological adaptation versus political appro-
          priation in the origins of India's cattle complex. Dialectical Anthropology
          3:221–38.
Dillon, Brian D.
  1975   Notes on trade in ancient Mesoamerica. Contributions of the University of Cal-
          ifornia Archaeological Research Facility, no. 24:80–135.
Dixon, Keith A.
  1959   Ceramics from two Preclassic periods at Chiapa de Corzo, Chiapas, Mexico.
          Papers of the New World Archaeological Foundation, no. 5. Orinda, CA.
Donley, L.
  1982   House power: Swahili space and symbolic markers. *In* Symbolic and structural
          archaeology. Ian Hodder, ed. Cambridge: Cambridge University Press.
Donnan, Christopher B.
  1976   Moche art and iconography. Los Angeles: Latin American Center, University of
          California at Los Angeles.
Doob, Leonard W.
  1935   Propaganda: its psychology and technique. New York: Henry Holt.
Drennan, Robert D.
  1976   Religion and social evolution in Formative Mesoamerica. *In* The early Meso-
          american village. Kent V. Flannery, ed. New York: Academic Press.
  1984   Long-distance movement of goods in the Mesoamerican Formative and Classic.
          American Antiquity 49:27–43.
Drucker, Philip
  1952   La Venta, Tabasco: a study of Olmec ceramics and art. Bureau of American
          Ethnology Bulletin 153. Washington, DC: Smithsonian Institution.

Drucker, Philip, Robert F. Heizer, and Robert J. Squier
1959   Excavations at La Venta, Tabasco, 1955. Bureau of American Ethnology Bulletin 170. Washington, DC: Smithsonian Institution.
Drucker, R. David
1974   Renovating a reconstruction; the Ciudadela at Teotihuacan, Mexico: construction sequence, layout, and possible uses of the structure. Ph.D. dissertation, Department of Anthropology, University of Rochester.
Dunning, Nicholas P., and Arthur A. Demarest
1990   Sustainable agricultural systems in the Petexbatun, Pasion, and Peten regions of Guatemala: perspectives from contemporary ecology and ancient settlement. Proposal submitted to the United States Agency for International Development.
Durham, William H.
1990   Advances in evolutionary culture theory. Annual Review of Anthropology 19:187–210.
Durkheim, Émile
1966   The rules of sociological method. George E. G. Catlin, ed. New York: The Free Press.
Duviols, Pierre
1967   Un inédit de Cristóbal de Albornoz: la instrucción para descrubrir todas las guacas del Pirú y sus camayos y haziendas [ca. 1582]. Journal de la Société des Américanistes, n.s. 56:7–39. Paris.
1976   Punchao, idolo mayor del Coricancha: historia y tipología. Antropología Andina 1–2:156–83. Cuzco.
1979   Un symbolisme de l'occupation, l'aménagement et de l'exploitation de l'espace: le monolithe "huanca" et sa fonction dans les Andes préhispaniques. L'Homme 19(2):7–31.
Eisenstadt, S. N.
1963   The political systems of empires: the rise and fall of the historical bureaucratic societies. New York: The Free Press.
Eliade, Mircea
1964   Shamanism: archaic techniques of ecstasy. Princeton: Princeton University Press.
Ellul, Jacques
1965   Propaganda: the formation of men's attitudes. Konrad Kellen and Jean Lerner, trans. New York: Alfred A. Knopf.
Elster, John
1983   Sour grapes: studies in the subversion of rationality. Cambridge: Cambridge University Press.
1985   Making sense of Marx. Cambridge: Cambridge University Press.
Fash, William L., Jr.
1982   A Middle Formative cemetery from Copan, Honduras. Paper presented at the American Anthropological Association Annual Meetings.
1983   Maya state formation: a case study and its implications. Ph.D. dissertation, Department of Anthropology, Harvard University.
1987   Maya statecraft in the Copan Valley: toward a millennial perspective. Proposal submitted to the National Science Foundation.
1988   A new look at Maya statecraft from Copan, Honduras. Antiquity 62:157–69.
Fash, William L., Jr., and David Stuart
1990   Interaction and political process in Copan. In Classic Maya political history: archaeological and hieroglyphic evidence. T. Patrick Culbert, ed. Cambridge: Cambridge University Press, School of American Research Advanced Seminar Series.

Feeley-Harnik, Gillian
   1985   Issues in divine kingship. Annual Review of Anthropology 14:273–313.
Feinman, Gary M., Stephen A. Kowaleski, Laura Finsten, Richard E. Blanton, and
Linda Nicholas
   1985   Long-term demographic change: a perspective from the Valley of Oaxaca, Mex-
          ico. Journal of Field Archaeology 12:333–62.
Finkelstein, Jacob J.
   1979   Early Mesopotamia, 2500–1000 B.C. In Propaganda and communication in
          world history, vol. I: the symbolic instrument in early times. Harold D. Lasswell,
          Daniel Lerner, and Hans Speier, eds. Honolulu: University of Hawaii Press.
Flannery, Kent V.
   1968a Archeological systems theory and early Mesoamerica. In Anthropological arche-
          ology in the Americas. Betty J. Meggers, ed. Washington, DC: Anthropological
          Society of Washington.
   1968b The Olmec and the Valley of Oaxaca: a model for interregional interaction in
          Formative times. In Dumbarton Oaks conference on the Olmec. Elizabeth P.
          Benson, ed. Washington, DC: Dumbarton Oaks.
   1972   The cultural evolution of civilizations. Annual Review of Ecology and Systemat-
          ics 3:399–426.
   1976   Interregional religious networks, introduction. In The early Mesoamerican vil-
          lage. Kent V. Flannery, ed. New York: Academic Press.
   1977   A setting for cultural evolution: review of Eric Wolf (ed.), The Valley of Mexico:
          studies in pre-hispanic ecology and society. Science 196:759–61.
Flannery, Kent V., and Joyce Marcus
   1976a Evolution of the public building in Formative Oaxaca. In Cultural change and
          continuity: essays in honor of James Bennett Griffin. Charles E. Cleland, ed. New
          York: Academic Press.
   1976b Formative Oaxaca and the Zapotec cosmos. American Scientist 64:374–83.
Flannery, Kent V., Joyce Marcus, and Stephen Kowalewski
   1981   The Preceramic and Formative in the Valley of Oaxaca. In Supplement to the
          handbook of Middle American Indians, vol. 1: archaeology. Jeremy A. Sabloff,
          ed. Austin: University of Texas Press.
Foncerrada de Molina, Marta
   1980   Mural painting in Cacaxtla and Teotihuacan cosmopolitism. In Third Palenque
          round table, 1978: part 2. Merle Greene Robertson, ed. Austin: University of
          Texas Press.
Fox, Richard
   1977   Urban anthropology. Englewood Cliffs, NJ: Prentice-Hall.
Freidel, David A.
   1979   Culture areas and interaction spheres: contrasting approaches to the emergence
          of civilization in the Maya lowlands. American Antiquity 44:36–54.
   1981a Civilization as a state of mind: the cultural evolution of the lowland Maya. In
          The transition to statehood in the New World. Grant D. Jones and Robert R.
          Kautz, eds. Cambridge: Cambridge University Press.
   1981b The political economics of residential dispersion among the lowland Maya. In
          Lowland Maya settlement patterns. Wendy Ashmore, ed. Albuquerque: Univer-
          sity of New Mexico Press, School of American Research Advanced Seminar
          Series.
   1986a Maya warfare: an example of peer polity interaction. In Peer polity interaction
          and the development of sociopolitical complexity. Colin Renfrew and John F.
          Cherry, eds. Cambridge: Cambridge University Press.
   1986b The Mesoamerican world. Latin American Research Review 21:231–41.

1986c   The monumental architecture. *In* Archaeology at Cerros, Belize, Central America, vol. 1: an interim report. Robin A. Robertson and David A. Freidel, eds. Dallas: Southern Methodist University Press.

1986d   Terminal Classic lowland Maya: successes, failures, and aftermaths. *In* Late lowland Maya civilization: Classic to Postclassic. Jeremy A. Sabloff and E. Wyllys Andrews V, eds. Albuquerque: University of New Mexico Press, School of American Research Advanced Seminar Series.

Freidel, David A., and Linda Schele

1988a   Kingship in the Late Preclassic lowlands: the instruments and places of ritual power. American Anthropologist 90:547–67.

1988b   Symbol and power: a history of the lowland Maya cosmogram. *In* Maya iconography. Elizabeth Benson and Gillette Griffin, eds. Princeton: Princeton University Press.

Fried, Morton H.

1967   The evolution of political society. New York: Random House.

Friedman, Jonathan

1974   Marxism, structuralism and vulgar materialism. Man, n.s. 9:444–69.

1975   Tribes, states, and transformations. *In* Marxist analyses and social anthropology. Maurice Bloch, ed. London: Association of Social Anthropologists.

Friedman, Jonathan, and M. J. Rowlands, eds.

1978   The evolution of social systems. London: Duckworth.

Friedrich, Paul

1986   Language, ideology and political economy. Paper presented at the American Anthropological Association Annual Meetings.

1989   Language, ideology, and political economy. American Anthropologist 91: 295–312.

Fritz, John M.

1978   Paleopsychology today: ideational systems and human adaptation in prehistory. *In* Social archeology: beyond subsistence and dating. Charles L. Redman, Mary Jane Berman, Edward V. Curtin, William T. Langhorne, Jr., Nina M. Versaggi, and Jeffrey C. Wanser, eds. New York: Academic Press.

1985   Is Vijayanagara a cosmic city? *In* Vijayanagara: city and empire. S. Dallapiccola and S. Zingel-Ave Lallement, eds. Heidelberg: South Asia Institute.

1986   Vijayanagara: authority and meaning of a south Indian imperial capital. American Anthropologist 88:44–55.

Fritz, John M., G. A. Michell, and M. S. Nagaraja Rao

1985   Where kings and gods meet: the royal center of Vijayanagara, India. Tucson: University of Arizona Press.

Fry, Robert E.

1979   The economics of pottery at Tikal, Guatemala: models of exchange for serving vessels. American Antiquity 44:494–512.

Furst, Peter T.

1974   Roots and continuities. ArtsCanada 184–187:33–60.

Gamio, Manuel, ed.

1979   La población del valle de Teotihuacan [1922]. Mexico, DF: Instituto Nacional Indigenista.

Garber, James F.

1983   Patterns of jade consumption and disposal at Cerros, in Belize. American Antiquity 48:800–807.

Garza Tarazona de González, Silvia, and Edward B. Kurjack

1980   Atlas arqueológico del estado de Yucatan, tomo 1. Mexico, DF: Instituto Nacional de Antropología e Historia.

Gay, Peter
1988   Style in history. New York: W. W. Norton.
Geertz, Clifford
1973   The interpretation of cultures. New York: Basic Books.
1980   Negara: the theater state in nineteenth-century Bali. Princeton: Princeton University Press.
1983   Local knowledge: further essays in interpretive anthropology. New York: Basic Books.
Gesick, Loraine
1983   Introduction. In Centers, symbols, and hierarchies: essays on the classical states of southeast Asia. Loraine Gesick, ed. Southeast Asia Studies Monograph Series, no. 26. New Haven: Yale University.
Gesick, Loraine, ed.
1983   Centers, symbols, and hierarchies: essays on the classical states of southeast Asia. Southeast Asia Studies Monograph Series, no. 26. New Haven: Yale University.
Gibson, Eric C.
1986   Diachronic patterns of lithic production, use, and exchange in the southern Maya lowlands. Ph.D. dissertation, Department of Anthropology, Harvard University.
Gillespie, Susan D.
1987   Distributional analysis of Chalcatzingo figurines. In Ancient Chalcatzingo. David C. Grove, ed. Austin: University of Texas Press.
1992   Power, pathways, and appropriation in Mesoamerican art. In Imagery and creativity: ethnoaesthetics and art worlds in the Americas. Dorothea S. Whitten and Norman E. Whitten, Jr., eds. Tucson: University of Arizona Press.
Gilman, Antonio
1989   Marxism in American archaeology. In Archaeological thought in America. C. C. Lamberg-Karlovsky, ed. Cambridge: Cambridge University Press.
Glassie, Henry
1975   Folk housing in middle Virginia: a structural analysis of historic artifacts. Knoxville: University of Tennessee Press.
Godelier, Maurice
1977   Perspectives in marxist anthropology. Cambridge: Cambridge University Press.
1978a   Economy and religion: an evolutionary optical illusion. In The evolution of social systems. Jonathan Friedman and M. J. Rowlands, eds. London: Duckworth.
1978b   Infrastructures, societies, and history. Current Anthropology 19:763–71.
1978c   Politics as "infrastructure": an anthropologist's thoughts on the example of classical Greece and the notions of relations of production and economic determinism. In The evolution of social systems. Jonathan Friedman and M. J. Rowlands, eds. London: Duckworth.
González Lauck, Rebecca
1988   Proyecto arqueológico La Venta. Arqueología 4:121–65. Mexico, DF.
Gossen, Gary H.
1974   Chamulas in the world of the sun: time and space in a Maya oral tradition. Prospect Heights, IL: Waveland Press.
Graham, John A.
1982   Antecedents of Olmec sculpture at Abaj Takalik. In Pre-columbian art history: selected readings. Alana Cordy-Collins, ed. Palo Alto: Peek Publications.
Griffith, Samuel B.
1963   Sun Tzu, the art of war. Oxford: Oxford University Press.

Grove, David C.
1968 The Morelos Preclassic and the highland Olmec problem: an archaeological study. Ph.D. dissertation, Department of Anthropology, University of California, Los Angeles.
1970 The Olmec paintings of Oxtotitlan Cave, Guerrero, Mexico. Studies in Pre-Columbian Art and Archaeology, no. 6. Washington, DC: Dumbarton Oaks.
1973 Olmec altars and myths. Archaeology 26:128–35.
1974a The highland Olmec manifestation: a consideration of what it is and what it isn't. In Mesoamerican archaeology: new approaches. Norman Hammond, ed. Austin: University of Texas.
1974b San Pablo, Nexpa, and the early Formative archaeology of Morelos, Mexico. Vanderbilt University Publications in Anthropology, no. 12. Nashville: Vanderbilt University.
1981a The Formative period and the evolution of complex culture. In Supplement to the Handbook of Middle American Indians, vol. 1, Archaeology. Jeremy Sabloff, ed. Austin: University of Texas Press.
1981b Olmec monuments: mutilation as a clue to meaning. In The Olmec and their neighbors. Elizabeth P. Benson, ed. Washington, DC: Dumbarton Oaks.
1984 Chalcatzingo: excavations on the Olmec frontier. London: Thames and Hudson.
1987a Chalcatzingo in a broader perspective. In Ancient Chalcatzingo. David C. Grove, ed. Austin: University of Texas Press.
1987b Comments on the site and its organization. In Ancient Chalcatzingo. David C. Grove, ed. Austin: University of Texas Press.
1987c Middle Formative serpent imagery: early symbols of rulership. Paper presented at the American Anthropological Association Annual Meetings.
1987d Raw materials and sources. In Ancient Chalcatzingo. David C. Grove, ed. Austin: University of Texas Press.
1987e Torches, knuckle dusters, and the legitimization of Formative period rulership. Mexicon 9(3):60–6. Berlin.
1989a Chalcatzingo and its Olmec connection. In Regional perspectives on the Olmec. Robert J. Sharer and David C. Grove, eds. Cambridge: Cambridge University Press, School of American Research Advanced Seminar Series.
1989b Olmec, what's in a name? In Regional perspectives on the Olmec. Robert J. Sharer and David C. Grove, eds. Cambridge: Cambridge University Press, School of American Research Advanced Seminar Series.
1992 Formative period horizons in Mesoamerica: the shared cosmology and evolving symbols of power. In Latin American horizons. Don S. Rice, ed. Washington, DC: Dumbarton Oaks.
Grove, David C., ed.
1987 Ancient Chalcatzingo. Austin: University of Texas Press.
Grove, David C., and Susan D. Gillespie
1984 Chalcatzingo's portrait figurines and the cult of the ruler. Archaeology 37(4): 27–33.
Grove, David C., and Veronica Kann
1980 Olmec monumental art: heartland and frontier. Paper presented at the American Anthropological Association Annual Meetings.
Grube, Nikolai, and Linda Schele
1988 A quadrant tree at Copan. Copan Notes, no. 43. Copan: Copan Mosaics Project and Instituto Hondureño de Antropología e Historia.
Haas, Jonathan
1982 The evolution of the prehistoric state. New York: Columbia University Press.

Hall, Robert L.
    1979   In search of the ideology of the Adena-Hopewell climax. *In* Hopewell archaeol-
            ogy: the Chillicothe conference. David Brose and Naomi Greber, eds. Kent, OH:
            Kent State University Press.
Hamell, G.
    1983   Trading in metaphors: the magic of beads. *In* Proceedings of the 1982 glass
            trade bead conference. C. Hayes III, ed. Research Records, no. 16. Rochester:
            Rochester Museum and Science Center.
Hammond, Norman
    1982   A Late Formative period stela in the Maya lowlands. American Antiquity 47:
            396–403.
Hansen, Richard D.
    1989   Las investigaciones del sitio Nakbe, Peten, Guatemala. Paper presented at the
            Tercer Simposio de Arqueología Guatemalteca, Museo Nacional de Arqueología
            y Etnología, Guatemala City.
Harner, Michael J.
    1973   The Jivaro: people of the sacred waterfalls. New York: Anchor Books.
    1977   The ecological basis for Aztec sacrifice. American Ethnologist 4:117–35.
Harris, Marvin
    1964   The nature of cultural things. New York: Random House.
    1968   The rise of anthropological theory. New York: Thomas Y. Crowell.
    1975   Cows, pigs, wars and witches: the riddles of culture. New York: Vintage
            Books.
    1977   Cannibals and kings: the origins of culture. New York: Random House.
    1979   Cultural materialism: the struggle for a science of culture. New York: Random
            House.
    1984   A cultural materialist theory of band and village warfare: the Yanomamo test. *In*
            Warfare, culture, and environment. R. Brian Ferguson, ed. Orlando: Academic
            Press.
Harrison, Peter D., and B. L. Turner II, eds.
    1978   Prehispanic Maya agriculture. Albuquerque: University of New Mexico Press.
Healey, Paul F.
    1974   The Cayumel caves: Preclassic sites in northeast Honduras. American Antiquity
            39:435–47.
Hellmuth, Nicholas M.
    1977   Cholti-Lacandon (Chiapas) and Peten-Ytsa agriculture, settlement pattern and
            population. *In* Social process in Maya prehistory: essays in honour of Sir
            J. Eric S. Thompson. Norman Hammond, ed. New York: Academic Press.
Helms, Mary W.
    1979   Ancient Panama: chiefs in search of power. Austin: University of Texas Press.
Hernández Príncipe, Rodrigo
    1923   Mitología andina [1621–22]. Inca 1:25–68. Lima.
Hester, T. R., ed.
    1979   The Colha Project: a collection of interim papers. San Antonio: Center for Ar-
            chaeological Research, University of Texas.
Heyden, Doris
    1975   An interpretation of the cave underneath the Pyramid of the Sun in Teotihuacan,
            Mexico. American Antiquity 40:131–47.
Higham, Charles
    1989   The archaeology of mainland southeast Asia. Cambridge: Cambridge University
            Press.

Hirth, Kenneth G.
    1987   Formative period settlement patterns in the Rio Amatzinac Valley. *In* Ancient
            Chalcatzingo. David C. Grove, ed. Austin: University of Texas Press.
Hirth, Kenneth G., ed.
    1984   Trade and exchange in early Mesoamerica. Albuquerque: University of New
            Mexico Press.
Hitler, Adolf
    1939   Mein kampf. New York: Reynal and Hitchcock.
Hocquenghem, Anne Marie
    1987   Iconografía mochica. Lima: Pontífica Universidad Católica del Perú.
Hodder, Ian
    1982   Symbols in action: ethnoarchaeological studies of material culture. Cambridge:
            Cambridge University Press.
    1983   The present past: an introduction to anthropology for archaeologists. London:
            Batsford.
    1985   Postprocessual archaeology. *In* Advances in archaeological method and theory,
            vol. 8. Michael B. Schiffer, ed. New York: Academic Press.
    1986   Reading the past: current approaches to interpretation in archaeology. Cam-
            bridge: Cambridge University Press.
Hodder, Ian, ed.
    1982   Symbolic and structural archaeology. Cambridge: Cambridge University Press.
Holmberg, Allan R.
    1950   Viru: remnant of an exalted people. *In* Patterns for modern living. Chicago: The
            Delphian Society.
    1952   The wells that failed: an attempt to establish a stable water supply in the Viru
            Valley, Peru. *In* Human problems in technological change: a casebook. E. H.
            Spicer, ed. New York: Russell Sage Foundation.
Houston, Stephen D.
    1987   The inscriptions and monumental art of Dos Pilas, Guatemala: a study of Classic
            Maya history and politics. Ph.D. dissertation, Department of Anthropology, Yale
            University.
    1989   Reading the past: Maya glyphs. Berkeley: University of California Press.
Houston, Stephen D., and Peter Mathews
    1985   The dynastic sequence of Dos Pilas, Guatemala. Pre-Columbian Art Research
            Institute Monograph 1. San Francisco.
Houston, Stephen D., and David Stuart
    1989   The way glyph: evidence for "co-essences" among the Classic Maya. Research
            Reports on Ancient Maya Writing, no. 30. Washington, DC: Center for Maya
            Research.
    1990   Resultados generales de los estudios epigráficos del Proyecto Petexbatun. *In*
            Informe preliminar #2: segunda temporada (1990) del Proyecto Arqueológico
            Regional Petexbatun. Arthur A. Demarest and Stephen D. Houston, eds. Report
            submitted to the Instituto de Antropología e Historia de Guatemala.
Isbell, William H.
    1978   Environmental perturbations and the origin of the Andean state. *In* Social ar-
            cheology: beyond subsistence and dating. Charles L. Redman, Mary Jane Ber-
            man, Edward V. Curtin, William T. Langhorne, Jr., Nina M. Versaggi, and
            Jeffrey C. Wanser, eds. New York: Academic Press.
Jones, Christopher
    1977   Inauguration dates of three Late Classic rulers of Tikal, Guatemala. American
            Antiquity 42:28–60.
    1990   Patterns of growth at Tikal. *In* Classic Maya political history: archaeological and

hieroglyphic evidence. T. Patrick Culbert, ed. Cambridge: Cambridge University Press, School of American Research Advanced Seminar Series.

Jones, Grant D., and Robert R. Kautz
1981 Issues in the study of New World state formation. *In* The transition to statehood in the New World. Grant D. Jones and Robert R. Kautz, eds. Cambridge: Cambridge University Press.

Joralemon, P. David
1971 A study of Olmec iconography. Studies in Pre-Columbian Art and Archaeology, no. 7. Washington, DC: Dumbarton Oaks.

Jowett, Garth S., and Victoria O'Donnell
1986 Propaganda and persuasion. Newbury Park, CA: Sage Publications.

Joyce, Rosemary A., Richard Edging, Karl Lorenz, and Susan D. Gillespie
1990 Olmec bloodletting: an iconographic study. *In* Sixth Palenque roundtable, Vol. III. Merle Greene Robertson, ed. Norman: University of Oklahoma Press.

Justeson, John S., and Lyle Campbell, eds.
1984 Phoneticism in Mayan hieroglyphic writing. Institute for Mesoamerican Studies Publication, no. 9. Albany: State University of New York.

Keatinge, Richard W.
1981 The nature and role of religious diffusion in the early stages of state formation: an example from Peruvian prehistory. *In* The transition to statehood in the New World. Grant D. Jones and Robert R. Kautz, eds. Cambridge: Cambridge University Press.

Kehoe, Alice B.
1975 Paradigmatic archaeology. Paper presented at the Society for American Archaeology Annual Meetings.

Keightley, David N.
1987 Archaeology and mentality: the making of China. Representations 18:91–128.

Kirch, Patrick
1984 The evolution of Polynesian chiefdoms. Cambridge: Cambridge University Press.

Knight, Vernon James, Jr.
1986 The institutional organization of Mississippian religion. American Antiquity 51:675–87.

Kohl, Philip L.
1978 The balance of trade in southwestern Asia in the third millennium B.C. Current Anthropology 19:463–92.

Kolata, Alan L.
1983a The south Andes. *In* Ancient South Americans. Jesse D. Jennings, ed. San Francisco: W. H. Freeman.
1983b Chan Chan and Cuzco: on the nature of the ancient Andean city. *In* Civilization in the ancient Americas. Richard Leventhal and Alan Kolata, eds. Albuquerque: University of New Mexico Press.
1986 The agricultural foundations of the Tiwanaku state: a view from the heartland. American Antiquity 51:748–62.
1987 Research objectives and strategies. *In* The technology and organization of agricultural production in the Tiwanaku state: first preliminary report of Proyecto Wila Jawira. Alan L. Kolata, Charles Stanish, and Oswaldo Rivera, eds. Report submitted to the National Science Foundation and the National Endowment for the Humanities.
1992 Understanding Tiwanaku: conquest, colonization and clientage in the south-central Andes. *In* Latin American horizons. Don S. Rice, ed. Washington, DC: Dumbarton Oaks.

Kolata, Alan L., Charles Stanish, and Oswaldo Rivera, eds.
  1987 The technology and organization of agricultural production in the Tiwanaku state: first preliminary report of Proyecto Wila Jawira. Report submitted to the National Science Foundation and the National Endowment for the Humanities.
Kroeber, A. L.
  1927 Coast and highland in prehistoric Peru. American Anthropologist 29:625–53.
Kubler, George
  1946 The Quechua in the colonial world. In Handbook of South American Indians, vol. 2: the Andean civilizations. Bureau of American Ethnology Bulletin 143. Julian H. Steward, ed. Washington, DC: Smithsonian Institution.
Kurtz, Donald V.
  1978 The legitimation of the Aztec state. In The early state. Henri Claessen and Peter Skalnik, eds. The Hague: Mouton.
LaBarre, Weston
  1971 Materials for a history of studies of crisis cults: a bibliographic essay. Current Anthropology 12:3–44.
Lamberg-Karlovsky, C. C.
  1974 Urban interaction on the Iranian plateau: excavations at Tepe Yahya, 1967–73. Proceedings of the British Academy 59:1–43.
  1975 Third millennium modes of exchange and modes of production. In Ancient civilization and trade. Jeremy A. Sabloff and C. C. Lamberg-Karlovsky, eds. Albuquerque: University of New Mexico Press, School of American Research Advanced Seminar Series.
Langley, James C.
  1986 Symbolic notation of Teotihuacan: elements of writing in a Mesoamerican culture of the Classic period. British Archaeological Reports, International Series 313. Oxford.
Laporte, Juan Pedro
  1986 El "talud-tablero" en Tikal, Peten: nuevos datos. Paper presented at the symposium "Vida y Obra de Roman Piña Chan," Mexico, DF.
  1989 Alternativas del Clásico Temprano en la relación Tikal-Teotihuacan: Grupo 6C-XVI, Tikal, Peten, Guatemala. Ph.D. dissertation, Departamento de Antropología, Universidad Nacional Autónoma de México.
Laporte, Juan Pedro, and Vilma Fialko
  1985 Reporte arqueológico: Mundo Perdido y zonas de habitación, Tikal. 10 vols. Guatemala: Instituto de Antropología e Historia.
Laporte, Juan Pedro, and Lillian Vega de Zea
  1987 Aspectos dinásticos para el Clásico Temprano de Mundo Perdido, Tikal. In Primer simposio mundial sobre epigrafía Maya. Guatemala: Asociación Tikal.
Lasswell, Harold D., Daniel Lerner, and Hans Speier, eds.
  1979 Propaganda and communication in world history, vol. I: the symbolic instrument in early times. Honolulu: University of Hawaii Press.
Lathrap, Donald W.
  1974 The moist tropics, the arid lands, and the appearance of great art styles in the New World. In Variations in anthropology. Donald W. Lathrap and J. Douglas, eds. Urbana: Illinois Archaeological Survey.
  1977 Our father the cayman, our mother the gourd: Spinden revisited, or a unitary model for the emergence of agriculture in the New World. In Origins of agriculture. Charles A. Reed, ed. The Hague: Mouton.
  1985 Jaws: the control of power in the early Nuclear American ceremonial center. In Early ceremonial architecture in the Andes. Christopher B. Donnan, ed. Washington, DC: Dumbarton Oaks.

Leone, Mark P.
1986   Symbolic, structural, and critical archaeology. *In* American archaeology past and future: a celebration of the Society for American Archaeology, 1935–1985. David J. Meltzer, Don D. Fowler, and Jeremy A. Sabloff, eds. Washington, DC: Society for American Archaeology and Smithsonian Institution Press.

Leone, Mark P., Parker B. Potter, Jr., and Paul A. Shackel
1987   Toward a critical archaeology. Current Anthropology 28:283–302.

Levine, Andrew, Elliott Sober, and Erik Olin Wright
1987   Marxism and methodological individualism. New Left Review 162:67–84.

Lewis-Williams, J. D.
1986   Cognitive and optical illusions in San rock art research. Current Anthropology 27:171–8.

Liverani, Mario
1979   The ideology of the Assyrian empire. *In* Power and propaganda: a symposium on ancient empires. Mesopotamia: Copenhagen Studies in Assyriology 7. Mogens Trolle Larsen, ed. Copenhagen: Akademisk Forlag.
1990   Prestige and interest: international relations in the Near East ca. 1600–1100 B.C. History of the Ancient Near East/Studies 1. Padua: Sargon SRL.

Love, Michael W.
1991   Style and social complexity in Formative Mesoamerica. *In* The formation of complex society in southeastern Mesoamerica. William R. Fowler, Jr., ed. Boca Raton: CRC Press.

Lowe, Gareth W.
1977   The Mixe-Zoque as competing neighbors of the lowland Maya. *In* The origins of Maya civilization. Richard E. W. Adams, ed. Albuquerque: University of New Mexico Press, School of American Research Advanced Seminar Series.

Lynch, Thomas F.
1983   Camelid pastoralism and the emergence of Tiwanaku civilization in the south-central Andes. World Archaeology 15:1–14.

MacNeish, Richard S.
1964   Ancient Mesoamerican civilization. Science 143:531–7.
1967   An interdisciplinary approach to an archaeological problem. *In* The prehistory of the Tehuacan Valley, vol. 1. Douglas S. Byers, ed. Austin: University of Texas Press.

Marcus, Joyce P.
1976a   Emblem and state in the Classic Maya lowlands. Washington, DC: Dumbarton Oaks.
1976b   The iconography of militarism at Monte Alban and neighboring sites in the Valley of Oaxaca. *In* Origins of religious art and iconography in Preclassic Mesoamerica. Henry B. Nicholson, ed. Latin American Studies Series 31. Los Angeles: Latin American Center, University of California at Los Angeles.
1976c   The origins of Mesoamerican writing. Annual Review of Anthropology 5:35–67.
1982   The plant world of the lowland Maya. *In* Maya subsistence: studies in memory of Dennis Puleston. Kent V. Flannery, ed. New York: Academic Press.
1983   Lowland Maya archaeology at the crossroads. American Antiquity 48:454–88.
1984   Mesoamerican territorial boundaries: reconstructions from archaeology and hieroglyphic writing. Archaeological Review from Cambridge 3(2):48–62.
1989   Zapotec chiefdoms and the nature of Formative religions. *In* Regional perspectives on the Olmec. Robert J. Sharer and David C. Grove, eds. Cambridge: Cambridge University Press, School of American Research Advanced Seminar Series.

Martínez Donjuan, Guadalupe
1982   Teopantecuanitlan, Guerrero: un sitio olmeca. Revista Mexicana de Estudios Antropológicos 28:128–33.
1986   Teopantecuanitlan. In Arqueología y etnohistoria del estado de Guerrero. Mexico, DF: Instituto Nacional de Antropología e Historia.

Matheny, Ray T.
1976   Maya lowland hydraulic systems. Science 193:639–46.
1987   Early states in the Maya lowlands during the Late Preclassic period: Edzna and El Mirador. In The Maya state. Elizabeth P. Benson, ed. Denver: Rocky Mountain Institute for Precolumbian Studies.

Matheny, Ray T., ed.
1980   El Mirador, Peten, Guatemala: an interim report. Papers of the New World Archaeological Foundation, no. 45. Provo, UT: Brigham Young University.

Mathews, Peter
1985   Maya Early Classic monuments and inscriptions. In A consideration of the Early Classic period in the Maya lowlands. Gordon R. Willey and Peter Mathews, eds. Albany: Institute for Mesoamerican Studies, State University of New York.
1988   The sculptures of Yaxchilan. Ph.D. dissertation, Department of Anthropology, Yale University.

Mathews, Peter, and Linda Schele
1974   Lords of Palenque—the glyphic evidence. Primera mesa redonda de Palenque, part 1:63–76. Pebble Beach: Robert Louis Stevenson School.

Mathews, Peter, and Gordon R. Willey
1990   Prehistoric polities of the Pasión region: hieroglyphic texts and their archaeological settings. In Maya archaeology and history. T. Patrick Culbert, ed. Cambridge: Cambridge University Press, School of American Research Advanced Seminar Series.

McLellan, David
1986   Ideology. Minneapolis: University of Minnesota Press.

Mead, Margaret
1979   Continuities in communication from early man to modern times. In Propaganda and communication in world history, vol. I: the symbolic instrument in early times. Harold D. Lasswell, Daniel Lerner, and Hans Speier, eds. Honolulu: University of Hawaii Press.

Meggers, Betty J.
1954   Environmental limitations on the development of culture. American Anthropologist 56:801–24.

Mercado R., Antonio
1987   ¿Una sacerdotisa en Teotihuacan? México Desconocido 121:6–9.

Mignon, Molly R.
1986   Review of Elizabeth Boone (ed.), Ritual human sacrifice in Mesoamerica. American Antiquity 51:199–200.

Miller, Arthur G.
1973   The mural painting of Teotihuacan. Washington, DC: Dumbarton Oaks.
1986   Maya rulers of time, los soberanos mayas del tiempo: a study of architectural sculpture at Tikal, Guatemala. Philadelphia: The University Museum, University of Pennsylvania.

Miller, Daniel, and Christopher Tilley
1984   Ideology, power and prehistory: an introduction. In Ideology, power and prehistory. Daniel Miller and Christopher Tilley, eds. Cambridge: Cambridge University Press.

Miller, Daniel, and Christopher Tilley, eds.
    1984   Ideology, power and prehistory. Cambridge: Cambridge University Press.
Miller, Mary E.
    1986   The murals of Bonampak. Princeton: Princeton University Press.
Miller, Mary E., and Stephen D. Houston
    1987   Stairways and ballcourt glyphs: new perspectives on the Classic Maya ballgame.
            Res: Anthropology and Aesthetics 14:47–66.
Millon, Clara
    1973   Painting, writing, and polity in Teotihuacan, Mexico. American Antiquity 38:
            294–314.
    1988   A reexamination of the Teotihuacan tassel headdress insignia. In Feathered ser-
            pents and flowering trees: reconstructing the murals of Teotihuacan. Kathleen
            Berrin, ed. Seattle: Fine Arts Museums of San Francisco and University of Wash-
            ington Press.
Millon, René
    1973   Urbanization at Teotihuacan, Mexico, vol. 1: the Teotihuacan map, part 1: text.
            Austin: University of Texas Press.
    1981   Teotihuacan: city, state, and civilization. In Supplement to the handbook of
            Middle American Indians, vol. 1: archaeology. Jeremy A. Sabloff, ed. Austin:
            University of Texas Press.
    1988a   The last years of Teotihuacan dominance. In The collapse of ancient states and
            civilizations. Norman Yoffee and George Cowgill, eds. Tucson: University of
            Arizona Press.
    1988b   Where do they all come from? The provenance of the Wagner murals from
            Teotihuacan. In Feathered serpents and flowering trees: reconstructing the mu-
            rals of Teotihuacan. Kathleen Berrin, ed. Seattle: The Fine Arts Museums of San
            Francisco and University of Washington Press.
Millon, René, and James A. Bennyhoff
    1961   A long architectural sequence at Teotihuacan. American Antiquity 26:516–23.
Millon, René, R. Bruce Drewitt, and James A. Bennyhoff
    1965   The Pyramid of the Sun at Teotihuacan: 1959 excavations. Transactions of the
            American Philosophical Society, vol. 55, no. 6.
Millon, René, R. Bruce Drewitt, and George L. Cowgill
    1973   Urbanization at Teotihuacan, Mexico, vol. 1: the Teotihuacan map, part 2: maps.
            Austin: University of Texas Press.
Mishkin, Bernard
    1946   The contemporary Quechua. In Handbook of South American Indians, vol. 2:
            the Andean civilizations. Bureau of American Ethnology Bulletin 143. Julian H.
            Steward, ed. Washington, DC: Smithsonian Institution.
Monaghan, John
    1990   Sacrifice and the symbolics of power in ancient Mesoamerica. Manuscript in
            possession of the author. Department of Anthropology, Vanderbilt University.
Morrison, Tony
    1978   Pathways to the gods: the mystery of the Nazca lines. Lima: Andean Air Mail
            and Peruvian Times.
Moseley, Michael E.
    1975   Prehistoric principles of labor organization in the Moche Valley, Peru. American
            Antiquity 40:191–6.
Murra, John V.
    1960   Rite and crop in the Inca state. In Culture in history: essays in honor of Paul
            Radin. Stanley Diamond, ed. New York: Columbia University Press.

1972   El "control vertical" de un máximo de pisos ecológicos en la economía de las sociedades andinas. *In* Visita de la provincia de León de Huánuco en 1562. Documentos para la Historia de Huánuco y la Selva Central 2. John V. Murra, ed. Huánuco: Universidad Nacional Hermilio Valdizán.

1975   The conquest and annexation of Qollasuyu by the Inka state. Paper presented at the Society for American Archaeology Annual Meetings.

1986   The expansion of the Inka state: armies, wars, and rebellions. *In* Anthropological history of Andean polities. John V. Murra, Nathan Wachtel, and Jacques Revel, eds. Cambridge: Cambridge University Press.

Nardi, Bonnie Anna

1981   Modes of explanation in anthropological population theory: biological determinism vs. self-regulation in studies of population growth in Third World countries. American Anthropologist 83:28–56.

Nations, James D., and R. B. Nigh

1980   The evolutionary potential of Lacandon Maya sustained-yield tropical forest agriculture. Journal of Anthropological Research 36:1–26.

Navarrete, Carlos

1969   Los relieves olmecas de Pijijiapan, Chiapas. Anales de Antropología 6:183–5.

1974   The Olmec rock carvings at Pijijiapan, Chiapas, Mexico, and other Olmec pieces from Chiapas and Guatemala. Papers of the New World Archaeological Foundation, no. 35. Provo, UT: Brigham Young University.

Netting, Robert McC.

1968   Hill farmers of Nigeria: cultural ecology of the Kofyar of the Jos Plateau. Seattle: University of Washington Press.

1977   Maya subsistence: mythologies, analogies, possibilities. *In* The origins of Maya civilization. Richard E. W. Adams, ed. Albuquerque: University of New Mexico Press, School of American Research Advanced Seminar Series.

Nichols, Deborah L.

1982   A Middle Formative irrigation system near Santa Clara Coatitlan in the Basin of Mexico. American Antiquity 47:133–44.

Norman, Garth V.

1973   Izapa sculpture, part 1: album. Papers of the New World Archaeological Foundation, no. 30. Provo, UT: Brigham Young University.

Núñez, Lautaro, and Tom D. Dillehay

1979   Movilidad giratoria, ármonia social y desarollo en los Andes meridionales: patrones de tráfico e interacción económica. Antofagasta, Chile: Universidad del Norte.

Orlove, Benjamin

1980   Ecological anthropology. Annual Review of Anthropology 9:235–73.

Packard, Randall M.

1981   Chiefship and cosmology: an historical study of political competition. Bloomington: Indiana University Press.

Pader, E.

1982   Symbolism, social relations and the interpretation of mortuary remains. British Archaeological Reports, International Series 130. Oxford.

Parry, William J.

1987   Chipped stone tools in Formative Oaxaca, Mexico: their procurement, production and use. Prehistory and human ecology of the Valley of Oaxaca, vol. 8. Museum of Anthropology Memoirs, no. 20. Ann Arbor: University of Michigan.

Parsons, Jeffrey R.

1976   The role of chinampa agriculture in the food supply of Aztec Tenochtitlan. *In*

Cultural change and continuity: essays in honor of James Bennett Griffin. Charles E. Cleland, ed. New York: Academic Press.

Parsons, Lee A.
1986 The origins of Maya art: monumental stone sculpture of Kaminaljuyu, Guatemala, and the southern Pacific coast. Studies in Pre-Columbian Art and Archaeology, no. 28. Washington, DC: Dumbarton Oaks.

Pasztory, Esther
1988 A reinterpretation of Teotihuacan and its mural painting tradition. *In* Feathered serpents and flowering trees: reconstructing the murals of Teotihuacan. Kathleen Berrin, ed. Seattle: Fine Arts Museums of San Francisco and University of Washington Press.

Patterson, Thomas C.
1971 Chavin: an interpretation of its spread and influence. *In* Dumbarton Oaks conference on Chavin. Elizabeth P. Benson, ed. Washington, DC: Dumbarton Oaks.

Paulsen, Allison C.
1976 Environment and empire: climatic factors in prehistoric Andean culture change. World Archaeology 8:121–32.
1981 The archaeology of the absurd: comments on "Cultural materialism, split inheritance, and the expansion of ancient Peruvian empires." American Antiquity 46:31–7.

Pearson, M.P.
1982 Mortuary practices, society and ideology. *In* Symbolic and structural archaeology. Ian Hodder, ed. Cambridge: Cambridge University Press.
1984 Social change, ideology and the archaeological record. *In* Marxist perspectives in archaeology. M. Spriggs, ed. Cambridge: Cambridge University Press.

Pease G. Y., Franklin
1973 El dios creador andino. Lima: Mosca Azul Editores.

Peebles, Christopher, and Susan Kus
1977 Some archaeological correlates of ranked societies. American Anthropologist 79:421–48.

Pendergast, David M.
1979 Excavations at Altun Ha, Belize, 1964–1970, vol. 1. Toronto: Royal Ontario Museum.
1981 Lamanai, Belize: summary of excavation results 1974–1980. Journal of Field Archaeology 8:29–53.

Peterson, Richard A.
1979 Revitalizing the culture concept. Annual Review of Sociology 5:137–66.

Pires-Ferreira, Jane W.
1975 Formative Mesoamerican exchange networks with special reference to the Valley of Oaxaca. Prehistory and human ecology of the Valley of Oaxaca, vol. 3. Museum of Anthropology Memoirs, no. 7. Ann Arbor: University of Michigan.
1976a Obsidian exchange in Formative Mesoamerica. *In* The early Mesoamerican village. Kent V. Flannery, ed. New York: Academic Press.
1976b Shell and iron ore exchange in Formative Mesoamerica. *In* The early Mesoamerican village. Kent V. Flannery, ed. New York: Academic Press.

Pires-Ferreira, Jane W., and Kent V. Flannery
1976 Ethnographic models for Formative exchange. *In* The early Mesoamerican village. Kent V. Flannery, ed. New York: Academic Press.

Plog, Fred T.
1975 Systems theory in archaeological research. Annual Review of Anthropology 7:207–24.

Plog, Stephen
1976 Measurement of prehistoric interaction between communities. *In* The early Mesoamerican village. Kent V. Flannery, ed. New York: Academic Press.

Polo de Ondegardo, Juan
1916 Relación de los fundamentos acerca del notable daño que resulta de no guardar a los indios sus fueros [1571]. Colección de Libros y Documentos Referentes a la Historia del Perú 3. Horacio H. Urteaga and Carlos A. Romero, eds. Lima: Sanmartí.

Ponce Sanginés, Carlos
1961 Informe de labores. Centro de Investigaciones Arqueológicas en Tiwanaku, Publicación 1. La Paz.

1969 Tiwanaku: descripción sumaria del Templete Semisubterraneo. 4th ed. La Paz: Los Amigos del Libro.

Pope, K. O., and Bruce S. Dahlin
1989 Ancient Maya wetland agriculture: new insights from ecological and remote sensing research. Journal of Field Archaeology 16:87–106.

Porter, James B.
1989 Olmec colossal heads as recarved thrones: "mutilation," revolution and recarving. Res: Anthropology and Aesthetics 17/18:23–29.

Porter, Muriel N.
1953 Tlatilco and the Preclassic cultures of the New World. Viking Fund Publications in Anthropology, no. 19. New York: Wenner-Gren Foundation for Anthropological Research.

Price, Barbara J.
1978 Secondary state formation: an explanatory model. *In* Origins of the state: the anthropology of political evolution. Ronald Cohen and Elman R. Service, eds. Philadelphia: Institute for the Study of Human Issues (ISHI).

1982 Cultural materialism: a theoretical review. American Antiquity 47:709–41.

Price, S. R. F.
1984 Rituals and power: the Roman imperial cult in Asia Minor. Cambridge: Cambridge University Press.

Prindiville, Mary, and David C. Grove
1987 The settlement and its architecture. *In* Ancient Chalcatzingo. David C. Grove, ed. Austin: University of Texas Press.

Proulx, Donald A.
1971 Headhunting in ancient Peru. Archaeology 24:16–21.

1973 Archaeological investigations in the Nepeña Valley, Peru. Research Report, no. 13. Amherst: Department of Anthropology, University of Massachusetts.

Puleston, Dennis E.
1977 The art and archaeology of hydraulic agriculture in the Maya lowlands. *In* Social process in Maya prehistory: essays in honour of Sir J. Eric S. Thompson. Norman Hammond, ed. New York: Academic Press.

1979 An epistemological pathology and the collapse, or why the Maya kept the Short Count. *In* Maya archaeology and ethnohistory. Norman Hammond and Gordon R. Willey, eds. Austin: University of Texas Press.

Pyne, Nanette
1976 The fire-serpent and were-jaguar in Formative Oaxaca: a contingency table analysis. *In* The early Mesoamerican village. Kent V. Flannery, ed. New York: Academic Press.

Rands, Robert L., and Ronald L. Bishop
1980 Resource procurement zones and patterns of ceramic exchange in the Palenque

region, Mexico. *In* Models and methods in regional exchange. Robert E. Frey, ed. SAA Papers, no. 1. Washington, DC: Society for American Archaeology.

Rappaport, Roy A.
1971   Nature, culture, and ecological anthropology. *In* Man, culture, and society. H. L. Shapiro, ed. Oxford: Oxford University Press.
1979   Ecology, meaning, and religion. Richmond: North Atlantic Books.

Rathje, William L.
1971   The origins and development of lowland Classic Maya civilization. American Antiquity 36:275–85.
1975   Last tango in Mayapan: a tentative trajectory of production-distribution systems. *In* Ancient civilization and trade. Jeremy A. Sabloff and C. C. Lamberg-Karlovsky, eds. Albuquerque: University of New Mexico Press, School of American Research Advanced Seminar Series.
1977   The Tikal connection. *In* The origins of Maya civilization. Richard E. W. Adams, ed. Albuquerque: University of New Mexico Press, School of American Research Advanced Seminar Series.
1983   To the salt of the earth: some comments on household archaeology among the Maya. *In* Prehistoric settlement patterns: essays in honor of Gordon R. Willey. Evon Z. Vogt and Richard M. Leventhal, eds. Albuquerque: University of New Mexico Press.

Rattray, Evelyn Childs
1981   The Teotihuacan ceramic chronology: early Tzacualli to Metepec phases. Manuscript in possession of the author.

Reichenbach, Hans
1968   The rise of scientific philosophy. Berkeley: University of California Press.

Reinhard, Johan
1987   Las líneas de Nazca: un nuevo enfoque sobre su orígen y significado. Lima: Editorial Los Pinos.

Renfrew, A. Colin
1982   Toward an archaeology of the mind. Disney Professor inaugural lecture. Cambridge: Cambridge University Press.

Renfrew, A. Colin, and John F. Cherry, eds.
1986   Peer polity interaction and socio-political change. Cambridge: Cambridge University Press.

Rice, Prudence M.
1987   Economic change in the lowland Maya Late Classic period. *In* Specialisation, exchange and complex societies. Elizabeth Brumfiel and Timothy Earle, eds. Cambridge: Cambridge University Press.

Riese, Berthold
1980   Katun-altersangaben. Baessler-Archiv, Beitrage zur Volkerkunde 28:155–80.

Ringle, William M.
1988   Of mice and monkeys: the value and meaning of T1016, the God C hieroglyph. Research Reports on Ancient Maya Writing, nos. 18–19. Washington, DC: Center for Maya Research.

Robertson, Robin A.
1983   Functional analysis and social process in ceramics: the pottery from Cerros, Belize. *In* Civilization in the ancient Americas: essays in honor of Gordon R. Willey. Richard M. Leventhal and Alan L. Kolata, eds. Albuquerque: University of New Mexico Press.

Robertson, Robin A., and David A. Freidel, eds.
1986   Archaeology at Cerros, Belize, Central America, vol. 1: an interim report. Dallas: Southern Methodist University Press.

Roe, Peter G.
1974   A further exploration of the Rowe Chavin seriation and its implications for north-central coast chronology. Dumbarton Oaks Studies in Pre-Columbian Art and Archaeology, no. 13. Washington, DC: Dumbarton Oaks.

Roscoe, Paul B., and Robert B. Graber, eds.
1988   Circumscription and the evolution of society. American Behavioral Scientist 31(4).

Rountree, Helen C.
1989   The Powhatan Indians of Virginia. Norman: University of Oklahoma Press.

Rowe, John H.
1946   Inca culture at the time of the Spanish conquest. In Handbook of South American Indians, vol. 2: the Andean civilizations. Bureau of American Ethnology Bulletin 143. Julian H. Steward, ed. Washington, DC: Smithsonian Institution.
1948   The kingdom of Chimor. Acta Americana 6(1–2):26–59.
1982   Inca policies and institutions relating to the cultural unification of the empire. In The Inca and Aztec states, 1400–1800: anthropology and history. George A. Collier, Renato I. Rosaldo, and John D. Wirth, eds. New York: Academic Press.

Roys, Ralph L.
1933   The book of Chilam Balam of Chumayel. Carnegie Institution of Washington Publication 438.
1965   The ritual of the bacabs. Norman: University of Oklahoma Press.

Rust, William F., and Robert J. Sharer
1988   Olmec settlement data from La Venta, Tabasco, Mexico. Science 242:102–4.

Ruthenberg, H.
1981   Farming systems in the tropics. Oxford: Oxford University Press.

Sabloff, Jeremy A.
1986   Interaction among Classic Maya polities: a preliminary examination. In Peer polity interaction and socio-political change. A. Colin Renfrew and John F. Cherry, eds. Cambridge: Cambridge University Press.

Sahlins, Marshall
1985   Islands of history. Chicago: University of Chicago Press.

Salomon, Frank
1985   The dynamic potential of the complementarity concept. In Andean ecology and civilization: an interdisciplinary perspective on Andean ecological complementarity. Shozo Masuda, Izumi Shimada, and Craig Morris, eds. Tokyo: University of Tokyo Press.

Sanders, William T.
1962   Cultural ecology of nuclear Mesoamerica. American Anthropologist 64:34–44.
1968   Hydraulic agriculture, economic symbiosis, and the evolution of states in central Mexico. In Anthropological archeology in the Americas. Betty J. Meggers, ed. Washington, DC: Anthropological Society of Washington.
1977   Environmental heterogeneity and the evolution of lowland Maya civilization. In The origins of Maya civilization. Richard E. W. Adams, ed. Albuquerque: University of New Mexico Press, School of American Research Advanced Seminar Series.

Sanders, William T., and Barbara J. Price
1968   Mesoamerica: the evolution of a civilization. New York: Random House.

Sanders, William T., and Robert S. Santley
1977   A prehispanic irrigation system near Santa Clara Xalostoc in the Basin of Mexico. American Antiquity 42:582–8.
1983   A tale of three cities: energetics and urbanization in pre-hispanic central Mexico. In Prehistoric settlement patterns: essays in honor of Gordon R. Willey. Evon Z.

Vogt and Richard M. Leventhal, eds. Albuquerque: University of New Mexico Press.

Sanders, William T., and David Webster
1988   The Mesoamerican urban tradition. American Anthropologist 90:521–46.
1989   The conjunctive approach revisited: the archaeology of Copan in the 1980s. Paper presented at the Society for American Archaeology Annual Meetings.

Sanders, William T., Jeffrey R. Parsons, and Robert S. Santley
1979   The Basin of Mexico: ecological processes in the evolution of a civilization. New York: Academic Press.

Sarmiento de Gamboa, Pedro
1942   Historia de los incas [1572]. Buenos Aires: Emecé Editores.

Schaedel, Richard P.
1978   Early state of the Incas. In The early state. Henri Claessen and Peter Skalnik, eds. The Hague: Mouton.
1985   Discussion: an interdisciplinary perspective on Andean ecological complementarity. In Andean ecology and civilization: an interdisciplinary perspective on Andean ecological complementarity. Shozo Masuda, Izumi Shimada, and Craig Morris, eds. Tokyo: University of Tokyo Press.

Schele, Linda
1976   Accession iconography of Chan-Bahlum in the Group of the Cross at Palenque. Segunda mesa redonda de Palenque, part III:9–34. Pebble Beach: Robert Louis Stevenson School.
1984   Human sacrifice among the Classic Maya. In Ritual human sacrifice in Mesoamerica. Elizabeth H. Boone, ed. Washington, DC: Dumbarton Oaks.
1985   The Hauberg Stela: bloodletting and the mythos of Maya rulership. Fifth Palenque round table, vol. VII:135–49. San Francisco: Pre-Columbian Art Research Institute.
1986   Architectural development and political history at Palenque. In City-states of the Maya: art and architecture. Elizabeth P. Benson, ed. Denver: Rocky Mountain Institute for Pre-Columbian Studies.
1987   Workbook of the hieroglyphic workshop. Austin: Department of Art, University of Texas.
1988a   Revisions to the dynastic chronology of Copan. Copan Notes, no. 45. Copan: Copan Mosaics Project and Instituto Hondureño de Antropología e Historia.
1988b   The Xibalba shuffle. In Maya iconography. Elizabeth Benson and Gillette Griffin, eds. Princeton: Princeton University Press.
1989   Brotherhood in ancient Maya kingship. Paper presented at the conference "New Interpretations of Maya Writing and Iconography," State University of New York, Albany.
1991   House names and dedication rituals at Palenque. In Visions and revisions. F. Clancy and P. Harrison, eds. Albuquerque: University of New Mexico Press. In press.

Schele, Linda, and David A. Freidel
1990   A forest of kings: the untold story of the ancient Maya. New York: William Morrow.
1991   The courts of creation. In The Mesoamerican ballgame. V. Scarborough and D. Wilcox, eds. Tucson: University of Arizona Press. In press.

Schele, Linda, and Peter Mathews
1990   Royal visits along the Usumacinta. In Classic Maya political history: archaeological and hieroglyphic evidence. T. Patrick Culbert, ed. Cambridge: Cambridge University Press, School of American Research Advanced Seminar Series.

Schele, Linda, and Mary Ellen Miller
1986 The blood of kings: dynasty and ritual in Maya art. New York: George Braziller.
Schele, Linda, and David Stuart
1986a Copan notes. Copan: Copan Mosaics Project and Instituto Hondureño de An-
tropología e Historia.
1986b Te-tun as the glyph for "stela." Copan Notes, no. 1. Copan: Copan Mosaics
Project and Instituto Hondureño de Antropología e Historia.
Séjourné, Laurette
1966 Arqueología de Teotihuacan: la cerámica. Mexico, DF: Fondo de Cultura
Económica.
Service, Elman
1975 Origins of the state and civilization: the process of cultural evolution. New York:
W. W. Norton.
Sewell, William H., Jr.
1985 Ideologies and social revolutions: reflections on the French case. Journal of
Modern History 57:57–85.
Shanks, Michael, and Christopher Tilley
1987 Social theory and archaeology. Albuquerque: University of New Mexico Press.
Sharer, Robert J.
1977 The Maya collapse revisited: internal and external perspectives. In Social process
in Maya prehistory: essays in honour of Sir J. Eric S. Thompson. Norman Hammond, ed. New York: Academic Press.
1978 Archaeology and history at Quirigua, Guatemala. Journal of Field Archaeology
5:51–70.
1982 Did the Maya collapse? A New World perspective on the demise of Harappan
civilization. In Harappan civilization: a contemporary perspective. Gregory A.
Possehl, ed. New Delhi: American Institute of Indian Studies.
Sharer, Robert J., ed.
1978 The prehistory of Chalchuapa, El Salvador. Philadelphia: University of
Pennsylvania.
Sharer, Robert J., and Wendy Ashmore
1987 Archaeology: discovering our past. Palo Alto: Mayfield.
Sharma, R. S.
1979 Indian civilization. In Propaganda and communication in world history, vol. I:
the symbolic instrument in early times. Harold D. Lasswell, Daniel Lerner, and
Hans Speier, eds. Honolulu: University of Hawaii Press.
Sheets, Payson D.
1979 Maya recovery from volcanic disaster. Archaeology 32(3):32–42.
1983 Summary and conclusions. In Archaeology and volcanism in Central America:
the Zapotitan Valley of El Salvador. Payson D. Sheets, ed. Austin: University of
Texas Press.
Sidrys, Raymond D.
1978 Notes on obsidian prismatic blades at Seibal and Altar de Sacrificios. In Excavations at Seibal, Department of Peten, Guatemala: artifacts. Gordon R. Willey,
ed. Peabody Museum Memoirs 14, no. 1. Cambridge, MA: Harvard University.
Simon, Herbert A.
1981 The sciences of the artificial. 2nd ed. Cambridge, MA: MIT Press.
Simoons, Frederick J.
1973 The sacred cow and the constitution of India. Ecology of Food and Nutrition
2:281–96.
1979 Questions in the sacred cow controversy. Current Anthropology 20:467–93.

Skocpol, Theda
1985   Cultural idioms and political ideologies in the revolutionary reconstruction of state power: a rejoinder to Sewell. Journal of Modern History 57:86–96.
Smith, Robert Eliot
1987   A ceramic sequence from the Pyramid of the Sun, Teotihuacan. Papers of the Peabody Museum of Archaeology and Ethnology, vol. 75. Cambridge, MA: Harvard University.
Sorokin, Pitirim
1941   The crisis of our age. New York: E. P. Dutton.
Spence, Michael W.
1984   Craft production and polity in early Teotihuacan. In Trade and exchange in early Mesoamerica. Kenneth G. Hirth, ed. Albuquerque: University of New Mexico Press.
Spencer, Charles S.
1987   Rethinking the chiefdom. In Chiefdoms in the Americas. Robert D. Drennan and Carlos A. Uribe, eds. New York: University Press of America.
Steward, Julian H.
1937   Ecological aspects of southwestern society. Anthropos 32:87–104.
1955   Theory of culture change: the methodology of multilinear evolution. Urbana: University of Illinois Press.
Stuart, David
1984a   Epigraphic evidence of political organization in the western Maya lowlands. Manuscript in possession of the author.
1984b   Royal auto-sacrifice among the Maya: a study in image and meaning. Res: Anthropology and Aesthetics 7/8:6–20.
1986   The step inscription of Temple 22 at Copan. Copan Notes, no. 18. Copan: Copan Mosaics Project and Instituto Hondureño de Antropología e Historia.
1987   Ten phonetic syllables. Research Reports on Ancient Maya Writing, no. 14. Washington, DC: Center for Maya Research.
1988   Blood symbolism in Maya iconography. In Maya iconography. Elizabeth Benson and Gillette Griffin, eds. Princeton: Princeton University Press.
Stuart, David, and Linda Schele
1986   Yax-K'uk'-Mo', the founder of the lineage of Copan. Copan Notes, no. 6. Copan: Copan Mosaics Project and Instituto Hondureño de Antropología e Historia.
Sugiyama, Saburo
1989a   Burials dedicated to the Old Temple of Quetzalcoatl at Teotihuacan, Mexico. American Antiquity 54:85–106.
1989b   Iconographic interpretation of the Temple of Quetzalcoatl at Teotihuacan. Mexicon 11:68–74. Berlin.
Sullivan, Lawrence E.
1988   Icanchu's drum: an orientation to meaning in South American religions. New York: Macmillan.
Tambiah, Stanley J.
1976   World conqueror and world renouncer. Cambridge: Cambridge University Press.
1977   The galactic polity: the structure of traditional kingdoms in southeast Asia. Annals of the New York Academy of Sciences 293:69–97.
1982   Famous Buddha images and the legitimation of kings. Res: Anthropology and Aesthetics 4:5–20.
1984   The Buddhist saints of the forest and the cult of amulets: a study in charisma, hagiography, sectarianism and millennial Buddhism. Cambridge: Cambridge University Press.

Tate, Carolyn E.
1986 The language of symbols in the ritual environment of Yaxchilan, Chiapas, Mexico. Ph.D. dissertation, Department of Anthropology, University of Texas, Austin.

Taube, Karl
1985 The Classic Maya maize god: a reappraisal. Fifth Palenque round table, vol. VII: 171–81. San Francisco: The Pre-Columbian Art Research Institute.
1991 The temple of Quetzalcoatl and the cult of sacred war at Teotihuacan. Res: Anthropology and Aesthetics. In press.

Tedlock, Dennis
1985 Popol Vuh: the definitive edition of the Mayan Book of the Dawn of Life and the Glories of Gods and Kings. New York: Simon and Schuster.

Tello, Julio C.
1960 Chavin, cultura matriz de la civilización andina. Lima: Universidad Nacional Mayor de San Marcos.

Thompson, J. Eric S.
1966 The rise and fall of Maya civilization. Norman: University of Oklahoma Press.

Tilley, Christopher
1984 Ideology and the legitimation of power in the Middle Neolithic of southern Sweden. In Ideology, power and prehistory. Daniel Miller and Christopher Tilley, eds. Cambridge: Cambridge University Press.

Tolstoy, Paul
1989 Coapexco and Tlatilco: sites with Olmec materials in the Basin of Mexico. In Regional perspectives on the Olmec. Robert J. Sharer and David C. Grove, eds. Cambridge: Cambridge University Press, School of American Research Advanced Seminar Series.

Tolstoy, Paul, Martin W. Boksenbaum, Kathryn Blair Vaughan, and C. Earle Smith, Jr.
1977 The earliest sedentary communities of the Basin of Mexico: a summary of recent investigations. Journal of Field Archaeology 4:92–106.

Tomoeda, Hiroyasu
1985 The llama is my chacra: metaphor of Andean pastoralists. In Andean ecology and civilization: an interdisciplinary perspective on Andean ecological complementarity. Shozo Masuda, Izumi Shimada, and Craig Morris, eds. Tokyo: University of Tokyo Press.

Townsend, Richard F.
1979 State and cosmos in the art of Tenochtitlan. Dumbarton Oaks Studies in Pre-Columbian Art and Archaeology, no. 20. Washington, DC: Dumbarton Oaks.

Tozzer, Alfred M.
1941 Landa's relación de las cosas de Yucatan: a translation. Papers of the Peabody Museum of American Archaeology and Ethnology, vol. 18. Cambridge, MA: Harvard University.

Trigger, Bruce G.
1982 Archaeological analysis and concepts of causality. Culture 2(2):31–42.
1985 Generalized coercion and inequality: the basis of state power in the early civilizations. In Development and decline: the evolution of sociopolitical organization. Henri J. M. Claessen, Pieter van de Velde, and M. Estellie Smith, eds. South Hadley, MA: Bergin and Garvey.
1989 A history of archaeological thought. Cambridge: Cambridge University Press.

Turner, B. L., II
1974 Prehistoric intensive agriculture in the Mayan lowlands. Science 185:118–24.

Turner, Ellen S., Norman I. Turner, and Richard E. W. Adams
1981 Volumetric assessment, rank ordering, and Maya civic centers. In Lowland Maya

settlement patterns. Wendy Ashmore, ed. Albuquerque: University of New Mexico Press, School of American Research Advanced Seminar Series.

Valcárcel, Luis E.
1946 The Andean calendar. *In* Handbook of South American Indians, vol. 2: the Andean civilizations. Bureau of American Ethnology Bulletin 143. Julian H. Steward, ed. Washington, DC: Smithsonian Institution.

Valdez, Fred, Jr.
1987 The prehistoric ceramics of Colha, northern Belize. Ph.D. dissertation, Department of Anthropology, Harvard University.

van Liere, W. J.
1980 Traditional water management in the lower Mekong Basin. World Archaeology 11:265–80.

Velson, Joseph S., and Thomas C. Clark
1975 Transport of stone monuments to the La Venta and San Lorenzo sites. Contributions of the University of California Archaeological Research Facility, no. 24:1–39. Berkeley.

Veyne, Paul
1976 Le pain et le cirque. Paris: Seuil.

Villagra, Agustín
1956–57 Las pinturas de Atetelco, Teotihuacan. Revista Mexicana de Estudios Antropológicos 14:9–13.

Vlcek, David T., Silvia Garza T., and Edward B. Kurjack
1978 Contemporary farming and ancient Maya settlement: some disconcerting evidence. *In* Prehispanic Maya agriculture. P. Harrison and B. L. Turner II, eds. Albuquerque: University of New Mexico Press.

Vogt, Evon Z.
1976 Tortillas for the gods: a symbolic analysis of Zinacanteco rituals. Cambridge, MA: Harvard University Press.

1983 Ancient and contemporary Maya settlement patterns: a new look from the Chiapas highlands. *In* Prehistoric settlement patterns: essays in honor of Gordon R. Willey. Evon Z. Vogt and Richard M. Leventhal, eds. Albuquerque: University of New Mexico Press.

1985 Cardinal directions and ceremonial circuits in Mayan and southwestern cosmology. National Geographic Research Reports 21:487–96.

von Winning, Hasso
1987 La iconografía de Teotihuacan: los dioses y los signos. Mexico, DF: Universidad Nacional Autónoma de Mexico.

Wachtel, Nathan
1982 The *mitimas* of the Cochabamba Valley: the colonization policy of Huayna Capac. *In* The Inca and Aztec states, 1400–1800: anthropology and history. George A. Collier, Renato I. Rosaldo, and John D. Wirth, eds. New York: Academic Press.

Wallace, Anthony F. C.
1956 Revitalization movements. American Anthropologist 58:264–81.

1966 Religion: an anthropological view. New York: Random House.

Webster, David L.
1975 Warfare and the evolution of the state: a reconsideration. American Antiquity 40:464–70.

1977 Warfare and the evolution of Maya civilization. *In* The origins of Maya civilization. Richard E. W. Adams, ed. Albuquerque: University of New Mexico Press, School of American Research Advanced Seminar Series.

Whalen, Michael E.
1981 Excavations at Santo Domingo Tomaltepec: evolution of a Formative community in the Valley of Oaxaca, Mexico. Prehistory and human ecology of the Valley of Oaxaca, vol. 6. Memoirs of the Museum of Anthropology, no. 12. Ann Arbor: University of Michigan.

Wheatley, Paul
1971 The pivot of the four quarters: an enquiry into the origins and character of the ancient Chinese city. Chicago: Aldine.
1983 Nagara and commandery. Department of Geography Research Papers, nos. 207–8. Chicago: University of Chicago.

White, Leslie
1949 The science of culture. New York: Grove Press.
1959 The evolution of culture: the development of civilization to the fall of Rome. New York: McGraw-Hill.

Wilks, Ivor
1989 Asante in the nineteenth century: the structure and evolution of a political order. 2nd ed. Cambridge: Cambridge University Press.

Willey, Gordon R.
1953 Prehistoric settlement patterns in the Viru Valley, Peru. Bureau of American Ethnology Bulletin 155. Washington, DC: Smithsonian Institution.
1976 Mesoamerican civilization and the idea of transcendence. Antiquity 50:205–25.
1977 The rise of Maya civilization: a summary view. In The origins of Maya civilization. Richard E. W. Adams, ed. Albuquerque: University of New Mexico Press, School of American Research Advanced Seminar Series.
1986 The Classic Maya sociopolitical order: a study in coherence and instability. In Research and reflections in archaeology and history: essays in honor of Doris Stone. E. Wyllys Andrews V, ed. Middle American Research Institute Publication 57. New Orleans: Tulane University.

Willey, Gordon R., and Peter D. Mathews, eds.
1985 A consideration of the Early Classic period in the Maya lowlands. Albany: Institute for Mesoamerican Studies, State University of New York.

Williams, Howel, and Robert F. Heizer
1965 Sources of rock used in Olmec monuments. Contributions of the University of California Archaeological Research Facility, no. 1:1–39. Berkeley.

Williams, Thomas
1870 Fiji and the Fijians. 3rd ed. London: Hodder and Stoughton.

Wilson, David J.
1983 The origins and development of complex prehispanic society in the lower Santa Valley, Peru: implications for theories of state origins. Journal of Anthropological Archaeology 2:209–76.
1985 Prehispanic settlement patterns in the lower Santa Valley, north coast of Peru: a regional perspective on the origins and development of complex society. Ph.D. dissertation, Department of Anthropology, University of Michigan.
1987 Reconstructing patterns of early warfare in the lower Santa Valley: new data on the role of conflict in the origins of complex north coast society. In The origins and development of the Andean state. Jonathan Haas, Shelia Pozorski, and Thomas Pozorski, eds. Cambridge: Cambridge University Press.
1988 Prehispanic settlement patterns in the lower Santa Valley, Peru: a regional perspective on the origins and development of complex north coast society. Washington, DC: Smithsonian Institution Press.

Wittfogel, Karl
1955 Developmental aspects of hydraulic societies. In Irrigation civilizations: a com-

parative study. Social Sciences Monograph 1. Washington, DC: Pan-American Union.

Wolf, Eric, ed.
1976   The Valley of Mexico: studies in pre-hispanic ecology and society. Albuquerque: University of New Mexico Press, School of American Research Advanced Seminar Series.

Wright, Arthur F.
1979   Chinese civilization. *In* Propaganda and communication in world history, vol. I: the symbolic instrument in early times. Harold D. Lasswell, Daniel Lerner, and Hans Speier, eds. Honolulu: University of Hawaii Press.

Wright, Henry T., and Gregory A. Johnson
1975   Population, exchange, and early state formation in southwestern Iran. American Anthropologist 77:267–89.

Wright, Rita P.
1985   Technology, style and craft specialization: spheres of interaction and exchange in the Indo-Iranian borderland, third millennium B.C. Ph.D. dissertation, Department of Anthropology, Harvard University.

Wyatt, D. K.
1984   Thailand. New Haven: Yale University.

Yamamoto, Norio
1985   The ecological complementarity of agro-pastoralism: some comments. *In* Andean ecology and civilization: an interdisciplinary perspective on Andean ecological complementarity. Shozo Masuda, Izumi Shimada, and Craig Morris, eds. Tokyo: University of Tokyo Press.

Yengoyan, Aram A.
1985   Digging for symbols: the archaeology of everyday material life. Proceedings of the Prehistoric Society 51:329–34.

Yoffee, Norman
1979   The decline and rise of Mesopotamian civilization: an ethnoarchaeological perspective on the evolution of social complexity. American Antiquity 44:5–35.

Zuidema, R. Tom
1964   The ceque system of Cuzco: the social organization of the capital of the Inca. Leiden: E. J. Brill.
1973   Kinship and ancestor cult in three Peruvian communities: Hernández Príncipe's account of 1622. Bulletin de l'Institut Français d'Etudes Andines 2(1):16–33.
1977a La imagen del sol y la huaca de Susurpuquio en el sistema astronómico de los Incas en el Cuzco. Journal de la Société des Américanistes, n.s. 63:199–230. Paris.
1977b Mito e historia en el antiguo Perú. Allpanchis 10:15–52. Cuzco.
1982   Bureaucracy and systematic knowledge in Andean civilization. *In* The Inca and Aztec states, 1400–1800: anthropology and history. George A. Collier, Renato I. Rosaldo, and John D. Wirth, eds. New York: Academic Press.
1983   Hierarchy and space in Incaic social organization. Ethnohistory 30:49–76.
1985   Llama sacrifices and computation: roots of the Inca calendar in Huari-Tiahuanaco culture. Manuscript in possession of the author. Department of Anthropology, University of Illinois, Urbana-Champaign.

INDEX

Abaj Takalik, 34
Altun Ha, 140
Amazon lowlands, 38, 52; Yanomamö, 45–48
Andes: connection with Amazon lowlands, 38; cults of the dead in, 167–68. *See also* Chavin; Moche state; Santa Valley, Peru
Appleby, Joyce O., 212–13
Arapa, 78
Architecture, public: Early Formative, 17–18; Late Formative, 35; of Maya, 120–21; Middle Formative, 32–34; in Santa Valley, Peru, 54, 56; of states, 216. *See also various headings under* Palenque; Teotihuacan; Tiwanaku site
Asante state, 217

Bloodletting, ritual: 23, 32, 33, 132n8
Bonampak, 183

Cacao, 34
Caracol, 140, 141, 144
Carneiro, Robert L.: circumscription model of, 25–26, 137, 187–88; coercive theory of warfare of, 52
Causality, 211–14
Ceramics: Early Formative, 24–25; Middle Formative, 29–30; Moche, 60; Olmec, 25; at Teotihuacan, 96, 98
Cerros, 139, 141
Chagnon, Napoleon, 45–48
Chalcatzingo, 18, 33, 35
Chalchuapa, 34
Chan-Bahlum, 123, 124
Chavin, 38, 39
Chazan, Naomi, 218
Chert, exchange of, 142–43
Chiapas coast, 21, 22
Chiefdom: ideology of, 198–99; Olmec as, 180–81; public architecture in, 18. *See also* Chiefs
Chiefs (Mesoamerican): exchange, control of, 19, 22; kinship networks of, 29; as mediators between society and supernatural, 26–27, 35; Olmec, 26–29, 31–32; sacredness of, 27; statuses of, 20; symbols of office of, 32; transfer

of office of, 31; underworld, as source of power of, 26, 31. *See also* Chiefdom; Elites; Shamanism
Chunchicmil, 121
Class structure: of Maya, 116–17, 128; role of ideology in maintaining, 72
Coca, 81
Coe, Michael D., 25–26, 105
Copan, 141; architecture of, 126, 133n16; defeat of, 144, 145; greenstone at, 30
Cuello, 119
Cuicuilco, 35
Cults of the dead, Andes, 167–68
Cultural ecology, and ideology, 3, 7
Cultural evolution, and ideology, 5
Cultural holism, 221
Cultural idealism, 65–66, 67, 177
Cultural materialism, 177–78; archaeologists' doubts about, 6–7; definition of, 65, 66–68; Harris's model of, 41; rejection of ideology in, 5
Cultural systems: Flannery's model of, 41–43; Harris's model of, 40–41; hierarchical models of, 40–41; Wilson's model of, 43–45

Dos Pilas, 140; defeat of Tikal by, 144, 145; expansion of, 155

Early Formative: ceramic motifs, 23–25; exchange, 19, 22; mirrors, 22–23; obsidian, 21; public architecture, 17–18; symbol system, 25. *See also* Olmec
Economy. *See* Exchange; Political economy
El Castillo, 58
Elites: alliances of, 33, 34; differentiated, 218
Elites, Maya: exchange, role in, 142–43; religious function of, 148; status goods of, 143
Elites, Olmec: ascribed status of, 31–32; authority over kin groups by, 30–31; control of exchange by, 30; interaction of, 26, 29
Elites, Tiwanaku: client-patron dyads of, 83; ideology, use by, 72; on public monoliths, 77;

SCHOOL OF AMERICAN RESEARCH ADVANCED SEMINAR SERIES

Published by the SAR Press

Chaco & Hohokam: Prehistoric Regional
Systems in the American Southwest
P. L. CROWN & W. J. JUDGE, eds.

Recapturing Anthropology:
Working in the Present
RICHARD G. FOX, ed.

War in the Tribal Zone:
Expanding States and
Indigenous Warfare
R. B. FERGUSON & N. L. WHITEHEAD, eds.

Published by Cambridge University Press

Dreaming: Anthropological and
Psychological Interpretations
BARBARA TEDLOCK, ed.

The Anasazi in a Changing Environment
GEORGE J. GUMERMAN, ed.

Regional Perspectives on the Olmec
R. J. SHARER & D. C. GROVE, eds.

The Chemistry of Prehistoric Human Bone
T. DOUGLAS PRICE, ed.

The Emergence of Modern Humans:
Biocultural Adaptations
in the Later Pleistocene
ERIK TRINKAUS, ed.

The Anthropology of War
JONATHAN HAAS, ed.

The Evolution of Political Systems
STEADMAN UPHAM, ed.

Classic Maya Political History:
Hieroglyphic and Archaeological Evidence
T. PATRICK CULBERT, ed.

Turko-Persia in Historical Perspective
ROBERT L. CANFIELD, ed.

Chiefdoms: Power, Economy,
and Ideology
TIMOTHY EARLE, ed.

SCHOOL OF AMERICAN RESEARCH ADVANCED SEMINAR SERIES

Published by the University of New Mexico Press

Director of Publications: Jane Kepp

Copy Editor: June-el Piper

Designer: Deborah Flynn Post

Indexer: Andrew Christenson

Typographer: G & S Typesetters, Inc.

Printer: Edwards Brothers, Inc.

This book was set in Linotron Berkeley Old Style Book.

The book paper is made from acid-free, recycled fibers.

Participants in the advanced seminar
Ideology and the Cultural Evolution of Pre-Columbian Civilizations
Seated, left to right:
Mary W. Helms
Robert L. Carneiro
Geoffrey W. Conrad
Jonathan Haas
Arthur A. Demarest
Standing, left to right:
David C. Grove
David J. Wilson
David A. Freidel
Alan L. Kolata
Robert McC. Adams
George L. Cowgill.